Forever ...and 365 Days

By

ULRIKE

MODERN THOUGHT
THEORIES

Troll River Publications
Los Angeles, CA

Troll River Publications

www.trollriverpub.com

Forever ... and 365 Days

<u>WARNING</u>

The author of this book does not dispense medical advice or prescribe the use of any technique as a form of treatment for physical or medical problems without the advice of a physician, either directly or indirectly. The intent of the author is only to offer information of a general nature to help you in your quest for emotional and spiritual well-being. In the event you use any of the information in this book for yourself, which is your constitutional right, the author and the publisher assume no responsibility for your actions.

Dedication

To my dear friend Virgil, who since has passed away into another dimension and probably knows the answers to his reincarnation questions by now. I am grateful for his wisdom and love.

Contents

Foreword

Is it right or is it wrong? Is it good or is it damaging? Why do we have to ask ourselves these questions all the time? We have double standards. We believe that evil is real. We believe that something can harm us. The truth is, however, that we are perfect beings of light, indestructible and pure. We have only fallen into the mist of misunderstanding and are acting according to our fears.

It is a lifetime task to sort out these wrong beliefs and teachings. We have to reeducate and retrain ourselves to think and act correctly. It is a daily task. Minute by minute we must be aware of our actions and make certain that love is our motive in everything we do.

Love, not emotion, is the key to our transformation from caterpillar to butterfly. Love is the motivating principle of all things and Love is the mother of our being. Let us return to this source of all bliss, let us enjoy our health, wealth and happiness - now and "Forever ... and 365 days".

Introduction

Last year, when I was just about ready to send the manuscript of my first book *"Better Living...Because You Can!"* to the publisher, I realized I had so much more to say. I love the daily discipline of writing, and even though I produce articles for magazines and quotes, and healing thoughts for my social media on a regular basis, I am always urged to write more by the higher self.

It dawned on me over New Year's Day that this was the opportunity to chronicle the unfoldment of a searcher's mind - my own - over the course of a full year. As a New Age teacher constantly searching for more enlightenment, it occurred to me that my own thoughts, my own challenges and solutions, my own applications of Truth, and my own searching for more Understanding would be of benefit not only to myself, but also help many others who are ready to tackle their own understanding of life and what it means to them. This was my concept in writing this book.

Life lives and will go on forever, but we are still dealing with 365 days a year with our human experiences, whether it be the joys and rewards of a life well spent, or challenges and tribulations from issues that arise day to day. We are still here - right now.

This book is a compilation of my thoughts and my daily diligent mental applications. They are my experiences, proving over and over again that thought is causative.

You will see the daily chapters at times jumping from one subject to another, but this is how my mind assimilated new ideas and has looked at fresh concepts. Being an avid reader, I have incorporated my findings after studying the texts of other metaphysical authorities, and it reflects the conclusions I came to and the mental growth I experienced.

Students, readers, and strangers alike have contributed their real life stories to make this a living document. It is a vivid picture of what happens to all of us in this stage of unfoldment. Characters and their woes in need of improvement, personal tests, and many valid inquiries are portrayed as practical as possible. I'm sure many of you may relate to more than one chapter and see your own life's reflection and experiences in the stories I have shared.

You are the "light that shines for all eternity" ... so make it the best 365 days you can, this year and every year, as long as you shall live on this plane!

Forever and 365 days

...a Year in the Life of an Inspirational Writer

Chapter 1: New Beginnings

January 1

Life is an adventure. Every day something new emerges; something else to solve or handle. Don't forget to enjoy the process. Turn challenges into possibilities. Let common sense, kindness, and love guide you!

Reflection: Letting go of residue

Waking up early on New Year's Day is nothing new to me. My husband and I usually don't choose to go out, avoiding the crowds and the driving conditions on a busy day like New Year's Eve. That evening, we walked instead to a local pizza place around the corner from our residence and enjoyed the familiarity of the little hole in the wall we've known for so long. Hollywood has been ravished by an arsonist for the past four days and this special night wasn't any different. Sirens and helicopters filled the night sky as law enforcement was trying to catch this deranged individual.

As 6:00 a.m. came around, the noise had quieted down and dawn was slowly creeping up. My first thoughts were reflective of 2011 and all the seemingly wrong that had been done to me by my previous long term employer. I promised myself over the past few months to let go of the lingering hurt feelings. However, I pondered the fact that I had lost my longtime job at the motion picture studio which I had worked for a total of

15

nearly twenty years. I grieved the loss of my beloved band, which was the house band for the studio that I had created five years earlier; all was gone, history in one month. But it was past. It was done. There is no use in holding on to hurts that have no substance; it was only a memory that needed to be looked at for what it was. A simple learning experience, designed to make me a better person, a stronger individual.

I am to step out of the past, and I have to shed the skin of yesterday. Renewal, rebirth - a daily ritual... I started feeling lighter, more inspired and full of anticipation. Hope and loving anticipation had once again entered my mind.

I shifted to being grateful for the new doors that had opened up to me. This was only possible because I was pushed by a higher power to make a change. A shift of awareness and priorities had occurred. New friends had entered the scene.

This morning I was thankful for the sunshine and blue clear skies that slowly started to lighten the horizon, and the ability to let our dog out the door in a T-shirt and shorts on a January morning. What a blessing to live in California I thought!

I was appreciative that the year had ended on such an up note and with so much hopefulness and I graciously committed myself to make every day of this year count. To look at each day as a new adventure and find one thing daily that is worthy of attention is what I will be reaching for.

As I started to jot my thoughts down on a piece of paper the words came easily. I am in the habit of writing by hand, in bed, under a side lamp. I do this mostly in wee hours while it is quiet and the daily noise has not set in yet. The thoughts come so quickly that I can't keep up writing them down. I can't write fast enough. It's like someone is feeding me the words. My mind is clear and precise. The truth spouts out. I am writing effortlessly.

After breakfast I was ready to walk back to the Zen Den, which is my pool house turned office, and to type up this first chapter. 364 to go!

January 2

All positive affirmations will not help you unless you act on them. Application is the key. You have to walk the talk!

Set your goals

One of my longtime habits is to write down my goals for the year. It helps me to focus and really look at what I think I want. Yes, what we think we want and what we really want is not always the same. It becomes apparent after a few months. Try it.

I usually choose goals from several categories. Work, home, relationship - you get the point. Here are some goals I set for myself for this year:

- Publish my second booklet, "The Seeds Will Sprout Somewhere"
- Increase my student base and start seminars and workshops
- Practice patience with my husband and allow the Law of Individuality to work
- Review our trust and legal papers and update accordingly
- Repave our driveway

These are just a few examples on my list. But it shows you, that some are basic day to day improvement projects that need to be followed through to better my living conditions. Some are mental adjustments like more patience and love, as well as success which acquire courage, a sense of abundance, focus and determination.

You can adjust these goals during the year accordingly, but it is your guideline and starting point to stay focused.

January 3

Don't block your senses with discouragement, negativity, and doubt. Leave the door wide open for love, success, and new adventures.

'Flow with life..."

Before I turned off my computer at the end of the day, I received a message on the Modern Thought Theories Facebook page from a male high school student. He was asking for advice, saying *"I find it so hard to 'flow with life' cuz all my time is spent doing things I don't wanna do."*

Yes, we all can agree that there are occasions in life that seem to be a waste of time. However, all experiences are lessons and therefore my response to him was as follows:

"Many times in life it looks like you have to deal with things, that you think you 'don't like to do', but you will find out that each experience is just a stepping stone and a way of learning. The truth is, that you will always 'flow with life' because you are life itself. You might stand in your own way sometimes, but you will always move forward and upward. Please know that in order to change any situation you need to start loving the things that seem not so fun or not so enjoyable. When you change your sense about them, they will change accordingly. Keep focused on what you want and you will get it. It's all about your dreams and your determination to achieve them."

What I loved most about this quest for advice was that it came from a young man who actually reached out on an inspirational website which is mostly frequented by females ages thirty-five to fifty-five, which make up 30% of my readers. The female group eighteen to twenty-four is also strong at 16%, however, as you can imagine, young male adults, especially under the age of twenty-five, are usually not interested in the subject provided by my site at this time in their life. Good for him!

January 4

Be persistent and do not give up or wander off your path easily. Insist and know that it can be done. Be determined to achieve whatever you've set out to do. Know and feel your desire so strongly that you can taste it. Sense it with all of your being and it will be yours.

Getting back to work

Yep … New Year, new goals, new hopes, new everything … Not sure why we always wait for a whole year to go by before we start new things that we've thought about for a long time? Is it fear of failure? Thinking we don't have the time? Is it an impossible dream or just sheer laziness?

Today is another great day as the sun is still high in the sky with record breaking, eighty-five degree temperatures, even by California standards. My husband made breakfast, yum! Full belly and all, I'm going back to my office to answer e-mails, research photos for flyers, and other work-related chores. Life is good!

My new business: How was it conceived?

To give you a quick recap of my state of mind in early 2010, and the events that followed, will help you to understand how my mind works.

After I was laid off from my big executive studio job I had to think quick and hard. I realized this was the opportunity to change my life experience. Being in the same job for nearly twenty years, the idea of quitting and doing what I really wanted to do was not an option. My past thinking would not allow such a luxury and adventurous undertaking.

This unexpected "woe" (and trust me it turned out to be the best thing of my life) pushed me to rethink my priorities. I didn't have to immediately worry about finances, I knew I would be OK, and I knew I didn't want to continue in the same field of expertise, which dealt with large-scale events for the movie industry.
I needed a change for a long time. So, I sat myself down and started to write in my journal. I asked myself "What do I really want to do?" Music is always on my list, working from home would be nice, didn't want to have to drive far to work ... think long and diligently and most of all be not afraid!

Personally, I have been a New Age student and teacher for over thirty years, always searching and looking for more Truth. It has been quite a journey looking under every rock and reading as many different authors on the subject as possible. My main background is Eschatology, the William W. Walter method, one of the many great metaphysical sciences from the early 1900ss. It's a small group of devoted people, mainly believing with all of their hearts in the Allness of Good. This is a great premise to start out from. How can you go wrong, knowing that all is perfect and good?

Today, this study when presented to new students is looked at as somewhat outdated and stuffy. It is mostly taught in small classes by private teachers and kept quiet. Too quiet for my taste, as I believe the Truth has to be spread, and all people on this Earth should reap the benefits. However, they are a good group of sincere individuals and I wish them all goodness and happiness.

I appreciate what I've learned and my heart will always cherish Mr. Walter's works. They are my cornerstone.

So here I was thinking that the time had come to make this my fulltime mission. I was so full of thoughts and ideas. I was so ready to share all I had proven to myself with everyone that wanted to listen. I had improved my life over the years tremendously and I loved teaching and counseling. I was bursting at the brim. Life couldn't get any more exciting!

The name *Modern Thought Theories* came to me in a flash. "Modern" for up-to-date and fresh; "Thought" because it was inspired, uplifted and active; "Theories" because it was proven to be true, it was scientific, and open to theorizing and brainstorming. It was a work in progress. Life is progress. Our individual life is a daily learning experience, a positive development, fit to flow with Universal advancement.

I had my name, my mission statement was next: "Modern Thought Theories is committed to teaching Universal Laws and the Truth of Being in plain language to help you and your fellow man to improve your life's experience. Make Happiness your Goal!"

Desire, imagination, courage, and action - that's how the journey began.

January 5

God is in the eyes of the beholder

In my networking efforts I connected with a group of writers yesterday. One of my goals for 2012 is to meet new people. I want to be more open to fresh connections. I'm one of those people who don't need a lot of friends. I have a few amazing ones and that is sufficient. However, I realize meeting new people that have common interests will be inspirational and infuse me with fresh ideas. Familiarity sometimes breeds stagnation.

I tend to be a hermit. I sometimes don't go out for days. Don't get me wrong, I'm outdoors most of the time. I created a garden, outdoor living space for reading and writing, large open windows to let the sunlight flow in, a music room, and wide open patio doors making me feel that the inside of the house is connected with nature at all times.

I have two fountains that are regularly frequented by the most colorful birds, plants, flowers, and my home grown vegetables are a staple that brings me continuous joy.

What I mean by "not going out" is I rarely socialize in groups, go to movies, and hang out in the mall or clubs. I only leave the house when I have a work commitment for my consulting business or necessary errands to run. I have had my years and years of parties, people, and fun. I was an event producer for a major Hollywood studio for nearly twenty years with an average of 300 events per year. Enough!

So going forward, meeting new people will be a very selective process and the group of authors I met online was delightful. The conversation about viral marketing quickly became helpful and supportive.

One of the authors, to my surprise, was a pastor from Northern California. He befriended my Facebook page and I thought about how I would answer him if he, being a man of God, would ask me:

"What is your idea of God and what does God mean to you?"

"God is Universal power, the Almighty substance that sustains all life. I am part of this substance called Consciousness. I can think, and thinking is the conscious

activity of this substance led by God's urge of expression.

God is Wisdom. So I, being part of this Wisdom, have to choose wisely as to what I think. It is my duty!

God is good. So I have to be and act of good to live up to God's standards. It is my duty!

God is Intelligence. So I, being part of this Intelligence, have to act intelligently and in accordance to the truth. It is my duty!"

Yes, this is how I would answer his question.

January 6

Have courage, show strength, and always trust in yourself.

Students come to me for different reasons

Today I was reminded about a previous student of mine by a mutual friend. Many students search for betterment mostly because they have financial troubles or difficulties in relationships. They know, or at least glimpsed at the possibility, that by changing their thoughts and their behavior improvement will occur. They know to a degree that they are in charge of their lives but haven't quite figured out how to apply the affirmations that ring true to them.

Most people equate bettering their life with acquiring material riches or improved relationships, a better job, avoiding a divorce and so on. They do not come and say:

"I want to find the Truth and I want to be more spiritually enlightened."

They haven't quite understood that this spiritual enlightenment is all that counts, and those material riches, improved relationships, a bigger house, etc., are natural outcomes or outflows of this new and improved SELF.

Affirmations are everywhere these days. People posting them on the internet, Facebook and well-meant e-mails accompanied with beautiful pictures are popping up every day. A few minutes later all those wonderful uplifting promises and positive commitments are all out the window ... forgotten!

Sallie's story

Today, one of my students came to me complaining that even though she was doing great in most of the areas of her life, she had not found her "man," her partner and soul mate. She was thirty-six years of age and felt that it was time to get married. She wanted children and in her mind the "time was running out."

We had a good hearty talk about her wishes, dreams, and expectations, and I told her that the general class teachings were about life itself and about how to change your thought habits. However, we could certainly weave her desire of finding a mate into this class work. I also told her that she needed to stop looking in faraway places as the right guy was already right around the corner.

In her desperation she had contemplated to move to a different city as she felt that Los Angeles was not a good "breeding ground for a husband." She continued to study with me for about a year and made great progress. Being a good thinker and reasonable individual, she quickly took responsibility and applied what she learned to her daily rituals.

At Christmas time she decided to go back to her home state to visit her family. As she arrived at her family abode, a young man was in the kitchen talking to her mother. She recognized him to be a childhood friend and he had stopped by not knowing that Sallie was on her way. He was not a regular guest; it was just a coincidence you might say. Ah! There are no such things as coincidences! It was synchronicity, perfect Universal timing. They quickly connected and, you guessed it, started to date, fell in love, and yes, they got married within the year.

He admitted to her later that he was smitten with her since he was a little fellow and that he had said as a child that one day he would marry her. Of course this statement was long forgotten until it became reality. She achieved exactly what she set out to do. She moved back to her home state and is happier than ever.

I haven't heard from her in a while. Many times a student moves on when they reached what they thought was their goal. But I rest in peace because I know that when the going gets tough she can go back to what she's learned. And I know she will!

January 7

Today I will watch my thoughts carefully. I will not allow pettiness, anxiety and worry to enter my mind. I will look for the good only.

In my first book, "*Better Living...Because You Can!,*" I addressed several illnesses and their relationship to our right or wrong thinking, i.e. being mental in cause. We will address this subject further as we go along, so it becomes natural for you to look at ailments and illnesses as dis-easiness rather than disease.

What caused my upset stomach?

Waking up, feeling good and rested, ready to tackle the day - that's what I expect every morning. It's my usual way of changing from dream world to now world. (I'm not calling it the real world, as this is not the real world ... whole other subject for a later date!)

Yesterday after dinner however, I felt heavy and somewhat uncomfortable. I went to bed early, waking up at midnight only to find myself feeling sick to my stomach and I spent most of the night in the bathroom doing rather unpleasant things.

Since I have studied the mental effects of all discomfort for a long time, and do not believe in so-called material causes like, for instance, food poisoning, I immediately went to the thought "What have I been thinking that is so repulsive to me that I have to get rid of it? What mistaken thoughts do I have to eliminate or empty out?"

I know that looking at the cause of my discomfort being in mind, rather than in the body, is necessary and is the key. This is because the ill reflection on your body will reveal to you your mistaken sense, feelings, and dispositions. Each illness has its origin in mind and can therefore be eradicated through thought correction.

I've been taught that the stomach represents reason and its proper use. Many times, when we reason about a problem, we allow too much emotions, and we run on and on about the problem. Sometimes we are too compassionate or concerned, and we go overboard with our feelings. Vomiting shows you that you are rejecting some idea in mind. Maybe you do not agree with something that happened and find it unacceptable and disgusting.

In my case, I reasoned, it was emotional residue from the loss of my job. I haven't finished grieving this so-called "loss." On top of that, I agreed to accept a temporary job which is employing me to do the same work as before. At this time I felt that the income would be helpful to our household. A job, I might add, I no longer want to do. I am rejecting the sense of "being stuck" in the same type of work environment I am trying to escape. The lingering sense of "loss" is a mere emotional hangover. Do you see how I reason things out?

Losing something

We say "I lost my job," "I lost my boyfriend"... but we should not think of it as losing, it's more like rearranging the furniture. You love to sit in this comfy old couch or worn out arm chair. It starts to sag and get uncomfortable, but you are so used to it you hang on to it. You just don't want to get rid of it, not yet ... but it's time. Replacing anything that you have outgrown, may it be a relationship or job, will make room for the new and fresh. It will be a breath of fresh air, necessary for your growth.

All is mental and that includes sickness and health. It would be easy to say that my discomfort came from the food I ate. However, that would make food *Cause or God*, which it is not. What I mean is that anytime you accept the thought that something outside of you can make you sick you give away your power to that particular belief.

We reverse cause and effect constantly in all aspects of life. It was my discordant thought, sense, and feelings that caused the discomfort. I made a mistake in my thinking (not fleeting thoughts, rather the ones that have lots of feeling and convictions attached) and I had to suffer the consequences. That is the working of the Law of Cause and Effect.

I had to turn it around by seeing the good only. So I made a list of gratitude that included: "I love my new friends at the Museum. They are lovely and good people. It's close to home, a three minute ride, unheard of in Los Angeles. On top of that it's only temporary; I am in charge if and when it is going to end."

But it was my lingering sense of bitterness (represented in the bile) and I still was hanging on to hurt feelings. I'm feeling better and better, as I am reasoning it out; only my emotions are still a bit raw from the experience.

Emotional pain brought on by a loss of job, loss of relationship or loss of anything can be healed by repeating: All is good, I am safe, I am well, I am happy; I am loved, and mean it.

As I pointed out before, in reality you cannot lose anything. You only shift things around to make room for new and improved experiences in all aspects of your life.

I am grateful that I have learned over the years of diligent study and observation to correct myself quickly, sometimes even instantaneously. If sickness would be understood as purely mental and not a physical condition, it could be healed by purely mental means.

Yes, I pop back up like a Yo-Yo, ready to face another day! Bring it on!

January 8

Harmony is the basic principle of all life ... focus on harmonious thoughts today and every day!

I realize that the world within me is becoming more and more apparent; I am in my own head most of the time. Meaning, I spend hours alone contemplating, reading, writing, imagining, and creating.

What's out there?

As I said, I don't go out much. Not because I can't, but because there isn't much "out there" that is of value to me. I pick and choose what I do carefully. The company of my husband and a few good friends is always enjoyable. A good dinner at a nice restaurant once in a while, or going to Farmers Market for fresh pastrami on rye and a glass of beer are highlights, when I have the urge to go out. But going to the malls shopping, hanging out in bars (whatever that means), and spending hours at the beauty salon is not appealing to me anymore. My perception has changed.

This doesn't mean it's wrong or that you can't do it. It might give you great pleasure to go to sports games or shop for that special something. It just means that my focus has changed.

We are all so different. We all need to do what makes us happy. It's an individual choice. You have the right to choose whatever it is that gives you a sense of fulfillment and happiness as long as it doesn't hurt anyone else or take from them. I just want to make sure, however, that I leave room for daily contemplation and meditation!

January 9

You have a choice. Yes, you've heard that a thousand times. So why are you still giving in to the victim's position? Why do you still think that the situation is out of control? Make a new choice; one that fits your new purpose and makes you happy.

Commitment: I will focus on my right and good choices today.

January 10

Word habits

Last night, a reader's comment reminded me of word habits and how important they are in communicating with each other but mostly within ourselves. The conversation went like this. I had posted the quote:

"Do not think you have to fight against the evil you see. Know that by changing your sense from negative perception to a positive sense of 'all is already good' your individual world will respond. Keep up with your good work!"

This reader responded to this statement of Truth, saying that "Mike Dooley, 'Notes from the Universe', recently said that we should replace the word 'evil' with 'ignorance.'"

So true! I rarely use the word evil, but chose it for this quote to relate to the "seemingly real" occurrences of "this" world. In reality all evil is only the effect of ignorance and therefore unreal. By changing cause, we change effect. By gaining wisdom, we replace ignorance.

I thanked her for sharing this piece of insight.

January 11

My daily prayer statement

All so-called material things are reflections of mind substance. They are mental in nature. I am the thinker, the creator of my life. I am the cause of everything I see and experience in my world.

Writing and teaching is a lifelong dream come true. I have been interested in all metaphysical studies for a very long time and have diligently searched for the Truth. There is only one Truth. All religions, the teachings of the East and West alike, culminate in one thing - the sincere quest to find God and the knowledge of who and what God is, and the unique relationship we have to this Universal all-power.

I am grateful to have glimpsed at the unlimited possibilities that this Universal all-power provides for all of us, and I am gladly taking its hand and walk with it through all eternity!

January 12

Let your star shine bright! Shed off all limitations, doubt and fear. Enter the realm of all possibilities. This is your true state, your spiritual heritage. Embrace this birthright and love with all of your heart.

January is the beginning of award season. Yes, I live in Hollywood, California, Land of the Glorified. There are two sides to Hollywood. Glitz and glamour, you say? Not so fast.

Homelessness versus glitz and glamour

About 50,000 youth in the U.S. sleep on the street for six months or more. Homeless youth face unique developmental challenges and vulnerability. They are easy prey on the streets, clinging on to anyone that gives them a feeling of "belonging." Many times this leads to drug abuse, prostitution, and in some cases, death. The United States homeless statistics reports that approximately 50% of all homeless women and children are fleeing some form of domestic violence.

How many in Hollywood? According to the Institute for the Study of Homelessness and Poverty at the Weingart Center, an estimated 254,000 men, women, and children experience homelessness in Los Angeles County during some part of the year and approximately 82,000 people are homeless on any given night. Unaccompanied youth, especially in the Hollywood area, are estimated to make up from 4,800 to 10,000 of these.

Behind the glamour and fame that surrounds Hollywood there is a growing population of homeless youth never discussed in the tabloids or recognized at any of the Hollywood awards ceremonies. These kids and teens, mostly runaways, come to this luring city to "make it big." With dreams and ideas, but no common sense, and

31

even less education, they end up lost. You find them sleeping next to the marble stars, laid on the Walk of Fame, a hard concrete reality.

You, as a parent, have to appeal to education first, no matter how scarce the financial situation in your household. Learning is everything. Teach them how to balance a check book, show them how to manage money first. It's amazing how many people are ignorant to basic accounting and day to day spending habits. Train your children from early age on to become responsible adults, and investors of the future of this country.

Hollywood is not bad in itself. It is a beautiful city and a wonderful place to live, if you are grounded and mature. There are two "realities," two perceptions, which is the glamorous world of TV and movies and the neighborhood next door.

It's been thirty-one years since I first came here and I call myself a true "Hollywoodian." There are many good people in this town, quite normal (yes, normal is in the eye of the beholder) and hardworking, like the rest of the country.

What's the difference between Hollywood and other cities? The difference is the perception of people, which, as we know, creates what you experience. More affluent people live in Los Angeles, Beverly Hills, and Hollywood area than in the rest of the country. The economy is driven by movie making and TV production. Most of the population, myself included, draws a paycheck from an entertainment industry related company.

But you have to be shrewd and careful. Again, it's all perception. You can get away with printing business cards with a swanky address to give an impression. Many work out of their cars or small homes. The iPhones, laptops and internet access make it all possible.

I have worked for, and with, the rich and famous for many years. I have enjoyed many of the experiences and I have loathed some of them. However, I am fully aware of the fact that life here is not what it looks like. And I have made a conscious decision to live according to Truth and Universal Laws, knowing that I have to look at the important and real things, and not the false and illusory.

January 13

We are masters but we are also servants. We are individuals, yet one. When we look at the other, we really look at ourselves.

How do you deal with others?

I, like all of us, know firsthand that everywhere in the world you will find people who are more demanding or arduous. Dealing with difficult individuals can leave you speechless, breathless, and stunned. You are trying to contain yourself; you are trying to not react. You are fighting to keep your composure, knowing that it would be for the best, but you feel the explosion inside of you and you react.

In your work environment, you have to deal with someone that constantly puts you down and reminds you that they are the boss. They have the last say, and you feel that you are in their hands as they are the ones signing your pay checks. You feel helpless. I have experienced this recently, but I have to remember that what I know about the workings of the mind is the honest Truth. However, my feelings have to be in agreement with this knowledge.

Reflections of another kind

Many of my ex-bosses and people around me have had an egocentric disposition. The "I am better than you," "I am richer than you," and "I am more powerful"

33

syndrome. It is, however, no matter how hard to accept, a reflection of something deep within you.

For example, what you see could be a reflection of what or who you are and what you like about you - i.e. strength, stamina, cleverness, good business sense; or a reflection of what you are lacking – maybe self-worth, patience, or common sense. It could be a reflection of what you dislike. Let's say you are seeing unpleasant traits, like rudeness, puffed up ego, indifference. You wonder why you are still seeing these traits. You reflect these dispositions back to you so you can either correct in self or be more acceptable in others. I know that my reflection is a mirror reflecting back to me exactly my beliefs and feelings.

The first question that needs to be asked, however, is: "Why do I work for someone that treats me like this?" Another question should be: "Why am I showing myself this picture?" and "What is it that I have to correct within myself?" As I am dealing with a very unpredictable employer at the moment, I have to ask myself these questions when doubt arises.

The truth is, however, we are not here to just learn and experience life as we originally are taught in our studies. We are here to remember, from within, what we already are by nature. The experiences on this plane help remind us that we already possess and know the Truth. Now that I am grasping this fact I have to remember, that my and your true spiritual inheritance is already that of perfection and godliness. We are already complete.

January 14

God's face has changed in my eyes. He has become "IT", the great "I AM"- this wonderful and uplifting power that sustains all Life. God's light shines at all times - it is Goodness itself and it is Wisdom.

My concept of God

God does not look one way or another, God is in everything and everywhere. Have you ever thought about this concept called God?

Being born in conservative Austria, I was raised in the Roman Catholic Church and taught from an early age that there is a place called heaven and hell, and a God that needed to be feared. I was told that "he" knows everything and would punish me for all my wrong doings. I had to go and confess my sins (wow - how many sins can a little girl have?) Religion was a grade-school class that was taught by a priest. We studied the Bible and talked about Jesus and all of his suffering, supposedly because we were sinners. We are at fault for his demise.

What I of course didn't know at the time was that this Bible studying would set the cornerstone of my knowledge about the scriptures. It also would educate me in one of the most closed-minded, mystical, and unreasonable religions in this world.

I was about eleven years of age when I started to wonder: "If God hears and sees all that I do and think, it seems that he would know me. I am, however, the only one who knows exactly what I think, feel, and want. So this "'God and I' know the same things about me." He felt very close at the time and I also realized that there was a special connection between me and this God, which was supposed to be mysterious and intangible.

I couldn't understand at the time however, that he also acted like a monster. He killed people, even little children and my pet rabbit. He didn't listen very well to what I or anyone else had to say. Just look at all the people praying for different things and never receiving anything in return!

As years went by I distanced myself more and more from the physical aspects of going to church. However, I started a journey of self-discovery that landed me where I am today; teaching me a new perspective of the Almighty power.

January 15

Animals represent character traits in us: The Lion or Cat, courage; the Cow, patience (chewing over her food many times); the Fox, wisdom and quickness; the Dog, obedience and loyalty. All of them have character traits that we should aspire to. We can learn from them.

Looking at my animals

The joy my pets bring has been an important part of my life. As they are getting older - they are twelve and sixteen - I reminisce on the fact that they will eventually leave this plane or "die." I am even uncomfortable to say this word "die" or "death" when it comes down to my beloved pets. It feels difficult to write it down, but yet it is inevitable.

How do you grieve for a pet that has been your companion for so many years? Even the kids moved out and on with their lives. But those lovable creatures, totally depending on you, waiting for your affection, have been by your side every minute, every step of the way.

I speak dog and cat language by now, and I'm sure many of you do too. There is no need for many words. But there is a look, a wiggle of the tail or a consistent purr that speaks volumes. There are different tones in the bark depending on the people that are visiting. A knock at the door can trigger happy anticipation or a deep-felt growl.

I still think about Pete my fish, my tiny little Beta fish that lasted nearly three years. A long time in fish years! My Guinea pig Miss Daisy, the beautiful little piggy with the long Elvis hairdo that graced me with her companionship for over ten years. Several dogs, each with their own personality and temperaments; and of course Sabrina, queen of the cats - in attitude that is. I have loved them all, and I will continue to love them - and the ones that will follow in years to come.

There is a trust that most humans are incapable of. There is persistence in asking for a toy or chewy bone where most humans give up too soon. What about the patience they display when they sit at the door faithfully awaiting your return or ready to go for a walk, but daddy or mommy are dragging their feet? Loyalty, courage, companionship, comfort … and most of all there is their love; unconditional, unwavering love. Yes, we can learn from them. I wouldn't want to miss a minute of our time together.

January 16

This morning I received a comment regarding this online quote I posted:

Healing thought
"Fear of any illness intensifies the symptoms. Say aloud: I am well, I am perfect, I am health, I am safe"

A comment from a reader read as follows:

"I prefer Paul: I can do all things through Christ who strengthens me."

Even though this comment from this reader was not criticism, it made me think. What about people of strong religious faith, like this lady, that read Modern Thought Theories writings? How will they react to some of the progressive ideas and concepts?

New Age thinking is not new. It has been around for a while, and especially since the early 1980s thousands of books have been written and published on the subject. The awakening of the masses has begun. But I wanted to clarify this question in my own mind and the answer came to me very clearly: Modern Thought Theories is a community of positive, spiritual, right thinkers.

Criticism or judgmental opinions of any kind are not acceptable or welcome. Even though freedom of speech and honesty is a cornerstone of this theory, it is loving, kind, and honest speech we are looking for.

This is a safe place. A place where all races, genders, political views, and religious beliefs are loved, honored, and embraced. We look only at true Spirit, the Soul, and not the visible "image" that you reflect. This "image" is what we are striving to correct; not the Soul - your Soul is already perfect.

I have attempted in my book "*Better Living...Because you can!*" to clarify the "Ten Commandments" in a common sense way, so everyone can make practical use of it. To mystify the Bible quotes and the Scriptures is of no use or benefit to anyone. It seems to me that many people are afraid to explore these ancient writings.

Why?

What will happen if you question the writings in your attempt to understand them? Nothing! Why not live by them in a more modern, progressive, and open way, rather than in ignorance?

The only thing that can happen is that you will improve your understanding of the Truth. It will bring you closer to God - the real God, the one that isn't a far off figure, unreachable and mysterious. This God is within you, the great "I AM."

To finish my daily thought, I must say: "Let us be good, kind, loving, and pure. We have plenty of work to do, improving ourselves. Waste no time criticizing or judging others.

January 17

Happy MLK Day!

Today is a day to remember: "Love everyone, no matter what race, color, gender, or religion. We are all One, all connected and worthy of the best possible Life we can imagine. Universal Unity should be our goal."

This says it all...

January 18

Love is a motivator. Love, makes you do things - so do the things you love!

Gratefulness

Gratefulness is always high on my agenda and you will see it woven throughout this manuscript. It is not any different this early morning as I am contemplating on the meaning of the word. The dictionary describes "gratitude" as "the quality or feeling of being grateful or thankful." Gratitude is not the same as indebtedness. Being grateful to a friend that has done you a favor is connected to "give and take." The gratefulness we are talking about here comes from the heart, without expectations of anything in return. It is appreciating anything and everything that you come into touch with.

I recently read a short story by Louise L. Hay, the founder of Hay House Publishing. She wrote: "I have noticed that the Universe loves gratitude. ... The Universe is a generous and abundant giver and likes to be appreciated." Well said!

When we choose gratitude our sense of well-being improves. When we continue to be dissatisfied we spiral downwards. We go back to the unpleasant experience that dissatisfaction brings. Gratitude is your life jacket - it keeps you afloat!

Just like a captain on a ship, you need to stir your life away from dangerous situations. You have to steer in high waters, i.e. high thoughts, and not run into low ground. Set your intent in motion; focus on your goal. Keep your thinking above the surface.

Can you be grateful for what seems to be negative? Letting go of painful experiences seems like a daunting task. It seems difficult to be grateful for the negative encounters we experience. And we don't know at first that this is a healing process. Often, a shift occurs because we have outgrown the old. We no longer belong in this lower frequency. Say "Thank you" to the Universe. Be grateful for what's in store next. New doors are ready to be opened. After some time has passed, you will gain a new perspective and see the light. You will once again feel grateful for your life.

Exercise your appreciation of people and see the face of God in everyone. This means that no matter how the individual appears or behaves, the truth is, that he/she is the same in substance as you. We are all Souls, Mind, and Spirit - nothing more, nothing less.

Look for the blessings all around you. Get busy looking for and seeing the good that engulfs you. Brush aside anything and everything that is less than loving, kind, generous, and beautiful. I certainly will!

January 19

You simply are the "I AM" ... The "I AM" contains all there is.

Thoughts on my birthday

The time before my birthday is always a reflective one. Going from the holidays into the New Year and right into the "Birthday" mode always has a "contemplating about my life" agenda. This year was no different. However, I was less anxious about the change in years. As a matter of fact, it didn't faze me at all.

Instead, I was giving thanks for the health and youthful appearance in this stage of my life. My unbroken spirit and my creative quests are intact; my new adventures and goals ready to come to fruition. I am giving thanks to all of my fresh ideas flowing from my mind through this pen onto a piece of paper. I give thanks to the anticipation of a new career, a lifetime dream come true. Limitless experiences are still in front of me, not yet conceived.

All of this is also available to you, as you are the creator of everything that befalls you, every day of your life! Think about this!

Yes, this special day has arrived again, marking the passing of another year. But this time I will look at it differently. I will embrace the wisdom I've gained this year. I will treasure the patience I have acquired. I will cherish myself. The positive or negative energy we bring to Life returns to us. This makes sense when we realize, that Life itself is energy.

January 20

Negative thoughts are like weeds. They spread quickly if you don't tend to them. Remove all weeds in your mind, especially fear and doubt.

Sin is ignorance; our sins are only our mistakes

It's a daily task. We have to get rid of our sins, meaning we have to gain wisdom in order to eradicate ignorance, which is a lack of awareness of the Truth. Ignorance regarding our spiritual heritage is the greatest sin, and from this lie about who we are all sin originates. A friend of mine just recently reminded me what "sin" really means. It merely means "missing the goal," remember that!

Don't call yourself a sinner; you will invite sin to enter your mind. Only define yourself in the highest sense you can. Don't focus on your shortcomings. Focus on your good qualities so they can multiply. Dig up this innate perfection, which is already eternally yours.

Don't condemn yourself for the mistakes of yesterday. I know this can be difficult; I've done it many times. However, the time has come to see things for what they really are. An experience, a test - nothing more and nothing less!

Enjoy yourself now. You will make more mistakes. As a matter of fact, we will always – for eternity – have to work on gaining a better and more advanced sense of ourselves. Evolution, progress, striving to walk towards the light … yes, there is a light at the end of the tunnel of this so-called Earthly life.

As Sri Yukteswar, Guru of Paramhansa Yogananda, so beautifully said:

"A saint is a sinner who never gave up"

Never count your faults, they are improvements in waiting!

January 21

Part of this journey, writing this book, is to show you by practical and real-life example how "mind" works. Not only my mind and your mind, but mind itself. The Law of Cause and Effect, Karma, and all the other Universal

Laws work at all times. They do not differentiate or pick one over the other. They simply "are".

Do not shove unsolved ill feelings behind you. Deal with them as they come along. Not facing the issues presented to you will manifest in back problems. Your body will reflect the aches and pains of your mind.

So here is part one of the Story of Dexter, a fifty-two year old African-American man, dear to my heart. He is a good-hearted person and has a great sense of humor. I've known him for many years and have watched his ups and downs.

Back problems

Day ninety-four of Dexter's disability: Back problems, seemingly incurred by pulling heavy wires on a rooftop at work. He slightly tripped and tweaked his lower back. It wasn't the first time.

Dexter has been working for the same company for twenty-eight years. He knows his job; he likes his co-workers. But he has his own opinion about how the company should be run. He disagrees with management's decisions and strongly opposes their style. Sharp, critical thoughts are on his daily agenda, just as his lower back feels sharp pain, every time he moves.

Not being able to voice his thoughts openly, he has been pushing the issues "in the back," rather than facing them and working them out. Feeling like he can't speak up, his frustration piles up. Tense and inflamed muscles are his rewards.

Healing thoughts

He has a choice. You have choices. We all have choices.

43

As a teacher I have advised him that he needs to face the issues at work and don't just let them fester and simmer in his consciousness. His job is to deal with the challenges in a professional way and to try to understand management's position. After all, it's their responsibility. Of course he has the right to disagree; but without anger and emotions.

Having said that, here is another choice: Either you like what you do, or get out of there. You can leave. Staying with something you dislike so much will eventually cause physical ill effects on your body and mind. It makes you sick and therefore is not an option.

If you worry about your paycheck, and the pay is more important than your physical well-being, you better change your sense about your job, and change your feelings about your boss, co-workers, environment, or whatever it is that upsets you so much. Start loving what you choose to do. Start loving the people you encounter every day. Again, if you think you cannot like the situation or people, at least take the feelings and emotions out of the equation. Physical well-being, as well as mental well-being, requires an easy, calm, and loving mind. Ease, not dis-ease, is the key.

January 22

Balance is the key to life. Your day should consist of part work, part play, and part rest and part meaningful contemplation. Please take time to enjoy yourself. Treat yourself well!

Anger

I haven't been that angry in a long time. I'm not saying that I don't get mad sometimes, especially at my husband's notorious lateness, but really "angry?" Not so much anymore.

I'm in a temporary work situation right now, reporting to a boss which I react negatively to. I could easily say: "She is mean, unfair, impossible, and difficult. She makes me so angry." But the truth is, and this is hard to swallow, I allow this feeling to arise. I react negatively to someone's (in this case my boss') opinion. In reality, she cannot do anything to me.

What I ought to do is look in the mirror and ask: "Why does she irritate me? Why is her criticism getting under my skin? What, or who, does she remind me of?"

I have to dig - deep, deeper, and deeper, until it hurts even more. I have to peel off the layers of old hurts and disappointments, until my Soul feels raw. Exposed. Honest.

I know that I know: The Soul is pure and perfect. Years of wrong learning and experiences have muddled and distorted my sense. I have to get back to what is true and good. Feeling anger is not good - obviously!

The punishment of chronic anger is severe. The unreasonableness and stubbornness anger requires will leave you in constant pain and discomfort. It goes for all of us. We feel right, they are wrong. We feel justified to feel bad; we think we have the right to judge them. We think we have to punish them. It's brooding within us.

The reward for this intense hateful feeling, called anger, will get you stomach troubles, ulcers, indigestion, constipation, tightness in muscles, and stiffness in the neck. Headaches, migraines, and high blood pressure; and in longstanding chronic cases it will develop into cancerous tissues that will eat you from the inside out.

Guess what? We are the ones in the wrong by feeling angry or hateful. We need to let go. The best of all is that the Universe and its Laws will take care of the punishing. It will reward their dispositions in due time.

45

Be assured, no one escapes the Law. So let go! Stop! I am talking out loud to myself. Breathe!

No more dwelling on the misconduct and ridicule. I remind myself to look at the person's face and know that all is good; at least in my world for now. I feel compassion, not anger; compassion, for their misguided disposition. Just imagine the pain they must feel to have the need to lash out so harshly at you and me.

So I am grateful for being a good person. I am grateful for the picture that is revealing itself to me. I am grateful for the lesson.

January 23

Gratitude is the healing balm needed to improve health, wealth, and happiness. This sense of gratefulness is your key to all the pleasures of life.

I wrote this article for an inspirational magazine. I love writing these assignments, they make me really dig deep.

How a positive attitude affects your overall health and reduces stress

You might say that right thinking is a supplement to your healthier diet and your daily exercise. It is a way of improving your health faster and with more pleasure, and best of all it's free!

A positive attitude always looks at the glass half full and knows that even if complications arise there is always a light at the end of the tunnel. A positive mind trusts that the outcome will be good. It's like waking up in the morning and saying: Hello world, here I am! I am going to have a wonderful day, I will be kind and loving, I will do the best job possible, and I will treat myself well.

A positive attitude includes gratitude. Appreciation for all that you have rather than complaining about what you don't have. Loving the fact that you are given the chance of a new day, a new promise, and the opportunity to grow and evolve. Your purpose is to enjoy your life, not dread it or just get by day by day. Your purpose is to grow as a person, as a spiritual being. Your purpose is to be you. You are unique. No one is like you. We know that no one has the same finger prints, no one's eyes are the same, and no one even speaks like you!

How does this positive attitude affect your health? Well, it invigorates you, gives you a feeling of wellness, because being well is your natural state. When you love life you will be more active, you will strive for reaching your goals, and you will certainly attract people that are on your frequency. All of a sudden you will see the smiles on people's faces; you will be invited to more functions because everyone wants to be in your presence.

I'm sure you have entered a room before and the air was so thick you could cut it. The people were tense, and even though no one was speaking a word, you could tell that something unpleasant just happened. But you also can enter a room and have a wonderful feeling of calmness or comfort; like your home should feel for you.

We all live in a world that has its challenges, but a positive thinker sees those challenges as tests or opportunities. They show up so you can improve yourself, fix your mistakes, and find the right path to happiness. Just imagine, if we wouldn't experience any challenges we would never know if we are on the right path or not! Life is good, it is a spiritual state, it's an era of awakening towards the light, and life is certainly to be enjoyed!

January 24

By giving birth to a child, you are multiplying pure life, goodness. You are an instrument of the Universe, supporting Life's urge for multiplication. You are a vehicle, able to have life express more of itself, through you. You are blessed.

Sons and Daughters

Today is my son's birthday, and many wonderful memories are accompanied by some funny and some not so funny stories.

One of the memories include his Baptism, or lack of. My son's paternal grandparents, being Italian, of course wanted us to baptize the baby in the Roman Catholic Church. At the time, twenty-six years ago, I had been studying for a while and anything to do with church or its rituals was out of the question. I defied my mother-in-law, although she sincerely was concerned about the baby 'hanging in purgatory'. In her mind the child could not go to heaven, and it was my fault entirely. But I stood my ground, and still to this day, my son and I joke about it with compassion.

Today, my view has changed. Knowing that all, including churches and their accompanying by-laws, demands, and sometime unreasonable standpoints are only the reflection of someone's life choices, opinions, and has nothing to do with me or my world. However, at the time, still early in my studies, I was not giving in to my mother-in-law's constant pleading and hell preaching at the time.

In fall of this year he will be married to a lovely young woman, in church and all - the wishes of her parents. Knowing a lot more, and having unfolded Universal Love and compassion, I have no objection. I will be there at his side.

48

January 25

If Universal Love would be practiced even in a small degree by everyone, we would not see the suffering that we see on this plane today. We all would be charitable entities and the world would heal naturally.

Today I had to meet with a difficult business person regarding a project we are working on. He is known to have poor relationships with people due to his constant criticism and outspoken rudeness. He knows it all, he's done it all, and he is the master of this Universe ... well, in his eyes.

Practice Love

I've dealt with this man for nine months now and it hasn't been easy, even for someone like me who, well, "should know better." It truly has been a workout. Grant you, I know in my heart that he is a good person. He is only blocked-off in Spirit, he is lonely and misguided. I felt compassion, trying to stick with the Truth that all people are good by nature. Only their actions are what are at fault, not their Souls.

I decided to conduct an experiment with him. Sitting across the table, faintly smiling at him and looking right into his eyes, I repeated mentally: "I love you" over and over again. At first, as I was listening to him complain about everything on the planet, including some of my work, it was difficult, and my attempt to feel love for him felt superficial. But soon this feeling gave way to the Truth: Yes, I loved him as much as I love all people on this Earth. Not an emotional love or affection, but a love that was pure and good and all encompassing.

I could feel him softening, and at one point I saw him twinge, ever so slightly, as my loving thought hit him with a vengeance. He didn't know what happened, but he unconsciously adhered to my loving thought.

49

He might not change, and it's not my mission to prove him wrong - he's very set in his ways - but for a brief moment he listened to the voice of the Universe. And since his experience is also part of my experience, I am using this exercise to learn more, and become more aware of how to handle those types of situations. Try it!

I love you!

January 26

Watch your word habits. You say: "I can't" or "I'm not able to." What about "I'm sick of it" or "I'm disgusted?" We say phrases like this all the time without noticing the damage they do. They are lies. You can, you are able to, you are not sick of anything that is lovely and good, and you are certainly not disgusted with your life if you live it righteously. Think about this!

Watch your language, I'm watching mine...

Positive talk is just as important as positive thought. Maybe being from another country, having learned English as a second language makes me appreciate "words" more. I cherish the fact that I can express myself better in English than German; I love playing with words and I look up the meanings frequently.

Your words and thoughts influence you but also influence others. They are not just your thoughts and words; they are your tool to communicate with people and the Universe. Vice versa, the words and thoughts of others influence you the same way, if you allow it.

If you are living without awareness and you are on autopilot, you will be more susceptive to this influence. These negativities will infiltrate your mind. You will start believing what others think and accept their opinions.

You know how powerful a smile can be. It can light up a room, get you to snap out of a bad mood or just make you feel appreciated. You know how hurtful a snide remark can be. You, accepting it as true will cringe and ask "what have I done wrong?", "Is it me?" or just feel guilty or hurt instantly. Just think of the impact the spoken word of a doctor or world leader has. It can literally change your life. It can be life-giving or life-destroying.

Watch your word habits for one day, from morning to night, and see how many negative words and phrases you use. How many doubts and fears are verbalized over the course of the day? From a simple "I dread going to work" to a passionate outcry, "I hate this traffic," all of them are designed to get you in a negative frame of mind. We have to snap out of this negativity and embrace the positive only.

January 27

Life is an adventure. Every day something new emerges; something else to solve or handle. Don't forget to enjoy the process. Turn challenges into possibilities. Let common sense, kindness, and love guide you!

Today's mantra: What I focus on expands. I am unfolding and expanding as we speak into a more loving and caring person. My business is unfolding and expanding into a respected community of likeminded, good people with the same goals of self-improvement, self-knowledge and self-sufficiency.

You are also unfolding and expanding all the time and will do so forever and ever. This is the Law of Progress in Unfoldment. Be thankful for everything, even if your good is not visible yet. It will manifest in due time. Patience!

51

January 28

This society wants instant gratification. There is no "patience" present in this kind of attitude. Good things come in due time and they are certainly worth the wait.

How grateful I am...

Gratitude is an abundant, peace-filled energy field. It is a loving sense. We can see this sense in someone that is filled with appreciation for life. True gratitude is felt despite unpleasant circumstances. A grateful heart will feel this sense no matter what the situation and will always find something to be grateful for.

What growth do we encounter through the experience of pain? Can you become grateful for your pains? What do they teach us? Do you see the lesson? Say to yourself: "May the lesson be revealed to me. May I become stronger, and may I learn from this experience."

Our culture has little patience; it wants instant gratification. But the spiritual process is not instant. It requires diligent thought and reason. It is an ongoing, evolving process with many ups and downs. Let God, the Universe, Almighty intelligent power know that you are happy to be alive.

January 29

Forgiveness is the generosity of the heart!

Forgiveness

I'm thinking about forgiveness. Forgiveness is the key to solving many of our problems. We need to be the first one to forgive. Let's make the first step. It doesn't matter who is right or wrong. Even if we cringe at the idea to forgive the person that has offended us, or treated us unjustly, our duty is to take the first step to make amends.

Why?

Because it heals our un-easy sense, it betters our experience. This forgiving feeling will lift us up and bring us peace and utter calm. Forgiving will be giving us more love and health and it will allow us to eventually also forget the so-called hurt. It is about all of us individually after all, isn't it?

January 30

If you dig deep down and listen to yourself, you will realize that the answers are already there. They are available to you, ready for you to grasp and apply, at any given moment.

Today I decided to resign from the consulting job I so reluctantly took nine months ago and the bossy boss I talked about earlier. It was no longer "joyful" to work under this management with all of its restrictions and power struggles, and it had become a stressful situation, chore, rather than a pleasant job opportunity. I said "adios" to the employees and waved good bye to a young man, whose story I want to share with you.

The story of Lucas

I met Lucas, a twenty-something young man outside a tourist attraction in Hollywood not too long ago. He had a friendly smile, sporting a baseball cap and a T-shirt with the company logo and greeting the people passing by.

He had moved from Idaho a few months back to leave his past behind. Some anger problems and youthful indiscretions prompted him to look for a new environment and life. He came on a bus like so many young men and women before him.

He found a job as a dishwasher and met a young lady, very quiet and shy, but the two bonded. His new job as a greeter was a step up from his previous dishwashing duties. The couple ended up in an old RV outside town, only part time work for the girlfriend and twelve dollars an hour for him. Not enough income for this high priced city. On top of this poor living situation they found out that Elma was pregnant.

Not being able to pay even the minimum living costs, they ended up as a homeless couple. Expecting a child, they did not know where to turn to. The only option was a "flea-bitten' Hotel, close to his job, so he could walk to work. Elma was patiently sitting in the Hotel room waiting, getting closer to giving birth. Where will she go I wonder? How will she get cared for without health insurance? No Hospital will take you in without proper certification.
He didn't complain. He didn't fret. He was quiet, but you could see the despair in his eyes.

Fact: A new baby will be born in the US every seven seconds, that's around twelve thousand children per day.

We have to realize that, while millions of people go homeless each year, millions of condos and vacant units stay empty because they cannot be sold for a profit. The "National Alliance to End Homelessness" says: 'Homelessness is a complex problem, fraught with many associated challenges and variables. But for all of its complications, the solution to homelessness is surprisingly simple – housing."

As of today Lucas and Elma are still waiting for the baby to be born. I will let you know when the day arrives.

January 31

Repeat after me: My life is full of Love. I love who I am. I love my life. I am Love.

My first day off and I am looking forward to a little meditation and some serious contemplation.

Meditation

Many people think that meditation has to be done in a certain place, position or go through a specific ritual. It seems sacred and spiritual but also difficult to achieve.

Not at all! Meditation means to take some quiet time to spend with your Self, focusing on your thoughts and feelings. It means to listen to yourself carefully and get in touch with your gut feelings, your instincts. You can do this anywhere and anytime.

I usually just sit in my favorite armchair (love that thing) and look out the patio doors into my garden. All noise, TV, radio is turned off. I make sure I am alone as I will hear many different noises. Until you train yourself to tune them out, they will cause distraction. Tune into yourself!

To get focused, start with a subject you want to explore. A certain feeling you want to appreciate or correct. Have a specific topic in mind that you want to get clear about. Then let yourself wander and feel. You can do this exercise little by little. Every time you can add a few minutes and soon you will not wander off the subject, but wander in this great mind of yours that already has the answers for you.

Chapter 2: Your Five Senses

February 1

Humility translates into "grounded" and "from the Earth" ... what a wonderful character trait. Be humble in your dealings with the Universe, be grounded in Understanding and embrace the Earth with Love.

What about Humility?

When you think about it, true humility is leaving the ego behind. As humble beings we look for the good and do not adhere to what ego dictates. Being humble, helpful, and kind, and serving the Universe and its inhabitants is true humility.

I thought the following examples of the meaning of humility were interesting:

Webster: Webster defines humility as the quality or state of being humble; and as the quality of being modest and respectful.

Wikipedia: The term "humility" comes from the Latin word *humilitas*, a noun related to the adjective *humilis*, which may be translated as "humble,", but also as "grounded," "from the Earth," or "low," since it derives from *humus* (Earth).

Christianity: Humility is defined as "A quality by which a person considering his own defects has a humble opinion of himself and willingly submits himself to God and to others for God's sake." St. Bernard defines it as "A virtue by which a man knowing himself as he truly is abases himself." Jesus Christ is the ultimate definition of Humility.

Buddhism: In Buddhism, humility is equivalent to a concern of how to be liberated from the sufferings of life and the vexations of the human mind. The ultimate aim is to achieve a state of enlightenment through meditation and other spiritual practices.

Hinduism: In order to practice humility and to get in touch with your true self, whether you call that God, Brahman, etc., one has to kill the ego.

In my experience, mingling with so-called important or famous people has been one of the more difficult exercises. I believe that all people are equal. I certainly know that no one's soul is superior or better than anyone else's. No one is superior or better than you or I - not even Mother Theresa.

Yes, there are some people that act better or act worse. The ones that act better give more, they are kinder, more loving, and generous and so forth, and they devote more time to the search for the Truth. The essence, however, of each person is the same. It is pure spirit, or mind substance.

What we do with this mind substance, since we have the ability to think, reason, and most of all make choices, is something else. Humility is a virtue, but don't mistake humility with low self-esteem.

February 2

Many times we have tough decisions to make. We are not certain if we are right or wrong. Listen to yourself. Is it good for you and all concerned? Is it lovely and kind? Is it helping your progress in unfoldment? If the answer is no, you know what to do. Be good to yourself!

February 3

Talk about what's good today, and limit all gossip and negative conversations. Catch yourself when you want to chime in. Hear yourself speak.

Kindness

Today I want to talk about kindness and compassion. In a world that runs mostly in survival mode, not losing these important character traits is of utmost important. Here is a question a member of a business networking group asked recently in open forum.

Is being nice a factor for success in business?

This was an interesting thought and even though it seems that in today's world everyone is out to challenge you, take from you, overpower you, and leave you behind, I believe that kindness still exists. Being "nice" doesn't just go for your personal life. It applies in all walks of life, including business. Being nice is more than being cordial. It includes a sincerity of loving thoughts, a compassion for all situations, and a harmonious temperament of the individual. Kindness is certainly a virtue, and a very powerful one at that.

You can be strong without intimidating others. You can show love without appearing weak.

Kindness goes a long way. How difficult is it to say "thank you," or compliment someone on their good work. A kind and loving gesture will make someone's day; you are sowing the seeds of more good and love. You are paving the way to a better world!

February 4

Fear of any illness intensifies the symptoms. Say aloud: I am well, I am perfect, I am health, and I am safe.

Thoughts on Healing

As Louise L. Hay states it, "Releasing resentment will even heal cancer." The little blue book "Heal Your Body" was written by her in the early 1980s and some parts were restated in the book "You can heal your Life" published in 1999 and reprinted as recently as 2011. She addresses the Mind/Thought/Body connection as to healing. Louise L. Hays was one of the early metaphysical teachers who were brave enough to actually put the discoveries into public print.

In the metaphysical field this discovery of mental health, cause and effect, is not new. My personal understanding, beliefs, and what I teach my students about mental healing, sickness and health, and this mind-body connection, was discovered by William W. Walter in the early 1900s. He wrote, but not published, the "Metaphysical Diagnosis."

This work explains in detail not only the health connection of the mind and the body, but it also correlates all symptoms to a specific body part. Each bodily organ represents a certain quality of mind. His work shows how your understanding of this Mind/Body connection can prevent disease in the first place if your thoughts and beliefs change to a better mind-model. In this extensive volume he addresses in detail all parts of the body and the effects our wrong and uneasy thoughts have. He also shows us how our right and good thoughts will heal all sickness and dispositions. Unfortunately, the world was not ready to accept this theory at the time of his discovery.

I will go deeper into the explanations as to what causes illness and diseases. I will make every effort to clarify in my own words the meaning during this year's diary. I hope the world is ready for some of it now. Using my friend Dexter as an example, he is one of the characters that will serve as an illustration on how each and everyone's mind works.

Dexter's progress ... or not?

Dexter talked to his counselor several times about his feelings toward his work environment. But no matter how it was explained to him, he didn't want to let go of his anger. He felt that he was right and they were wrong.

Instead of letting go and focusing on his recovery, healing his back injury, he went to meet up with his work buddies every day at lunch time. He was still on disability, but he wanted to be filled in on the happenings and the misery at the work place. He wanted to hear the gossip and the gripes, and commiserate with his peers. They met daily at a local bar, drinking beer and focusing on the wrong.

No progress was made, no change in his thinking and attitude occurred. Even his wife tried to reason with him several times, telling him that his behavior was not appropriate for someone on disability. He needed to focus on healing and getting better, so that he could return to work. Dexter shrugged her off, saying: "It's a man thing ... that's what the boys do."

One Friday, after work, his wife came home to find him in agony. He had climbed up a ladder in an attempt to trim a tree, trying to surprise her. Instead, reaching for the last small branch, he overextended and fell six feet onto the rocky ground. Lucky to be alive, having missed a large rock and a metal bench, he broke a rib in three places and was bedbound. He was in excruciating pain and barely could move. He needed help with everything; even the smallest tasks were too painful. And of course, he couldn't continue his behavior.

Do you see the point?

Synchronicity, the Universe's perfect plan, had shown him the way. Granted, a very painful way. However, the lesson presented shows you that we must listen, learn, and do what's right. His bouts with alcoholism were addressed at the same time. It literally was a "sobering up" in all aspects of his life.

As I am writing this, Dexter is still very much in pain and I will report on his progress and recovery as we go through the chapters.

February 5

My writing assignment is waiting. Large cup of coffee, still dark and quiet in this early morning hour, I mosey on into my office and accomplish the task at hand.

Discover the Female Element

What is the difference in the mental in regards to men and women? Why are we females seemingly unique? Why do we think and react differently, what are our issues, and what are our strengths? Better yet, what makes us so resilient and strong?

Many studies suggest, and psychologists have proven, that women are better communicators, nurturers, and caretakers. Men (and of course there are exceptions) mostly rule with their intellect, they reason with fewer emotions, and are more controlled in many situations. However, this is not a psychology paper or medical research study. This is a purely metaphysical look at our differences in the mental; an examination of the female mind.

What does this mean to the metaphysician? How does this seeming diversity relate to our thoughts and our daily experiences?

Consciousness consists of the male and the female element. When used in mind the elements are also called "reason" and "feeling". The male element or reasoning ability does the analytical chores, while the female element or feeling ability does the nurturing, loving, and reacts emotionally. We, both men and women, are comprised of both elements. We are male and female; however, we express what we have "more off." I am a woman because I have more female present, and so forth.

An excerpt of my book *"Better Living...Because You Can!"* will explain the connection in a more traditional way. The chapter is called: "What Does Marriage Represent in the Mental?" The concept of marriage in the mental represents the blending together of the male and female elements in mind. This is not a physical action, but a mental one.

It takes the male and the female elements, knowing and feeling, to create anything. What is made, or appears in the visible world, was conceived in the mental, nurtured by good thoughts, and born through your conclusion or conviction, which is a feeling of certainty. It is an extension of your consciousness.

The birth of a child is the visible expression of this mental process. The visible symbol of Earthly marriage is the coming together of a man and woman to create more life. As we explored earlier, we are all composed of the male and female elements. We are a complete whole, and we give birth to more wholeness. We are multiplying life into its visible form. The focal point of our journey is to unfold and gain an understanding of the truth of life and how the creation or birth process works. All else will fall into place naturally.

So how does the male and female element affect our daily lives?

Our thoughts are the creators of our experiences. We can think as many good and right thoughts as we want to, but unless we feel these thoughts as true, we will not manifest our desires. Feeling is the mother of all creation. Giving birth does not only mean giving birth to children to replenish the Earth, it means giving birth to ideas and everything that exists in our wonderful realm. Everything you see is a specific idea and was conceived by a thinker. It was not only conceived, but also nurtured and carried in mind until it was time for the idea to be born and manifested into this world. It could only be born if a feeling of certainty - the conviction that "it is so" - was reached. This full understanding of the specific idea brought forth the experience, or manifestation.

What makes a woman strong?

I'd like to point out why being the mother or feeling/female element is most important. Our children are actually thought children or ideas, as mentioned earlier. Children born reflect life's urge to express more of itself – which could not be done without the feeling/female element. The idea of birth would be trapped, just sitting there as an idea in mind conceived by reason or the male element.

The reflection or picture in the material world shows forth as the male being equipped, yet trapped, with all if his potential. However, he would not be able to produce more life of his own. Reason, thoughts, potential ... the male comes first, the feeling of certainty or conception and the creation of all, including more life, comes second. This process clearly shows that life consists of both, male and female –elements – as neither could produce without the other.

A baby's sex is determined at the point of conception, depending on the dominant mental element present. This is a progressive idea and most likely will meet with some resistance. But I have observed this concept over many years. When I first read about this discovery I was pregnant myself and I was not surprised that we produced a son. The theory is that if the parents are more on the analytical side they conceive a boy child, but if the parents imbue more feelings, the child conceived is most likely a girl. This is also the reason that most "planned" children are male and most surprises, conceived with lots of emotions, are females. Again, these are metaphysical theories and not backed up with medical studies.

A word of advice and loving guidance

God, Universal Intelligence, created all things from within. They are not created from nor are they of the material world. All creatures and things stem from this godly source and are projected out into the visible world. However, the substance of you, us, and all things remain of Universal Intelligence and are of mental origin.

In my world, there is only me and my sense of me. In your world, there is only you and your sense of you. No one knows how you feel and what you think deep down in your heart, not even your family or closest friends. Your feelings, emotions, and thoughts are your own; they are your secret.

Therefore I ask of you: Don't see yourself as being a man or woman. Don't buy into being black or white, or whatever color your skin exhibits. Do not think that your sexual orientation is who you are. Do not use the country of your birth as your identity. All of these are only perceptions. They label you to act one way or another. See yourself as a mentality, a soul. Free yourself of the sense of racial, cultural, and sexual limitation. Act as the free Spirit you are. Your soul does not have a specific color or race; it is not only a man or a woman. It contains ALL.

February 6

Use your words wisely. Speak with from your heart.

The spoken Word and your verbal ID

I just had an epiphany and my thoughts are racing. It occurred to me, reading as I usually do in the early morning hours, that if I take any book and rewrite it in my own words it would sound and feel differently. It would reflect a different sense; my own personal sense.

Not only is our DNA different, and our fingerprints, but also our communications style, word usage, and individual sense varies from each other. There is no one alike. The individual sense we put into writing a letter, blog, or manuscript can be felt by the reader.

Out of billions of people, I, as well as you, have a specific style of the spoken word, our "verbal ID." My sense, my communication ability is in my mind. This thought ability can also reach out and touch another, and therefore you can also heal by mental means alone.

The English language is so wonderful, expressive, and full of word choices. Even though it is my second language, with German being my first, I communicate much easier in English, verbally and in writing. The German language has less vocabulary and is a more straightforward, harsher language. It is black and white. No beating around the bush, no softening of the tone. I am very grateful for having the English language.

February 7

No matter where you came from, what your background is, or who your parents are – it's up to you, what you make out of your life. You are the maker of your own destiny, not some other circumstance or cause.

Complaining

Our journey from our worldly ego sense to Spirit is important; it's what you are doing right now, and it's what you will do for the rest of your life. Ego has needs, constant wants, and expectations. Spirit only wants what is naturally good and loving; not more, not less - only the discovery of its inherent perfection and goodness.

Think of the sun for example. Some complain it's too hot, it'll burn your skin, and it will cause cancer. Yet the sun is the core, life sustaining, and source of existence. Like water, we could not exist without the sun. Cherish and embrace it. Give it thanks and be grateful for the warmth it provides.

Some groan about the rain, yet we couldn't live without the water it provides to nurture all plant life and creatures, including humanity. Cherish the water. Do not be wasteful and careless with its resources. Cherish the Earth and all the goods it provides.

Complaining about anything only focuses your mind's attention on what's missing. It shows us a glass half empty, instead of half full. I first was tempted to say: "There isn't anything you can do with the empty side of the glass," but a wise friend of mine pointed out that even the empty side of the glass contains air, which is one of our life sources. And I just read about a great third option: "What about a refill?" Yes, let's refill the glass of life with love, gratitude and forgiveness when it looks half empty!

Life is always full - not empty. It is full of opportunities, ideas, and the capacity of fulfilling your dreams. Start seeing the good and full life only! Thank you Mother Earth!

February 8

The truth is that you are not labeled this or that, not Mr. VP or Mrs. Superwoman. The fact is that you simply are, the "I AM," nothing more, nothing less. "I AM" contains all there is.

Fear and its role as an actor

How is Dexter doing? Dexter's pain intensified and even the hardcore pills prescribed didn't do their job for long. I could see the fear in his face and so I suggested going back to the hospital for more x-rays. Dexter chose a different facility, one he was more familiar with and in which he trusted the doctors and staff. The doctor on staff promised to call with the results. In the meantime I continued with my silent treatment, sending him lots of healing thoughts of perfection and wholesomeness.

His Spirit needed to remember that he was already well. Sickness is only a self-induced shadow. Shadows are not real. They are reflections. When you take away the cause, the shadow will disappear. So Dexter went on to get another diagnosis and the x-ray revealed a shadow over his left lung and heart. Dooms Day had arrived!

He called and we talked, all the while his imagination went to the worst possible outcome. At the same time I held in mind perfection as the principle thing and kept emotions as far away as possible.

A couple of hours later the radiologist phoned with news he wanted to share immediately. The shadow was nothing more than a touch of pneumonia, easily healed with the proper dose of medication. The injured ribs were also healing nicely, and the bruising incurred by the fall had started to vanish.

Hearing these positive findings, and explained to Dexter in an uplifting and encouraging tone of voice, made all the difference in the world. He would live! The pain lessened within minutes. It was remarkable to see that this great bully of fear, which is always the main culprit in most cases of pain, had lost its grip. That night he needed only half of his meds and he slept comfortably, able to get in and out of bed without assistance. Half of the battle was won.

Now, he has to start working on his change of behavior, and attitude, towards the real issues. The underlying wrong, habitual thoughts that caused the injuries and miseries in the first place need attention and correction. The real work is still in front of him.

February 9

Always be honest with yourself and with others. Honesty is the most important part in your search for truth and self-improvement.

It is important for you to understand that each of the chapters, days, in this book are my thoughts. These are the topics I think about, either when I first wake up or what comes my way during the day. It's my journal, my day to day encounters - my life. Yes, there is also cooking, cleaning, yard work, and the laundry, but the bulk of the day is spent with thinking, writing, and teaching.

You have your own life; your own thoughts and daily dealings. Do you observe these happenings? Do you analyze and dissect these thoughts? Do you see the improvements that need to be made? Why don't you start writing your own thoughts down? Why not see what's in your heart?

You have to start somewhere

If this is something that interests you and if you're not sure where to start with your thought improvements, make a list. Start with the easier corrections. Doing so will give you the confidence to keep on working towards your goal. And point out the good you have already accomplished - don't forget to love yourself.

In this exercise, however, we are talking about improvement of thought habits. For example, a longstanding resentment might take some time and some diligent analysis. An ungrateful spontaneous notion, however, can be corrected more quickly. Moods are established over time, so they will require repetition of an improved attitude. A careless or thoughtless behavior will improve if pointed out to you, accepted by you, and if you have the desire to change your part.

In my case, many years back, I was told that I come across firm and stern. Many of my employees were scared of me, as my manager informed me. I was shocked and surprised at this discovery, as my true "inside'" was neither firm, stern, nor scary.

However, this provided the opportunity to take a good look at my demeanor. I found that my extreme sense of responsibility to the company and my work habits, coupled with my German accent – and my usage of the English language that had not been refined yet – reflected to others as stern and inflexible.

I had to accept this perception in order to correct myself without any emotions or hurt feelings. I had to make a conscious effort to soften my demeanor. I wanted to reflect the goodhearted and kind person I am. It took some time to fully develop this quality, but I soon found out that you can be strong without intimidating others. You can show love without appearing weak. My personality became more openly caring, kinder, and more all-inclusive!

February 10

God looks at you without judgment or favoritism. He does not punish or reward. He only acts according to Universal Law.

I'm not afraid to call him God.

For many years, when I realized God wasn't an old man with a beard sitting on a gold throne way up in the sky, I wasn't sure what to call him. Could I even call him a "him?" It became a serious question. It might be a "she." What if it was an "it.? I knew there was a power - a source of strength and wisdom - but it took time and sincere studying to find the answers.

Today I can speak the word "God" easily and without discomfort. I know what it means. I associate myself with "IT," my father, my mother, my creator, and my source.

Born of "IT," I have to be "IT." I am a child of God, as you are also the children of this God substance, perfect and good. Let's do "IT" justice by living righteously and by spreading this goodness to every corner of this wonderful planet Earth.

February 11

When you read this book, I want you to remember:

I am not asking you to blindly believe. I am asking you to keep an open mind, test the principles for yourself, and come to your own conclusions. I am asking you to focus on yourself, and improve your thoughts one at a time. Your results will speak for themselves.

Here is another article I wrote not too long ago on the idea of ego, which we all know can be a great deterrent in the search for truth.

Let Go of E-Go!

Your self-image, what and who you think you are, including your personal appearance, is only a reflection of your ego. It is not your true self. Your true self is Spirit. It is formless, without race, color, and gender. You are "all of this;" not just one thing or another.

Ego constantly wants approval. Ego lives in fear and doubt. It looks outside of itself and believes what the perceptive sense tells it. It doesn't question or reason about Truth, it only follows what it perceives and what it thinks it wants. Always more and more, nothing is ever enough. Ego also needs control. It is like a shadow that lurks over your shoulder and whispers in your ear. It is that little negative voice that accompanies you wherever you go and whatever you do. "I have to be better, bigger, and more beautiful" it cries. "I need to have more money and more power!"

Ego is a prison, built by you over years of neglecting your Soul. You have allowed the walls of ego to encase you and you didn't question its validity. How do we escape? Where is the key? How can we unlock this harmony destroyer?

Take a look at your wants and desires. Are they ego based? Is status important to you? Do you want more and more of material goods without spending time on your mental well-being? Sincere honesty is important to unlock your internal chamber of your subconscious. It's not wrong to have everything you need and live a life of abundance. You are born to enjoy the goods of the Universe. You are meant to be a harmonious, peaceful, and loving spiritual entity.

What is wrong is the constant focus on Earthly material goals and goods and the neglecting of your Soul. To the "true you," your spiritual awakening is of utmost importance. It is not important what your neighbor thinks - or anyone else for that matter. It is important what you think and how you feel! Are you truly happy and fulfilled? Are you as good as you can be and as loving as you could be? Do you care about others and do you see your connection to all living things?

You are neither beneath nor above anyone. You just are. You don't have to defend your viewpoints to anyone. You don't have to make excuses or be apologetic for not fitting into the mold of society. All you have to do is act good, do good, and think good – at all times. Your Soul is the source of all Universal qualities. Peace, harmony, love, creativity, happiness – all of these are natural and given freely to you. They are available for the taking.

The world of ego is bound by time, place, status, stress, and all Earthly limitations. It is destined to create fear. It is self-centered and self-absorbed. It is shallow and destructive, clingy and demanding.

We have to go beyond the ego and allow the light of eternal peace and love to shine upon us! We have to recondition our subconscious mind with truth and guard our conscious mind from false impressions.

So be still, and remember: Let Go of E-Go!

February 12

During the process of writing this manuscript I thought it would be very helpful to tie real-life stories and characters into the text. You have already met Dexter. Please meet Ilene Waters, a woman who has battled weight issues all of her life.

Don't give up so easily. Stick with it. Whatever it is you want: be determined, focused and patient.

72

Your desire already exists in the next dimension. You only have to bring it into your NOW experience.

The Creation of Ilene Waters

It's all perception. Anything you see, including people, are made up images, stemming from Mind. You can create a new persona anytime you want to.

Actors are a good example. They slip into different roles as easily as into a new outfit. Then they identify themselves with that persona and" become" them. It's called character acting. Unfortunately the fine line between their real ID and the new persona sometimes becomes blurred. This next story of recreating a new image for yourself will inspire you.

Ilene, a woman in her mid-fifties, took a good look at herself and her life, and decided it was time to recreate her image. She had been battling her weight problem all of her life. Her ups and downs, ranged between twenty to fifty lbs., not just a couple here and there, as for many of us. She is an attractive woman, very smart, and a sweetheart of a Soul, but she carries everyone's load - literally. We can all relate to this. We've all had our doubts and fears about aging without fulfilling our dreams and not living to our full potential. We fear that through this lack of self-fulfillment we miss out on Life in general.

She has contributed her tale in her own words and we will follow her story throughout the year.

Weighting for Change

"I've spent the better part of my adult life living in extremes – living with a sense of urgency while waiting for change. It's been an eternal moment of going nowhere, or so it seems many times. I'm tired of it. And I know much of it has to do with the weight I carry

73

around – emotionally and physically. Losing the weight will free me – I get that. It's the dieting that holds me back.

Denying myself whatever it is I'm lacking. I'm trying to figure out all my lacks and fill them with purposeful intentions. Maybe then I will be free to step into a new moment. I just looked up the word "diet" in my 1913 Webster's Dictionary. The first definition of diet reads "Course of living or nourishment." I like their old school take on it. It's right on. And it occurs to me that my diet has never really been on a directed course of anything substantial enough to nourish my life's purpose, whatever that is. I've stumbled and rambled on so many paths to nowhere that, when I was reading the song title of one of George Harrison's tunes on his last record called "All Roads Lead to Here" I laughed at the irony. Yeah, here is my dumping ground alright. Fifty-four years and I'm right at the site called my life.

I started dieting when I was a teenager in the '70s. I was probably 150 pounds when most my girlfriends were 110. Looking back at those pictures I think I looked pretty good – I always thought I was a pretty girl – but I was always the "eternal best friend" – never the main event. It's a role I grew into and learned to perfect – disarmingly humorous charm coupled with being the "smart one." Yeah, I was fat, but two out of three wasn't bad. I was always popular so it worked for me. In my twenties, aside from the extreme partying I partook in from that decade of decadence and debauchery, I pretty much maintained a weight of 215 or so. It scared me when I first hovered over that 200 mark. I recall someone once telling me that once you passed over that edge, there was no turning back.

I visited many a diet doctor and got a handful of pills to curb my appetite. I was working a switchboard in a record store and recall pacing nonstop around my work area square in the middle of the store like a caged panther. Anything set me off and I stayed in a perpetual state of uneasiness and aggression. I joined gyms and, after a hefty workout with my girlfriends, went to lunch or dinner and pigged out and then would go to Swenson's ice cream and reward myself with a huge towered dripped in hot chocolate sundae sauce.

I always thought I'd get married and have three kids. I never really had a plan for it. I just thought it "would happen" because that was the way life worked. You know that saying "Life Happens." That's been my mantra. I thought some force called "Life" made stuff happen and I reaped the rewards. I didn't understand fully that the "I" of my life was always in control, for better or worse. Many folks never get this. I'm glad it finally clicked with me. So no kids, no real relationship, and fighting the battle of the bulge...

And so her story began...

February 13

A dream is not elusive or just imagination. It is a solid goal, achievable through your desire, determination and want.

I will play and think about my dreams all day today. I will pamper myself, by allowing myself the time to visualize, idealize, and outline my biggest desires. Today will be a fun-filled day!

February 14

Take time to enjoy yourself. Treat yourself well. Be your best friend.

More thoughts on the mind-body connection

How many of you are familiar with the concept of the mind-body connection when it comes to health? Most of you probably will agree that positive thinking works and affects our daily life, but what about health?

First of all, we have to understand that our thoughts are influenced by our belief systems. Those belief systems in turn affect our attitudes, our emotions, behaviors, and habits such as hurry and worry, which are all connected within us through mental energy and our own individual frequency.

And because we are all individuals and unique, our thought convictions and beliefs are reflected onto our bodies. The connection to having a healthy body starts with understanding and managing our thoughts first. It is like doing a mental housecleaning, then going on a mental diet, and retraining ourselves with new thought habits – all at once. It all starts in the mental, not the physical.

I will give some examples about the obvious ones like being angry. Being angry always affects the stomach. If it's an occasional outburst of anger it might just be some stomach acids, maybe an uptight feeling in that area or a loss of appetite. But if you are habitually angry, hot tempered, or easily irked, your stomach problems will show habitual illnesses such as irregular bowl movements, ulcers, or even stomach cancer.

Think about the number one disease in the USA today, called stress. Again, the symptoms start slowly with headaches, nervousness, later migraines or a nervous breakdown, leading into more and more severe illnesses when not addressed. Now you can swallow every pill there is and it will temporarily relive the pain, but what after? You have to go to the root of the problem. You have to address the real issue.

In the mid-'80s, working for a large corporation, I had what you could call a "mean" boss. This lady was demeaning and demanding and I felt she really didn't know what she was talking about. That was my judgment call and my first mistake. I was upset every day and started to dread going to work, even though I loved my job. After a few weeks I developed a rash in my face. Right there for everyone to see. It was severe and wouldn't yield to any medications. So the doctor put me on stress leave for three weeks. Even though the rash subsided somewhat it didn't go away. I knew I had to go back to the same situation and I wasn't looking forward to it. But then a miracle happened only a couple of weeks after I had returned to work. The woman was let go and I was healed within a couple of days. Can you imagine?

Another example of the mind-body connection was reflected in my intense desire to get a promotion. I had worked for the company for over fifteen years and was overlooked several times when it came to more money or a better title. My male counterparts would always win out. I started to stress and get resentful. I felt I deserved the advancement.

The migraines I developed weren't a pretty picture and I suffered immensely. For three years I continued to feel this way and no pill would solve the issue.

However, the day I finally was put in charge of my area and I received what I thought I deserved, my migraines subsided. In a short period of time they totally disappeared. Needless to say, that with my newly gained understanding of the workings of the mind, I never head a migraine or a headache again. This was nearly twenty years ago and I am so grateful that I can see the benefits of right thinking. We are so wrapped up in our daily lives that we don't realize how much mental clutter we accumulate and how many wrong and painful thoughts we think every day. So lift the negative expectations and look for the good only, because after all, you deserve a better life worth living!

February 15

The world is better because of you. It wouldn't be complete without you, or any one of us. You are part of the Universal puzzle.

Think before you criticize

I said to my husband this morning, finding him in the kitchen making breakfast: "Why are you using this pan for the bacon. It's too small. You know better." Instead of appreciating the fact that he was trying to surprise me with a meal, I criticized his choice of cooking utensil. I expected him to do what I would have done.

What was it to me? Did it make a difference? Of course not!

We constantly criticize and judge others, they are not good enough, and it's not the way we would do it. Habitual comments of criticism are so subtle; we don't notice them often. We just are in the habit of blurting them out. I am sure everyone has their own little story...

February 16

Intelligence, not intellectuality, is the key. It's not what you know from an Earthly perspective. It's what you intuitively know, and understand, drawn from your internal intelligence that counts.

Everything happens in perfect order. In my case, when I'm done with a specific experience, let's say writing this book, I will be able to look back and see this point clearly. The picture will show that it was the right goal, at the right time, falling into place and into the greater picture. It will be a stepping stone to what's yet to come.

At dinner, with friends last night, I was asked, "How can you think about all those things you write about? You post new quotes every day. You write teaching materials and articles frequently. Where do those ideas and thoughts come from?" The answer is I don't have to think and struggle. It just flows easily and effortlessly from within. It's as if an inner voice dictates the words. I already know what I want to say and write about. It feels like a message that needs to be broadcast to the world, an internal dialogue - ready to be externalized.

See, all there is to know already exists. We just have to remember. Once you tap into this vast ocean of Truth and Knowledge it comes out effortlessly and endlessly. This is only the tip of the iceberg for me. I only have just begun to consciously recognize this "iceberg" of information and potential.

There is no specific plan in my writing, no pre-set structure. No ulterior motive or intent. There is only the purpose of positive, life changing, and helpful information. A sharing of Truth and Love, you might say. I'm taking you on this journey with me. Let's travel!

February 17

Regarding the Hereafter: All you can take with you are your values, your character, and the knowledge you have unfolded at the time of your passing, or transition to the next dimension. Your Earthly belongings will be nothing more than a dream.

Thoughts on reincarnation

One of my very good friends has been asking me questions about reincarnations, revealing that he tends to believe in this theory. His letter read:

"Where are you on the subject of reincarnation? We touched on the subject briefly one time. It just seems to me that reincarnation explains so many things in our world, not the least of which is the difference in people's

79

spiritual awareness or willingness to be open to spiritual thought. Our physical existence on this planet is quite short at this time in Earth's history. If one had hundreds of years, which according to the Bible and other texts was our life span in a different era, it would allow one the time and experience to understand and reach spiritual enlightenment. Without a lengthy life span, reincarnation seems the only explanation of how some can be spiritually aware to varying degrees while others can't even grasp awareness beyond what they see as our physical reality. Even the Bible refers to a belief by the Jews during Christ's time of reincarnation. Anyway, I am just curious about your current thoughts on the subject."

"Dear Virgil,

In the last couple of months several articles and reading materials have appeared in front of me, in my metaphysical research, suggesting I should look into the subject more closely. And so I did. However, I have not come to a sound conclusion at this point. There are still so many open questions in my mind.

I agree that the time on Earth seems limited, but since life is endless it stands to reason that this life continues in other "places," dimensions, or whatever we call this "next" state of being. I think reincarnation on this Earth is not necessary. However, I'm not ruling it out, as I had several experiences that suggested I have been here before.

We all know about sensing a familiarity with someone we just met, or remembering a place that we've never been to. I, for one, have been drawn to the Western History movies and Indian legends; even though I have never experienced any of those places and obviously am born one-hundred years too late, not to mention on a different continent.

We can read in the scriptures that people lived hundreds of years, and even though science has been theorizing that we have the potential to live up to 180 years, I'm not sure if we can take these biblical statements literally, or if it is only a metaphor for something more important. Here are some reasons why I am still questioning this theory even though many circumstances point in the direction of reincarnation.

Why would you want to come back to a plane that wasn't that great in the first place? Do you think you are forced to return? You are a Soul, part of the Almighty power; you would be in charge - even regarding the return to Earth.

I have read in my eastern studies that we, our Souls, have a choice and actually choose to come back over and over again. With each return we learn (and remember) more and different things, until we decide to move on to a higher plane; state of being. This seems possible. However, why would it be necessary for us to forget our past experiences and be born again as infants - starting from the same point of unfoldment? It doesn't make sense to me. So, if I am a somewhat metaphysically educated individual, working on my unfoldment and on my way to a higher dimension - why start from scratch? I understand that the soul has to evolve, as it is a Universal Law, but why on this plane when we have limitless dimensions to work with?

I understand these concepts could apply to people that haven't had a chance in this life. Deaths of small children, people that just live without knowing the true goal in life and other persons that do not contribute to this ultimate goal of bliss. Maybe they need another awakening. But, someone who has studied, learned, and gained even a small amount of understanding shouldn't have to go over it again and again; instead they should be able to see 'more light.' Of course, this is just my humble opinion!"

Still so much to ponder and think about, but then that's what's so fascinating about this life!

And so I went on to give this subject serious thought and attention. I'm sure you'll hear much more about it before the year is over.

February 18

There is a fine line between being focused or obsessed, being relaxed or lazy. It is a balanced drive, just right, that's needed to achieve what you set out to accomplish, and finish what you have started. Stay on course!

Desires and Dreams - dream big and expect it to happen!

Whatever you put after the "I" becomes the command to the Universe. You can say "I am rich" or you can verbalize it as "I want to be rich." There is a big difference. The latter suggests that you only "want to be," meaning you are not - you only desire to be without action, not actually 'being it'.

"I am rich," means you already are rich, which is the truth, even though the appearances in your life may appear to the contrary. However, the "I am" is your command - and it "shall be."

Remember, "being rich" means many things, and material riches should not be your number one goal. There is nothing wrong with "being rich" as long as you don't forget to also enrich your Soul.

Most of us believe that we have to "earn" a living. This is what we have been taught. You also have been taught that you have to earn your way to heaven, depending on the specific religion you adhere to. Nevertheless, the goal is the same: You have to earn happiness and eternal bliss. The truth is, you don't have to "earn" anything. You simply have to "be" abundance, love, or anything you want to experience in order to express these qualities.

February 19

Desire, imagination, and a huge amount of self-confidence will get you to your goal every time. Do not waver or doubt. Stick with it. Focus, and most of all, love what you are trying to achieve. Everything is possible in the realm of the unseen, the vast ocean of Universal Consciousness.

My interview with Oprah

We are sitting on stage, white couches and the lights glaring. It's a clean look and a smiling audience greeted me, making my heart pound less. Oprah, elegant as ever, makes me feel at ease with her great smile and open arms. The audience sits in anticipation of her first question.

"Where did you come from, seemingly out of nowhere?"

"I've been around for a while"- I say, smiling sheepishly - "at least in my mind. My interest in all metaphysical started over thirty years ago. I was on my path, but like everyone else, felt that I had to have a career, raise my child, marriage, and just deal with day to day survival issues. I've known for a long time that eventually I would end up writing and teaching about my findings, and hopefully contribute to a better world."

"When did you decide to start writing, when did you know the time had come?"

"I lost my job of nearly twenty years seemingly out of the blue. No warning signs, at least I didn't see them, and I had a real awakening on what was important in life and what was fluff. I lived in the world of Hollywood, and as you well know there is a lot of superficial living going on. I wasn't willing to participate anymore and I think that was part of the experience of 'losing'. In reality you can't lose anything. It's more like a rearranging of your life. Going to what is necessary to improve your true path."

"So you sat down and started to write your thoughts down every day? What were you trying to accomplish?"

"First of all I had to take a deep look into who I was, and who I wanted to be. It's like shedding off all that you have been, and starting fresh. My first action was to go back to my birth name ULRIKE. It was my first ego-id that my parents had given me. During my life I had changed my name, just as I changed my hair color ... whatever worked at the time. So with this pure name and good intention, I created the brand Modern Thought Theories. It stood for fresh, up to date language-creative thoughts and ideas - and openly discussing and theorizing about those ideas. I wanted to create a community of likeminded people that could talk and support each other, and share similar stories showing their growth. The writing part came easy. It was all pent up in my mind, ready to be expressed."

"What would you like to see happening?"

"I would like to be able to continue to write and teach. I like to engage with my readers. I answer every e-mail and every online post in person. I'm not one to travel, nor do I want to be in the limelight and meet important people. I've done that. It wasn't always pleasant and it would put me right back to where I was; right back to the ego world.

Don't get me wrong, I absolutely understand that in order to get the message out, we need to use media and that's a blessing, like this conversation with you. I am very grateful for this opportunity. However, I would like to have other people, which love this type of business, carry out those networking tasks. I will provide the necessary written and oral materials.

No doubt, we will always have 'some ego' on this plane. It's part of this journey here. But our efforts should be focused on letting go of all superficial, pretense, and imaginary that is less than good, learn to balance."

"So you think you have a calling as an inspirational writer?"

"We all have a calling. Some have an enormous one, like you Oprah, some have a smaller one - but we all are here for a purpose; and we are all necessary to complete this puzzle of life. This purpose is to contribute to Universal Love Consciousness in any way we can. Just by being a good person – you are contributing. It's that simple!"

And so our talk ended on a loving note. Of course, this interview hasn't happened yet. It is a figment of my imagination.

February 20

Physical vitality is the result of healthy, vital and vigorous thoughts. Physical weakness is the reflection of worn out, tired, vulnerable, and confused thoughts. Think strong and healthy thoughts; love life. Health comes from within, never from without.

February 21

Now is the time, and always has been. Stay right here, in the now ... and see everything around you perfect and good ... now!

Your old thoughts are gone. There is nothing you can do about them. No need to hang on to them, or trying to get them back. They are past. But you can do something about the "now" thought - the one you are having right now, this minute.

For example, I was frustrated a minute ago. But now I realize, and I reminded myself, that I am only in control over my own life. So now, I let go of the frustration, and the want, of trying to change the other person. My "now" thought acknowledges the truth, embracing the Law of Individuality and moves on to forgiveness. I forgive myself for the mistake, and the need of meddling into someone else's life. I forgive the other for their behavior.

I remember that all is good.

February 22

Negative thoughts are like weeds. They spread quickly if you don't tend to them. Remove all weeds in your mind, especially fear and doubt.

My question of the day is: "Why do I still feel unsettled at times? What makes me uneasy, worried, and rattled? Why do I react when I know better?"

We have to keep our frequency in balance. Have you ever listened to and observed your frequency? You can actually hear it, feel it.

Lie still, especially when you are upset, and listen to the buzzing of your whole being! It feels unnatural when you are riled up; your "engine" is running too high.

Stop it with the command: "All is well, I am calm, I am safe"- and mean it!

February 23

The present is eternal; nothing else is real but the NOW. The past has been thought and the future is still in the making. Your focus has to stay right here, right now.

Hear, see, touch, taste, smell, and its correlating manifestations:

More than just five senses

The five senses help us to understand our "perception" of the physical world. But what about the mental meaning or the relation to our spiritual understanding of what we call hear, see, touch, taste, and smell? In the mental world there is also "reason." When understood correctly, all of these abilities and the faculty of "reason" culminate in Understanding. Let me explain.

Humans have five senses that are based on signals we receive through the ears, eyes, skin, tongue, and nose. Scientists are still working to understand all of the complicated tasks these senses accomplish. As we know today, the brain takes these signals and makes logic of them, and this in turn creates our interpretation of the world. Yes, our interpretation of what we think this "world" consists of. Everything we've ever come to know since we were born, including our time in the womb, has been based on sensory experiences. How can we really be sure that this so-called "world" we perceive actually exists outside of our own imagination? Why is it important to understand the effect our imagination has on our experience of this "world" and our daily living?

I loved the example I read in a blog from 2008. The writer said to "Turn off all the lights, electronics, or other contraptions in your room, close your eyes, sit very still and, if you can, try to imagine that you cannot see, hear, taste, smell, or feel. You would be nothing but a brain hovering in the middle of an endless abyss of space." Think about this. Your consciousness would still exist, but the abilities to experience your "world" would have been taken away. It's like being in a deep coma you might say.

Therefore, we can deduce from this test that the senses are part of your consciousness. They are the activity of mind, not a physical sensation.

As the brain, speaking in metaphysical terms, is the seat of individual intelligence, or the picturing forth of this Universal, absolute, and limitless Intelligence, it is clear that the five senses are directly connected to the brain's activities. This individual Intelligence is sending out signals of "hearing" (hearing the truth), "sight" (seeing the truth), "touch" (being in touch with the truth), "taste" (taking in the truth and digest it) and the "smell" (differentiate between right and wrong, ultimately coming to a conclusion based on truth).

The world and your personal existence has meaning through your understanding of this seemingly outward perception, identified through your faculties and your abilities. We form memories through our senses; we envision the future through our senses, our day to day experience depends on our senses, and all in accordance with the inert knowledge of being a full and perfect Soul, even though most individuals haven't gained this insight at this stage of their lives.

Our body responds to every thought we think. The body always "speaks" to us and we have to listen to its messages. In reality, we think first - the body responds. However, we are not always aware of our habitual thoughts, so by listening to our body, we can interpret the thoughts we have thought of in the first place. Every cell in our body responds to every thought!

If you don't like the reflection on your body, your thought improvements will do the trick! Tomorrow let's look closely at our five senses and the meaning of the symbols.

February 24

All things are really "thinks;" they are ideas formed in mind, expressed into the visible by your desire to enjoy these goods.

Hear

When we are born our hearing is a precise instrument, being able to differentiate between thousands of sounds. However, after the exposure to noise and every day loud tumultuous sounds the hair cells in the inner ear flatten and make us less sensitive to the surrounding commotion. Our brains process sounds faster than images. Hearing allows us to listen to music, to the voices of loved ones, and many other wonderful things. In fact, humans wouldn't have developed language without the ability to hear. Our sensitive ears are the tools which are not only capable of gathering sound, but we are also able to make out volume, pitch, direction, and distance of noise. Metaphysically "hearing" is the ability to hear the Truth about our true spirituality.

On the other hand, constant noise is an unhealthy contributor to your nervous system and robs you of mental rest and vitality. Noise is what keeps you from meditating deeply and from connecting to your life source, Universal consciousness.

The ears are the symbols of the sense of hearing. They represent our ability to hear. We can see that "hearing" relates to listening as well as to hearing. We should only listen and hear the truth of being. So what happens if we listen and hear other untrue, hurtful, angry, or un-easy words?

Anytime you experience an earache, you need to take a look at what's going on around you. What don't you want to hear? When pain is present you can be sure that you are also angry or hurt about what you hear. Many small children manifest earaches due to fighting between parents, loud arguments, and other verbal household miseries.

John, who came to me for advice, couldn't get rid of this dull feeling in his ear. It wasn't so much painful as it limited his hearing. He said to me, "it seems I can't hear on my left ear anymore" – and I asked him: "What don't you want to hear? Is what you are hearing uncomfortable to you? Are you trying to block what you hear out of your consciousness?"

The situation was this: His boss, an extremely opinionated fellow, who constantly talked and expressed his point of view with no room for negotiation, had called meeting after meeting with John. He made him sit next to him and listen hour after hour, day after day, to the business woes and how they had to do better. The boss was very wealthy and didn't have a care in the world, but he wanted to make sure that the employees didn't think they could slack off. John knew that the speeches were just a repetition of this man's insecurities and egocentric character. So, not being able to speak up or leave the room in fear of losing his job, his subconscious blocked the words. He was literally going deaf.

You can see this frequently in old couples that bicker at each other all the time. It's mostly the husband that can barely hear anymore, especially his wife's excessive babble. Deafness occurs when there is a longstanding refusal to listen to someone. One talks and the other can't hear!

Women have a greater tolerance for words. They love talking to each other, while men mostly hold words in. They digest internally before they speak. So listening is less natural to them. Of course I am generally speaking.

February 25

We learn to do things well when we identify ourselves with them. Loving what we do and creating what we love will give us a sense of being the creation itself.

See

Seeing, which is a gathering of light, appears to be a function of the brain. Again, in the mental realm, it is a visible symbol of the mental ability to "see" the Truth. Seeing also means understanding. "I see," as so many of us reply when in a conversation with someone trying to explain our point of view.

Vision demands that the brain, which as I pointed out earlier is the visible picture of Universal Intelligence, differentiates the background from the foreground and edges from lines. Your brain makes sense of shapes and symbols. Your brain is the most intricate and powerful tool you have. Even computers have not been able to figure some of this out.

Universal Intelligence knows all, it does not have to learn anything – it already understands. You only have to tap into this vast sea of conscious energy and pull the information you need.

In the mental, the eyes represent our ability to see clearly. You can see the truth with clear vision, or you can look at the imaginary and lose focus. Vision is the capacity to see your past, present, and future - as you sense it, or as it should be. It is an expression of your understanding.

When you experience eye trouble ask yourself: "What don't I want to look at in my life, and around me?" "What is my vision of life?" "Is my vision of myself blurred or clear?"

91

The farsightedness that comes later in life stems from your belief in aging. Mentally speaking, you are not able to focus as quickly as you once did. You are looking at things a little bit "stiffer" these days.

February 26

Many people are afraid to learn new things because they fear failure. There is no failure in trying; there is only failure in giving up.

Touch

We do not realize how strange it would be to live without the sense of touch. It's really difficult to imagine. What we don't realize is that the skin is considered to be the body's largest organ.

Touch, for instance, is associated with comfort. Sitting in a soft chair, touching a lovely fabric, or caressing a baby or a loved one are all feel-good touch senses. Some of the most sensitive parts of the body are the lips, finger tips, and the sole of the feet. Being touched can reduce stress, being held makes you feel safe, and babies need the touch in order to survive and grow into a healthy human being.

Metaphysically, "touch" symbolizes your ability to connect to all of life. It connects you with the other person's life, your daily experiences including the handling of daily issues, and it symbolizes to be in touch with life itself. Being in touch with life's energy - and there is not one tiny space in this Universe that is not absorbed with life energy - will surely make you realize that you (your skin) are surrounded by this energy at all times.

The ability to handle your experiences, and to "touch" someone's life, as well as to grasp onto an idea, is what's represented with touch. Your hands are handling your affairs; they reach out to greet someone, they wave at a friend or they write a note to a loved one. You use them as a tool to express yourself when trying to get a point across. You caress, you hold on, and you feel.

February 27

Surrender to the Allness of Good, the true state of conscious living; all else will naturally fall into place. Your ultimate goal will be obtained by allowing the Universe to do its job, which is manifesting your good desires. Don't stand in your own way.

Taste

Taste and smell are perhaps the most important senses as they cause us to want to eat, and help us know what we should be eating. Smell actually works with taste to help us decide whether we're eating something pleasing or disgusting, which can save our lives in case of spoiled foods or poison.

We have over 10,000 taste buds which are spread over the tongue, palate, and inner cheek. The taste buds send signals to the brain, which is the mental seat of intelligence, which will determine if the food is acceptable or not.

However, there is a much greater meaning to this sense of "taste." Taking in food represents "taking in ideas," digesting them, and either keeping or eliminating them. So it is with our thoughts. We have to take in only the good, the right, and the lovely - the good tasting thoughts of life - in order to digest properly. This will benefit the body, or temporary vessel of ours, in many ways.

You are here to taste the good things in life. You are to enjoy the flavors and the varieties of living. Goodness is limitless. Be careful what you take into the chambers of your Soul!

February 28

Become a channel of the Universal Mind. Creativeness and energy will flow through you easily once you have opened yourself up to this cosmic power.

Smell

We respond to smell with a greater intensity than to the other senses. Smells will trigger a pleasant experience or appall us immediately if recalling a nasty encounter. The nose can also determine from where the smell is coming from. Our sense of smell is deeply individual – we smell things uniquely and perceive what's nice or nasty in different degrees.

Smell represents our natural ability to differentiate between right or wrong in our mind. It is this differentiation that puts us on the right path to everlasting happiness, or on the road to unpleasant life experiences.

We take in different smells all the time and we differentiate by what we smell. In the mental, a runny nose will signal a sense of overload, and running on and on about something. Being stuffy, stuffed up about something - all clogged up about an issue. See it's all in the mental and you can see it clearly by observing the signs.

During the holiday season you can see many more people having colds. It's not because of the winter season, the snow, or a rainy day. It's not because the co-worker or the kids have "given it" to you - it's because you are busy running around, trying to get your shopping done, fretting about having to "get it all done" and "how will I pay the bills" - too much of everything,

94

not enough rest and still time. Of course your belief of being able to contract any illness from another is a belief strong enough to exhibit this illness. Thinking so makes it so – you get what you are convinced of.

February 29

Start being what you want to be. Start living how you want to live. Start loving how you want to be loved.

And lastly, our faculty of "Reason"

Your five senses are very important in showing you what you have to apply in order to find the truth. Hear only the good. See only the good. Touch only the good. Taste only the good, and smell or take in only the good.

Taking in all of these impressions is the starting point that needs to be monitored and regulated by right reason. Your reason is your Christ or Savior. Your reason is represented in the stomach. It digests your ideas. It assimilates the new and it sorts out the useless waste and discards what is no longer necessary.

A stubborn or angry mental attitude only can be healed by reason. You might have ulcers and stomach bleeding. Before you do so, however, the fact remains that all is mental and all can be healed by mental means alone.

You have to reason on the right side, the side of Truth. You have to obey Universal Laws.

The moral of the story

Be very careful using your senses properly. What you perceive in this so-called material world is most likely a distorted image of the Truth. We are only at the beginning stage of understanding the workings of the mind. Use your faculty of reason correctly to discern right from wrong, the true from the imaginary. It's a wondrous and exciting time, and to be part of this process produces an immense sense of gratefulness in my consciousness.

Chapter 3: People and You

March 1

Knowing what lies behind the idea of transition to the next dimension, will take the sting away of so-called death. Life cannot die, life lives. Your Soul is the unbroken connection to the Almighty universal source.

Chew on that statement for a while...

March 2

Let me ask you a question:

Do you feel alone, like you fight the battle by yourself? Always carrying the burden? Is it that we separate ourselves from God, this Universal power that sustains all? Does this separation – which only can be an illusion, as it is impossible to separate from your life source – leave us feeling empty and in a constant struggle?

We have to remember that are never alone, but always all-one. When we grasp this fact of oneness, we will always have strength, support and we will always feel loved and cared for.

Here is a response to the above statement from a reader:

"You may not know how profoundly this thought has struck me today, the coincidence is not coincidental ... we truly are ALL ONE not Alone ... that space and extra L makes all the difference!"

Yes, adding that 'L' into the word alone, (all-one) does make a difference. When you realize that you are OK and safe, this newfound strength will reflect onto others. It will inspire them. Live by example and bring your awareness and knowledge to others. Share your blessings and celebrate life.

March 3

A little slice of quiet time

My husband is visiting his twenty-three year old son, who lives about fifty miles from our town with his mother. Once a month, he likes to spend the weekend with him, and just 'hang' like the guys do - his words. Luckily, they have established a great relationship despite the rocky earlier years.

This absence of a spouse provides me with the opportunity to enjoy alone time and tranquility. I love my husband and enjoy his company, but I look forward to these 'me-me' days. No TV, no music, no noise, no interaction with people and no phone calls. Just 'little old me' - and my animals. They also seem to enjoy the quiet time, both sleeping calmly and relaxed in the same big comfortable chair I'm sitting in. Dog, cat, me, - a big pile of happiness!

March 4

Good company is essential to your spiritual path. Choose your friends wisely - like attracts like. Look for likeminded people that share your positive conversations, and leave the negative squawkers behind.

Positive friends

Since I've been working from home many of my previous acquaintances have changed. I realize that it's easier to keep my positive attitude when I'm not confronted with tons of people every day. My job included many nights of networking and keeping my attitude right about everyone I met had its challenges.

The company you keep is very important. When you hang around a pessimist, in due time, you will acquire a pessimistic attitude yourself; if you allow it. Doubt and fear will quickly creep into your mind and soon you will chime in, and join this cesspool of negativity.

Tune into the vibration of positive thoughts as much as you can. Teach yourself to rise above likes and dislikes, and distance yourself from worldly dramas and emotions. Even if our reasoning ability is very well developed, our feelings always get the best of us. Watch your feelings, see how fast you jump to conclusions due to a feeling that crept up quickly, and make sure they are in tune with your reason.

March 5

I see people suffering from depression, even though they seemingly have everything...

Depression is a lack of interest in Life; a shortage of appreciation of the goodness around you. Start seeing love and get interested in living. As difficult as it might seem, keep moving toward the light. Step by step the darkness will disappear; true Life will be yours again.

Loving Life is the essence of living.

March 6

Parallel Dimensions

My good friend and business associate posted this question onto our LinkedIn group this morning.

Parallel dimensions, nutty thoughts or another fact, just like the Earth IS round?

"I hope this discussion is not too far-fetched for the group and you don't think I'm nuts. A personal experience keeps me wondering if there is such a thing as parallel dimensions and if it is possible for us to 'sneak' into another dimension, in other words to switch from a life happening in one dimension into another one happening parallel, kind of time traveling. Sounds nutty and impossible but not so long ago the thought of the Earth being round was considered nutty and impossible too. And it is round after all. What do you think? I would love to hear opinions from people who share these thoughts with me."

I was so excited. What a great question and inquisitive mind!

Yes, yes, yes on the parallel dimensions! And NO you are not nutty! You have a wonderful inquisitive mind. Where would Einstein be if he hadn't asked all the questions? Deepak Chopra addressed this topic in his books. However, Neville Goddard was a metaphysician that actually experimented with this concept. Research his works (he writes under 'Neville') - his results are fascinating!

Think about it. We slip into parallel dimensions all the time, even here in this 'lower' level. Doesn't your mind wander and explore? Don't you feel transported into a different dimension when you are engulfed in thought- imagining a place you'd like to be right now?

When we pass on from this life, as we know it, we are only transitioning to another dimension. A dimension that will suit our new concept of ourselves, ready to make another journey of self-discovery... I guess book #5

Thank you for the morning thoughts! I sincerely hope some of the members of this group will chime in!

March 7

Brain storming is one of my favorite things to do.

Be open-minded. Allow others to be themselves. Embrace the new and the unusual. You will be surprised how much more interesting your life will become.

What would you choose as your next reality?

Think of your life right now. What would you change if you could do it all over again? Can you truly say nothing? Maybe a few things, but most of your life was satisfactory? If so, congratulations to you! You have a choice again, and again. I'm not talking about your next life either. I'm talking about NOW.

Today, and any day, you can look at your experience and say: 'I will change my (blank) to (blank).' Fill in the desire you have outlined for yourself. Reason about it and come to a conclusion that reflects your new style of living. In my case, I am currently thinking about moving to another city, creating a special retirement place for my husband and I. Together we chose the location, Palm Springs, and are remodeling a home which we bought several years ago to fit our needs. We decided to leave the bustling city of Los Angeles that no longer serves our life style. As I visualize and mentally picture this improved state of being, I will improve my state of mind, and my outer scene will change accordingly. What

I create in my mind will become my new, or next, reality.

Think about the days, way back in time, when you thought of yourself a certain way. Hasn't it all changed? Aren't you a different being now? Imagine making this transformation consciously and planned. Planning a better future for your self is vital. No one wants to be stuck in the old ways of living, especially when they are not working for them. Going over and over the same woes and problems, not making any progress whatsoever, seems not only redundant but also excruciating. Who doesn't want a better, more harmonious life?

Well, I do. Therefore I have committed myself to a rigorous mental work out. I faithfully go to the mental gym and practice diligently, by repeating statements of truth, applying what I know and practicing right thinking on a daily basis. What about you?

March 8

See only the good and beautiful. Turn away from all appearances that are less than good. See your world as perfect, because in reality it already is.

Response to the above quote from a reader:

"It's hard to do, especially if that aggressive person goes out of their way to make sure they make their mark ... physically yelling at you, have other people call you to tell you how beautiful that person is, promoting mixed signals, one day speaking normally, the next day walking by as if they're looking into outer space. How do you ignore someone who is obviously going out of their way to try to get a reaction from another person? (Can I also say they are 40-50 year old women?) How do you remove yourself, mentally, when you're in a work environment?"

Great question! Having worked with, and for, many ego-centric people I understand what you are talking about, especially in the work environment. I think you can turn it around by feeling compassion towards people that lash out, treat others unkind, unfair or have a mean attitude in general. When you realize how terribly unhappy, insecure, unfulfilled, and tormented they must be in order to feel the need to act this way you will muster up all the love and forgiveness you can. It will help you to stay on course with your own spiritual unfoldment, and you can be certain the Law will take care of them.

March 9

Healing thought:
Bitterness, an attitude of envy or jealousy, is poison to your health. The bile, produced in the liver and stored in the gallbladder, represents this bitterness. Let go of all bitterness in your mind. Allow love to flow freely through your consciousness and heal this poisonous sense.

March 10

It's not about changing who you are; it's about bringing the best out of you. You are already good by nature; you just have to make better choices.

Let's check in with our friend Dexter

Dexter was healing nicely and ready to go back to work in a couple of weeks. As he felt better his attitude improved and his demeanor lightened up. He called and we talked about his general health issues. I explained to him that all illnesses are related to his mental beliefs about health, and his habitual wrong thoughts. We agreed that he would take classes twice a week to talk about healing.

Dexter, being African American, has several racial beliefs taught to him by his parents, the medical profession and his general cultural heritage. Hypertension, heart issues and sickle cell anemia are said to be 'black people's' woes. They are more prone to develop these diseases.

However, the mentality does not differentiate between your skin color or religion or any other racial diversity! Your mentality is pure Spirit, not black, white, and purple or polka dotted!

You did not inherit your mother or father's disposition – it is your 'belief' that makes it so! It is your, and all of our, immature and wrongly taught thought that causes the sickness. I know this is a hard concept to grasp at the beginning stage of your study, however, the fact remains that all is mental and all can be healed by purely mental means.

The correct diagnosis of a doctor is necessary to pinpoint your mistake. Take this knowledge and transform it into the mental aspects of this theory. It will show you where the mental corrections need to take place. The medications of this world can only heal you temporarily. A correction of your wrong and habitual thoughts, mental attitudes and feelings, need to be achieved if permanent health is your goal. If you do not correct your state of mind, the disease will re-appear to reflect the mental mistakes.

You can and will prove it to yourself many times, if you give this theory a chance. Practice it, live it, and you will see clearly the healing effect your new and improved thought, imbued with Truth, will have on your health. I've been applying this Truth for over 30 years and have proved it to myself over and over again. Let's take a look on what Dexter's health issues represent in the mental. What is really going on in his heart...

104

March 11

I'm doing research on health issues this morning and wanted to share my findings with you. Here is a general overview on what hypertension and heart issues represent in the mental:

Hypertension:
Hypertension is the term used to describe high blood pressure. Blood pressure is a measurement of the force against the walls of your arteries as your heart pumps blood through your body. Blood pressure readings are usually given as two numbers -- for example, 120 over 80 (written as 120/80 mmHg). One or both of these numbers can be too high. If you have pre-hypertension, you are more likely to develop high blood pressure. The National Library of Medicine says
You have a higher risk of high blood pressure if you:
• Are African American
• Are obese
• Are often stressed or anxious
• Drink too much alcohol (more than one drink per day for women and more than two drinks per day for men)
• Eat too much salt in your diet
• Have a family history of high blood pressure
• Have diabetes
• Smoke

Here you go, they said it...and, you believed it.

The blood, in the mental sense, represents Love. Love flowing through and through you. You cannot live without Love. Love for yourself, love for others, love for everyone and everything- Universal Love. But instead you react to your work environment and close associates, being irked all the time about everything. You get yourself all riled up and the pressure goes up. You are a living pressure cooker, instead of healing your longstanding emotional problems.

Heart Issues

The heart, in the mental sense, represents self-sufficiency. It is your ability to cope with your life; the heartbeat of your life, ever pumping blood (the symbol of love) through your arteries. You must maintain "thoughts of life" and feel fully self-sufficient to maintain a healthy heart.

Heart issues come in many forms. It always will depend on the wrong sense someone has regarding life. Depression and a sense of a desperate "end of all things" also contribute to heart problems. A fear of death of course plays a role. Add a "lack of joy" for life and a so-called hardening of the heart will ensue. The heart is your spiritual center of love and emotions. Treasure it!

March 12

Putting yourself down is letting God down. We constantly put ourselves down. I'm not good enough, I'm not capable enough, I'm not smart enough, I'm too old for this or that ... always something that isn't in conformity with the Truth. Do you think God is less than or not good enough?

Nothing in Life is permanent

It constantly changes. Every minute of our lives we encounter a shift, a ripple in the fabric of Consciousness. It's all individual, yet the ripple effect flows through all life and perfectly ties all individuality together.

The material body, or shell, is an imaginary solid corpse, a vehicle for this plane, guided by the Soul. We wouldn't be seen, or have an ID without it. So it is necessary in this stage of unfoldment. However, do not "become" the illusion. This body is the only one we have right now. Why don't we take better care of it? It's the temporary home, house, of your Soul. Make it livable; keep it clean and healthy so the Soul can expand and thrive.

The question begs an answer: Why do we abuse the body? By abusing your body, your mind cringes and stiffens. The Soul part of you (your spiritual self) wants to become free. It wants to return to its true home, the realm of Universal Consciousness, where it can regroup and reincarnate to another experience.

Last month, one of the greatest singers of all times died due to an overdose. She had been tormented for a long time, all of her "Earthly" wealth and status could not prevent her from destroying herself, proving again that your focus should be on a healthy mind. Material riches, as comfortable as they might seem at the time, have no lasting value. The Soul always yearns for the spiritual values and will leave the body when the enjoyment of this Earthly life has vanished.

The unenlightened mind is deceived by likes and dislikes and shaped by past habits and old ways of looking at things. It seeks fulfillment and ecstasy in superficial endeavors. It looks in all the wrong places.

The enlightened mind is searching for the truth and looks at it with indifference. It knows the truth is constant and unchangeable. The Understander will nourish the Soul and enjoy life to its fullest, always appreciating what he has at the time. Striving for more understanding, rather than material riches is the goal of a true searcher. Being wealthy is not bad - it is very, very good as long as you do not mistake it for "important" and "necessary" and know that you would be just as happy without it. This knowledge is true wealth.

March 13

Can I truly say I respect every aspect of myself?

Self-Respect and respecting others

From a reader, thoughts about self-respect:

"I come from a family where addictions run rampant - alcoholism, drug addiction, and obesity have had free reign over my family tree past and present. These addictions have killed and hurt and tormented those closest to me. I have felt the sting of betrayal, and time and time again suffered loss and respect for those I love.

Today I feel anxious. Anxious because I know one brother is in the middle of an alcoholic meth binge and the other seems to be over medicated on various meds prescribed for his bi-Polar/Hepatitis C/psychiatric issues. I try to put the worry and fear out of my mind yet again and again it creeps to the forefront of my mentality; the blackness of all this blocks out the bright sun of a beautiful day.

I know I cannot control their lives. I know I should think and know they are the controllers of their own destiny - I should respect the Law of Individuality and just know in my heart that they will be fine. This same scenario has played out more times in my life than I care to admit.

Where is my SELF respect, I am wondering today? Where is my love for myself to not waste one second more on someone else's problems? Why is my lovely Saturday afternoon not spent on my own happiness - my own enjoyment - my own life? Why do I continually choose to throw the focus off myself and worry about other people's lives and problems that I have no control over? Where is the "I" in ME? The all-powerful, self-assured, in control of my own life and steering a course for happiness woman I know I can be and have shown myself to be?

The little "me" is an eight year old girl trying to hold a family together ... trying to be the communicator, the peace maker, the middle-child syndrome in full swing as I try to right all the perceived "wrongs" my family experiences. I assumed this role many years ago and have yet to fully shed the heavy cloak I wear.

I love myself and loathe myself simultaneously for who I have become rather than the possibility of who I aspire to be. Where is my self-respect? Is it wrapped up in being perceived as the eternal good-girl caretaker of others? Is it buried deep in my overweighed body from swallowing years of anger, sadness, hurt and regret? Is it in seeing the words I write this minute - coming clean on a blank piece of paper for all the word to read? It is, most likely, all of the above. I am trying to find my way and some days I falter. Other days I fly freely and reach new heights of self-awareness. At this moment I'm simply humming Aretha's anthem: R-E-S-P-E-C-T ... find out what it means to me ... R-E-S-P-E-C-T ... find out what it means to me."

Remember: Respecting others means to allow them to be themselves, and continue their journey through their own choices, even if it hurts.

March 14

It's OK to make mistakes. This is how we learn to do better. It doesn't make us bad, stupid, or less than. We are here to unfold our innate perfection and to remember who we are.

I was thinking today that in life you do not have "to do" anything - it's a matter of what you are "being." Who am I choosing to be? Who are you choosing to be? "Being" implies that you already did what's necessary to get to this state of "Being" what you want to be.

109

This is a higher sense and takes time to understand. We always expect "having to act" and "to do" – however the more advanced sense is to feel "being" your desire. I had to sit on it for a while, if you join me – you will see the point.

March 15

My thoughts on single-mindedness

Be of One Mind and good purpose. Be single-minded. Don't switch constantly between one thing and another, being wishy-washy all the time. Doubting your decisions and straying off your path will get you nowhere. Focus and stay on course. Single-mindedness is different from being able to see another person's point of view.

Single-mindedness is the roadmap to success. It implies courage, focus, and the conviction that you are powerful within yourself. It shows that you know what you want.

The above quote brought up a good point:

Reader: *"Thank You, the word 'stubborn' has such a closed minded sound to it"*

Me: *"Oh yes it does ... and it creates constipation ..."*

Reader: *"Please explain this one; I am not sure I agree ..."*

Me: *"Would love to! When someone is stubborn for a long period of time, or unmovable in their opinion, it is reflected in constipation. The stomach represents 'reason' - being stubborn also means being unreasonable at times. All mental attitudes eventually reflect on the body. Hope this helps!"*

Reader: *"It does and Thank You I am going to share this one and Yes I agree!"*

I want to point out that single-mindedness has nothing to do with being stubborn. Stubbornness means you will not budge from your opinion, right or wrong. Single-mindedness means that you know what is true and what you want to achieve. It makes you stay on course and go forward whole-heartedly in your quest to achieve your goal.

March 16

Healing thought:
I am a complete and perfect Soul. I am well, and prosperous, and I know it!

More thoughts on reincarnation

As I said earlier, I agree with the concept of reincarnation, but struggle with: Why back to this planet? No doubt, we can and will meet in different dimensions. As life is unlimited, I expect "dimensions" to also be unlimited and co-existing. The Soul is connected to only one source and that is Universal Consciousness, which is all there is, with its infinite possibilities, limitlessness, and all-containing.

Nothing has power over us. Our subconscious acts upon our choices. If you believe that there are other powers that can affect you, and all of us for this matter, you make those influences God. Even the true God, Universal Consciousness, when understood and used correctly, has no "power," *per se,* over us - he/it only reflects and carries out our thoughts and convictions. This is not blasphemy; this is God carrying out God's plan. He is indifferent; he is cause and effect - guided by our individual mind patterns. He is the Law.

The Soul has no beginning and no end. The concept of "no beginning" is difficult to understand in our realm of being. It seems easier to agree that there is "no end" because it is a comforting thought. You and I like to believe the fact that there is no end to our being. "I AM" forever and ever more...

Many unanswered questions remain to be solved. Why did we come here in the first place? What is our purpose? Maybe life is simpler than we think? Maybe we take ourselves too seriously?

Let's say, for example, I was born into this world to remember or learn something; for instance, to remember my God-being. In reality I am already the ALL that there is. Adopting this theory, I, my Soul, came here and forgot who I was (or still am). I came here as a mental infant, and I came to a dimension, or Earth life, with the Law of Cause and Effect already in place. So my Soul ("I") started to experience this belief-world and bought into all that is presented to me during my upbringing.

Then an inert urge of self-knowledge and self-discovery sparked the search for truth. Since there are so many different levels of Soul-awareness on this plane of being, it doesn't puzzle me to think that some individuals come back to Earth as teachers and guides, supporting and teaching others. Your Soul remembers everything, and even though you have forgotten this vital point, and only remember what is stored in your memory, the question remains: Why start as an infant again and again? Going through another forty years of experiencing woes and tribulations in order to recall "who" and "what" I am seems to be wasted time. (Ooops, there is no time!)

This is definitely a topic for the next book. Let's keep it real and simple for now. By working out the basic life challenges, we will naturally develop the higher ideas of mind.

March 17

The Soul loves to think quietly. It cherishes the comfort of solace, relief from emotional distress. The hustle and bustle of this world belongs to the ego. The beauty and silence of Nature belongs to the Soul.

Thoughts on "All-Good"

William Walker Atkinson (writer and metaphysician 1863 – 1932) wrote in 1908, on the last page of his book "Reincarnation and the Law of Karma" as a finishing statement to believers or unbelievers alike:

"... Sees in everything as the working out of a great Cosmic Plan whereby everything rises from a lower to higher, and still higher. To it Karma is but one phase of the great LAW operating in all planes and forms of life and the Universe. To it the idea that 'The Universe is governed by Law' is an axiom – generally accepted truth. And while to it Ultimate Justice is also axiomic, it sees not in the operation of penalties and reward – merits and demerits – the proof of that Ultimate Justice; it looks for it and finds it in conception and realizing that ALL WORKS FOR GOOD – that everything is tending upward – that everything is justified and just, because the END is ABSOLUTE GOOD, and that every tiny working of the great cosmic machinery is turning in the right direction and to that end.

Consequently, each of us is just where we should be at the present time – and our condition is exactly the very best to bring us to that Divine Consummation and End. And to such thinkers, indeed, there is no Devil but Fear and Unfaith, and all other devils are illusions, whether they be called Beelzebub, Mortal Mind, or Karma, if they produce Fear and Unfaith in the All Good.

And such thinkers feel that the way to live according to the Higher Light, and without fear of a Malevolent

Karma, is to feel one's relationship with the Universal Good, and then to live 'Live One Day at a time – doing the Best you Know How – and Be Kind' – knowing that the All-Good you live and move and have your being, and that outside of that All-Good you cannot stray, for there is no outside – knowing that which brought you Here will be your There – that Death is but a phase of Life – and above all that There is nothing to be afraid of – and that ALL IS WELL with God; with the Universe and with YOU! – Finis."

Wonderfully expressed!

March 18

It is our responsibility to contribute to the awakening of the masses; the journey has begun. Be good, act good, and do good. Be a contributor to this universal awareness that has started to grow and blossom.

We are all responsible for the awakening that is taking place right now. You can see it everywhere. Like little flowers in the spring, sprouting and pushing up their tender heads through the snowy fields. Fragile, barely born seeds of good thoughts – growing stronger and determined to reach the light are bursting out all over the world. What you see happening in this day and age are "good thoughts" searching for the Truth and Souls longing for their ultimate state of perfect being.

March 19

Every Wednesday is teaching class day. My longtime friend, and student, arrives every week faithfully at 4:20 p.m. and we both look forward to digging into what matters. Here is an interesting article she wrote, and I want to share it with you - looking at this subject from a mental standpoint:

AI & KI

"Much has been written about 'Artificial Intelligence' - the fostering of robots, computers, and machines having the ability to think and reason just as we do. Even better than we are able to, science fiction proclaims, because computers can reason with 100% accuracy based on data, not emotions. Yet, as many of the movies based on AI play out, the closer the machines come to actually being on par with us, the more emotionality they exhibit. Go figure ... in the end, they really just want to be as human as we are.

Well, in my mind's view, that's really not so hard to figure out, seeing as how they are the products of our own mentality. In the big scheme of things, they are our creations. Anything we can think of is already in mind; it just has to be exported into the visible via reason and feeling. We give birth to 'Artificial Intelligence' through our own natural Intelligence. It's ironic, isn't it?

In our quest for more self-unfoldment, we mistakenly think we give life to inanimate things, yet we are really giving birth (becoming aware of) to more of our own Intelligence. It's like the mirror within a mirror within a mirror image. More of our self is really less, when you come to realize what self is. It's invisible Universal Consciousness. I'm ok with my own version of AI. It's called KI, or Karen's Intelligence."

March 20

My garden inspires me on a daily basis ... poetry in motion!

Planting new seeds of lovely and good thoughts in your mind will bring you the blossoms and blessings you are yearning for.

Some unattended seeds will sprout quickly and wilt away. Some are nurtured and cared for; some seeds put

115

in fertile soil. Flowers bloom beautifully for your enjoyment, and even after they are done blossoming, reaching full fruition, they turn into more seeds, ready to produce more beauty. So it is with your thoughts also.

Flowers reproduce more after their own kind – just like your good thoughts produce more good thoughts. See, everything is mental - and flowers, blooms in their brilliant colors, symbolize "kind thoughts." Look deeply at the blossom and see its wondrous design and beautiful color. Have you ever seen such glory?

March 21

Healing thought:
The skin represents your reactions to close associates, family, environment, and daily work. Dealing with skin troubles shows that you literally let things get "under your skin." It's a surface type situation; you are over-sensitive, distressed, irritated, or feel harassment. Sooth yourself and praise yourself; know that no one can hurt or anger you unless you allow it. You are a reasonable, calm, forgiving individual and you are goodness itself.

Skin issues

When you think about skin, the word "sensitive" will most likely come to mind. The skin covers the whole body, representing that you are in touch with Life itself.

Skin troubles showing up on your hands indicate that the way you "handle" things need to be dealt with. When the affliction appears on the face, it reflects a "confrontation" of a situation that is right in front of you; it is not hidden or held back. However, if it shows up on your back, you can be assured that you have pushed the issues to the back. You don't want to deal with it. Whatever the situation is in your life, this irritation will be reflected on the part of the body that symbolizes the correlating circumstance.

March 22

Healing your Soul will naturally heal your pocket book.

Healing your Soul will not only heal your ailments in the areas of sickness, loneliness, misery, and any negative situation, it will also heal your lack of abundance. It will heal your world.

Let's work on achieving one of your goals that is "pocket book" related. Let's say you want to change careers. What do you need to fulfill this want? Well first of all, you will need to know what you want.

Focused thought

Here is a great example from my experience that will show you how focused thought works:

After I had finished my first book and had sent it off to the publisher, and was also dealing with the web design, branding, marketing, and all the other tasks that come with the publishing process, I also wanted to create a gift store.

The store had to include only beautiful, inspirational and healing gifts that were affordable for anyone. It wasn't about "money" *per se* – it was another avenue to share my book, my thoughts, and teachings with the world and at the same time have people enjoy a new line of especially designed inspirational gift items.

One day during this time period, I received an invite to a social networking group from a lady that was a fellow Austrian inviting me to join her business group – and I did. In the process of communicating, I found out that she was a designer of small, pretty inspirational gifts as well as many other fun store items.

At the time I was helping a tourist store in Hollywood to find merchandise and I invited this woman, Susan, to come and present her inventory, which she did. But what happened next was amazing.

Sitting in a small diner, sipping iced tea, she looked at me and said, "You don't remember me?" I was embarrassed and said "No, should I?" She smiled and reminded me of an incident that happened over ten years ago. Susan and her husband, pastry chefs at the time, had baked and delivered a retirement cake to the studio I worked for as the Events Director. Something had gone wrong with the spelling and I didn't call them back for additional orders after this incident. I had totally forgotten about it - it wasn't a big deal to me. There were many more bakers out there.

Poor Susan, however, was still mortified and apologetic. I laughed and assured her that it was much better to let go of the "cake memory" – she was only hurting herself, keeping negative memories with her for such a long time; especially when the other party hadn't given it another thought. Quickly we bonded, and instead of talking about the gift store we instantly conversed on a metaphysical level. I found out that she also was a sincere seeker of truth. We agreed that this was the "real" reason why we reconnected.

Of course the mutual "gift store," The Thought Broiler, was up and running in a few weeks and since then we have partnered and developed an additional gift line, available to everyone that enjoys pretty and loving presents; always keeping in mind that we want everyone to be able to enjoy and afford them. See, you have to know what you want and you have to believe that it already exists. The right circumstance will present itself to you. Keep your thoughts focused and be single-minded, stay on course, and keep your eye on the prize. Just look and listen!

March 23

Healing thought:
Let go of resentment, it will stiffen your bones.

Always look for people that are on your wavelength, the ones that easily tune into your radar, someone loving and kind; a person that reflects your good character.

Don't attract so-called "evil" people into your reality by accepting and dwelling on their dispositions and being outraged by their behavior. Your judgment and criticism will lower your frequency and it will draw those individuals back to you.

When you do experience unpleasant people in your life, it is only a lesson – teaching you to make the choice of kindness, forgiveness, and compassion; allowing you to correct your own wrong sense. As long as you see them and their behavior as something wrong, or evil, it will reflect back to you. Declare: "I do not accept any behavior that is less than good in my reality!"

March 24
Thoughts from a dear friend regarding her focus:

Under the Microscope

"Every morning I wake up with good intentions. I make a to-do list to help me stay on course and I vow to do a little something every day on a lot of different aspects of my life. Some of the stuff on my to-do list consists of chores - other parts of it are focused on health, happiness, and my general well-being. It's a medium to long list and I've tried many different approaches to actually staying on target. I shorten the list and vow to do 'something' on a particular thing - this takes the pressure off a little and I feel like I'm actually accomplishing some forward momentum.

This approach seems to work the best for me. Or I prioritize and only tackle one task. This works too, except I usually choose the easiest task and know in the back of my mind there are many, many more. The more I think of everything else I need to tend to, the more anxious I become; so much for a less stressful approach.

The bottom line is this: I'd really accomplish more if I just focused. I mean really focused ... like when you look under a microscope and give minute attention to a magnified image brought full scale to your senses. You can't ignore it if you bring it full screen ... really pay attention in detail to what it is you are examining, do what you need to do with it, then move on to another slide. It sure seems simple enough, but often it is the most difficult thing to do.

Other stuff seems to get in the way. 'Like what?' you ask. Well, anything and everything. A phone call is a great way of stalling or thwarting a good intention. I lose momentum after a lengthy chat. I can always find something more important to do which is more appealing than anything I actually NEED to do. You know the excuses. We use them every day.

I read a sign on a dance instructor's door many years ago that read: 'Do what you say you will do.' It had a profound impact upon me because it made me accountable to myself. Focus is the key in life to accomplishing anything and everything you want. The most accomplished and successful people have all confirmed that they are driven by focus and passion to realize their dreams. As for myself, I'm fifty-fifty these days in really focusing on what it is I want and dare to dream for myself. I am a work in progress and I know I can achieve more. I don't need a focus group to tell me that. I just need to focus on self."

March 25

God is my idea of myself.

What Is Meditation?

According to the Self-realization Fellowship, founded by Paramhansa Yogananda in 1920, it is stated this way:

"Meditation is the science of reuniting the soul with the Infinite Spirit or God. By meditating regularly and deeply, you will awaken your soul — the immortal, blissful divine consciousness at the innermost core of your being."

The true science of meditation is not for everyone as it requires full concentration, long periods of undisrupted time, focus, wanting to know the Truth and God, and the commitment of a Saint.

However, let's take a look at a more practical approach that anyone wanting to reap the benefits of this ancient practice is able to accomplish. Everyone can spend at least ten minutes in the morning of quiet contemplation. Thinking calmly about your day and it's routine, planning the most efficient and pleasant way of dealing with daily duties and the affirmations of better mental attitudes will certainly give you a right start. Maybe you are an evening person and you can spend that time in a pleasing environment to reflect back, and correct, some of the thoughts that needed improvement during the day. Focus your thought calmly, a few minutes is really all it takes.

March 26

Healing thought:
Fear of death is a stifling and terrifying experience. We will succumb to this fear until we realize that Life is not a sorry joke that can be taken away in a moment's notice. Life lives and

steadily moves forward towards its true origin. Life is eternal, and only looks limited and short, if we believe this Earthly experience to be more than a dream.

I'm an avid reader. Not of novels or fiction, but of everything on this planet that has to do with metaphysics, mind, spirit, and anything that relates to finding God in the true sense.

There is a wonderful parable by Paramhansa Yogananda. He explains that electricity doesn't "die" when withdrawn from the light bulb. You can clearly see that when the light bulb shatters, the electricity is still there. This light bulb is your body, or Earthly vessel. Your Soul is the electricity or animating substance that energizes the bulb.

Life energy – your soul – is not annihilated when it wishes to withdraw from your fleshly body, i.e. bulb. Your energy will continue, returning to a higher, a different form and state of existence, and will continue being aware of your individual ID. Ignorance of this fact doesn't alter Universal Law. The Law is just, fair and, indifferent. The Law is also exact.

"Be not deceived; God is not mocked: for whatsoever a man soweth, that shall he also reap." (Galatians 6:7)

March 27

Frustration easily turns into anger if you don't deal with it immediately. Don't hold it in; address the cause, and see what needs correction in your mind. A quick outburst of annoyance, a slight sense of disappointment, and easily irritated thoughts become a habit; and a habitual thought becomes your reality.

Pain reminds us that we have made a mistake in our thinking. Without it we would live comfortably and coast rather than look for improvement. There has to be duality, so to speak, in order for you to want better. We have to be pushed toward the business of the mind rather than staying in the realm of materialism.

Most mornings, I restate to myself that we are the Children of Light, Consciousness, and we will not sleep forever in this delusion we call life. This Life experience is a movie, and just like the movie screen it can be turned off - just like a dream, you can wake up. This movie is made by you. Each and every one of us produces their own version of the movie of Life. You are the producer, the writer, the director, and the actor!

March 28

Healing thought:
Tumors are pictures of festering thoughts, boils within your mind. Tumors are an exaggeration of your perception, not Truth. Release the festering anger and temptation to exaggerate your problems - and the tumor will shrink away into the eternal nothingness it came from.

Growths and Tumors

Growths and tumors reflect a sense of exaggeration, a festering of a long held misconception in your mind. Depending upon the location of the tumor on your body you will be able to diagnose your mental mistake that needs correction.

For example, in my case, an unhealthy attitude towards men and relationships in general during my younger years, and fostered by a distant and emotionally unavailable father in my childhood, lead to the manifestation of a large cyst on my ovaries. This went on for many years until I was diagnosed at a point at which I was seemingly beyond operative repair. The cyst had ruptured and the fluids had already poisoned the blood stream. Doctor's did not want to risk an operation.

Fortunately, the step-father of my best friend was a surgeon and she convinced him to save my life by performing the operation needed (even without health insurance). At the time I had only studied for a short period of time and only had glimpsed at the cause and effect theory. But I knew enough, and believed that my thought was causative and therefore the source of my predicament. I immediately went to the right idea of "I am healing quickly," "I am well, and I know it," and most of all I was not afraid. I knew that since I caused the illness I must have the power to heal it. I knew that this ordeal was a blessing in disguise and I quickly learned the necessary thought corrections that led to a speedy recovery. I have learned my lessons over the years and I am grateful that as my understanding unfolds so does my health and my overall well-being. All this time I remembered the words that I live by:

It's good, nothing than good can come, it's in my mentality.

I am born out of Goodness and I am Goodness itself...

March 29

Healing thought:
Fear of any illness intensifies the symptoms. Say aloud: I am well, I am perfect, I am health, I am safe.

Heal not only your illnesses and dis-eases; heal your emotional dispositions, your lack of abundance, your relationships, and your character flaws. Heal your world!

March 30

The Law of Individuality is a Universal Law that is broken by all of us most of the time. We are individuals and need to be able to express ourselves individually. No one should demand,

control, or plan for us. No one should judge our actions, not even our loved ones.

Maria

Since her early teenage years, Maria has chosen men that are hardworking, blue-collar guys with a temper. She has been through several incidences of abuse. Not that they were bad men, they loved her in their own way, cared for her and provided for her, but there was always a hot-tempered and violent side to them.

Many, many moons ago, she was only seventeen when she got engaged for the first time. It was more an escape from an alcoholic mother and unpleasant step-father.

She has bettered herself over the years by not allowing this kind of behavior anymore - she "graduated" to verbal abuse ... she herself can be verbally abusive when she feels helpless or powerless. After a period of verbal batter, but with serious intent to better herself, she found a new husband that is kind, reflecting her improved sense of relationship.

She has been married for twenty-one years now, a long time for today's standards and the relationship has been tumultuous, yet good in so many ways. They sincerely love each other, but both have much baggage and deep sadness from childhood not yet resolved. They are each other's mirror. It weighs on their togetherness and their communication styles. They do not always see eye to eye.

Maria has become controlling over the last many years, always telling her husband what to do and what not to. Always worrying about him and his immature actions; gambling, drinking, and wasting funds they could use for a better purpose. However, she knows that even though he makes wrong choices, she needs to allow him to do so. They are his choices. It is his life after all. She is still growing and learning with an open heart. As they improve their actions and love for each other, so the reflection in the mirror changes to reflect this new light.

You belong to no one and no one belongs to you.

I'm sure many people can relate to Maria's story. We all have our own way of dealing with relationships which is a bit more challenging since there is another person involved.

How do you act in a situation that is not ideal? Divorce is not always the answer, even though most people these days just pack up and leave, which the high divorce rate in this country sadly proves. It is obvious that a marriage enduring physical abuse is not a marriage. It is an unacceptable situation that needs to be resolved immediately. Please, find help through a counselor or therapist.

In the unions where love and caring is present, but one partner is more mature than the other, let communication between the two parties rule. If there is a sincere heart and the want for the continuation of the relationship, all differences can be healed.

First, remember, the "other" is only a reflection of you. Good or bad. It is a picture of your sense of the other combined with your sense of yourself. A reflection of all of your likes, dislikes, needs to improve, or already established goodness. When you look at your relationship with your partner from a distance, and not from a personal view point, you can see these observations, and they will make sense.

Not blaming the other for their so-called shortcomings but a patient and supporting role is commendable. Remember, they are perfect beings – it's only their actions that need improvement. Their "shortcomings" are only mistakes, wrong choices and immaturity. Finally, you have to be good and loving first, before you can expect the other to reflect these character traits. Look in the mirror, what do you see?

March 31

A few days ago I read: "Live in daily forgiveness!" What a powerful thought. To have the sense of "forgiveness" in the forefront of your mind all day, every day, and for everyone, is a wonderful application of thought. Cleaning out those pesky feelings of hurt, anger, and, resentment immediately and on a constant basis surely will heal your sense quickly.

Chapter 4: Application and Choices

April 1

We fool ourselves by thinking that we can get away with lesser thoughts and then we act surprised when unpleasant action follows. "Poor me" we say, and wonder why ... The remedy is simple. Improve not only your thoughts, but also your habitual demeanor. Good feeling is the key.

April Fool's Day!

Let's talk about fooling ourselves, and playing tricks ... aren't our perceptive senses always playing tricks on us? Don't you feel solid when you touch your body? Don't you see others as separate from you? Don't your ears deceive you when you hear your increased heartbeat with anxiety and fear instead of perfect calm? Doesn't your taste trick you when you swallow the bitterness of envious thoughts instead of the sweet fruits of joy?

We are to see our true being, pure Soul, we should feel our eternal being and hear the sweet sound of Nature. No trick to the Truth. Always reliable and always dependable!

April 2

Change your sense from "I have to earn money to live" to "I am abundantly provided for." Your wealth does not consist of money alone. Money is only the visible symbol of your abundance, which is produced in mind. Stop blocking your natural flow by limiting yourself to such restrictive thoughts as "I don't have enough," "I need," "I am broke," and replace them with "I have everything I need" and feel it as strongly as you can. And crown it with gratitude for what you already have.

Affirmations

From a reader, commenting on one of my daily inspirational postings:

"These are very good tips and I am sharing them. Do you have to speak these statements out loud or can you just think them in your head for them to be effective also. I am normally a very quiet person and don't talk much, but every morning before I get up I say my affirmations and prayers. After that I normally don't say much anymore, but I do listen to affirmations and brainwave entrainment audio throughout the day on my mp3 player when I get a chance."

My answer:

"What you think is more important than what you speak. However, if the verbalization helps you to really, really mean it, then that is fine.

Words spoken aloud are often just an added impress on your mind. It's like looking in the mirror while you are saying these affirmations - it will actually make it more personal to you.

You seem to have a very good habit of tuning into the Truth on a regular basis. Just make sure that you sincerely feel what you are thinking and saying. Feeling is the creative mother element, which gives birth to our ideas."

April 3

We cannot force anyone to understand or to want to learn about the Truth. We can only live by example.

I somewhere read the phrase "spiritually fertile hearts," what a wonderful way of saying that the heart has to be ready to receive. Fertile soil is needed when you plant a seed, so it is necessary to fertilize your heart with love and spiritual desire.

April 4

Healing thought:
The stress I am experiencing is self-induced. Therefore, I have the power to release this unnatural tension. Say: I am strong, I am self-sufficient, and I am a complete particle of the Universe. I can handle anything that is brought to my attention.

We constantly stress ourselves out with unnecessary fears and evil expectations. Why do we expect the bad all the time instead of the good results that comes from good thoughts? Why do we buy into the false advertisements of the media and the local or world news every day? They are designed to get us involved and emotionally distraught. They hype and entangle us in: "Look how terrible," "see what horrific accident," "observe these unspeakable crimes..." Where are the good news?

The media has to sell papers and get audiences for their shows; and outrageous news sells. So why do we watch? Do we realize that if we all would turn off the TV and only turn it back on to watch "good" programs the media executives wouldn't have a choice but to change the programming? It's us, the audience, which decides what is being broadcasted.

April 5

Do you deceive yourself by thinking you are a material being with a short time to live? Do you think that you are powerless over the many afflictions and illnesses just waiting outside the door? Why not wake up and see the mentalness of all, the limitless power your thought has over all that comes your way every day, and the beauty that escapes you only because your eyes are closed to the Truth.

April 6

Thoughts of a mother, called "me"

My son is getting married in a few months. It is a bittersweet time and even though he has been living on the East Coast for a while, and has served in Iraq for a year, including having been an avid traveler for most of his young life keeping him away from home, it is a new chapter in his life and in our relationship as mother and son.

I now have to accept the fact that he is grown and ready to create a family of his own. I shouldn't be surprised. He has always been an "old" soul. Very bright and curious, always involved in world issues, politics, and very well informed in all economical agendas.

He knew from an early age on what he wanted to be, never swayed in his decision to serve his country. At the tender age of eight years old he had told me that he wanted to be a special forces agent or with the military in some aspect. As a mother I wasn't always too thrilled about his career choice, but I respected his determination and, after all, it is his choice, his life.

Letting go as a mother is not always easy, but it can be very rewarding if done correctly. The daily phone calls I receive and the honesty that exists between the two of us prove that this approach works. All it takes is love and understanding. How blessed am I?

April 7

We cannot force anyone to understand or to want to learn about the Truth. We can only live by example.

What Easter means to me

Being raised Roman Catholic the story of Easter was always a sad and joyous one alike. As everyone knows, many religions teach that Jesus died on Ash Friday at exactly 3:00 p.m. and resurrected on Easter Sunday. The story is all about the suffering this man endured for "us."

I will not forget the processions I attended as a young girl, carrying the Virgin Mary with my school friends, and singing in church choir to celebrate this momentous occasion of Jesus' resurrection.

Now being all grown up my perception and beliefs have changed. Well, they started to change a long time ago – step by step. And not just a little bit.

The fears and threats of religious organizations do not have a hold on my persona and thoughts anymore. The days are gone that I think my sins have to be forgiven by another person, called priest, who then prays to God to forgive me, kind of like a buffer … how insane!

Don't get me wrong. I adore Jesus, but as a man, like you and me, with just a lot more knowledge of the

Truth. A man that lived and preached what he understood to be true, telling us that the kingdom of heaven was within us – not in a faraway place.

His wisdom misunderstood by so many. Like all great seers, East and West alike, he was showing the masses what needed to be done in order to find God.

And so on this Easter weekend I will remember that life is eternal. That we do not die and that through finding God and becoming "like him" we will find eternal bliss. We, like Jesus, are able to make this transition to the next plane consciously. We do not have to fall into deep sleep in order to rise to the next dimension.

We are all his children and so I rest assured that I am made of the same substance, perfect intelligence, goodness and wisdom as this great Universal power that we call God.

Have a wonderful and uplifting Easter Holiday!

April 8

Conscious transition

I'd like to talk about this "conscious transition" for a minute. We've heard about Jesus' resurrection, we know that Enoch walked with God "and was not," we read about the "chariot of fire" that transported Elijah into the heavens and about the Virgin Mary - she experienced a bodily ascension without the experience of physical death.

There are many others, gurus, and yogis that are documented to have risen after so-called death. One of the great reports of 1952 was the transition of Paramhansa Yogananda, who accomplished this in front of a room full of people. Here is a short version of the account that took place on March 7, 1952:

After returning to America, Paramhansa Yogananda continued to teach, write, and establish the Self-Realization Fellowship in southern California. He had a faithful following and many devoted disciples.

In the days leading up to his death, he began hinting that it was time for him to leave the world. On March 7, 1952, he attended a dinner for the visiting Indian Ambassador to the U.S. in Los Angeles. At the conclusion of the banquet Yogananda spoke of India and America, their contributions to world peace and human progress, and their future cooperation, expressing his hope for a "United World." ("Autobiography of a Yogi" by Paramhansa Yoganada.)

According to eyewitnesses, Yogananda ended his speech, he read from his poem "My India," concluding with the words "Where Ganges, woods, Himalayan caves, and men dream God — I am hallowed; my body touched that sod". As he uttered these words his body slumped to the floor.

As reported in Time Magazine on August 4, 1952, Harry T. Rowe, Los Angeles Mortuary Director of the Forest Lawn Memorial Park Cemetery in Glendale, California, where Yogananda's body was embalmed, wrote in a notarized letter sent to Self-Realization Fellowship:

"The absence of any visual signs of decay in the dead body of Paramhansa Yogananda offers the most extraordinary case in our experience... No physical disintegration was visible in his body even twenty days after death... No indication of mold was visible on his skin, and no visible drying up took place in the bodily tissues. This state of perfect preservation of a body is, so far as we know from mortuary annals, an unparalleled one... No odor of decay emanated from his body at any time..."

I am sure he joined his guru Sri Yukteswar on the astral planes per his belief.

April 9

**You constantly make choices. You say: "I don't
know what choice to make." Even doing nothing,
or not acting on something you should be doing, is
a choice. Feeling good is a choice. Being miserable
is a choice. I can go on and on ... isn't it time to
make the right choices?**

Do we have a choice?

We have the ability and freedom to choose. Choice is
one of the most important privileges given to us. It
ranks right up there with Reason.

Per William W. Walter, the Walter Method my original
long time studies, "choice" is represented in the spine.
The spine is the visible picture of this ability. We have to
make sure to use choice correctly. What we think, what
we do, and how we act are all the results of the choices
we make. We should only choose the good and make a
conscious effort to eliminate all wrong. We must stay on
the side of right in our mental activities. It's interesting
to note that when we speak from a place of confidence
and honesty we straighten out our spine and sit more
upright.

But if we feel that we "have no choice" in any matter,
and our shoulders slump in defeat, we are allowing our
power to be taken away or to stay inactive. We always
have to keep our power active.

Remember, you always have a choice, but sometimes it
can be an easy cop out to allow others to make choices
for you. It is extremely important that you are the
choice-maker in your life.

It is so important, that when a person "gives up," in
many cases their spine collapses and they end up in a
wheel chair. Not using your abilities always results in a

"loss of" something physical that represents this faculty or capability.

April 10

Healing thought:
Alcoholism is an immaturity of the mind. The sufferer avoids dealing with every day challenges and hides, not wanting to face growing up. The unholy ghost of emotions has taken over the fragile ego not governed by reason. It is time to mature and know that everyone is self-sufficient and capable of change. The only requirement is the desire to do so.

A drink, or two, or three, or...

One of the most detrimental choices is the obsessive use of alcohol and its effects. It seems that most every family has an alcoholic amongst them. Unfortunately, not everyone can have one or two drinks and call it a day. As I am not a doctor or health professional I can only strongly recommend seeking professional help. Alcoholism stems from very early childhood experiences, a not wanting to grow up, and a clinging on to childish behavior. Individuals who have this affliction do not want to take responsibility for adult living. They desperately hang on to the past and have a tremendous fear of failure.

The desire to change is a distant vision and in their minds a huge task. The pain has to become greater than the pleasure of being intoxicated before they even admit to the fact that a change in their behavior is necessary. I have watched closely and with astonishment, willingly or not, and I must say that tremendous will-power is necessary, but it can be done. No one can find true life by being intoxicated.

To the one that struggles I say: Wake up and allow the fresh healing waters, your yet unsolved thoughts, to enter your mind. Purify those thoughts with sound reason and understanding. Come back to the true meaning of Life!

April 11

Morning thoughts

I know many metaphysical writers have talked about the "unconscious" mind. However, there is no "unconscious" mind because all "mind" is active. The better expression would be subconscious mind. How it works is described as follows:

The conscious mind is your awareness of what you experience during waking hours. It's the part that reasons, assimilates what you take in through your five senses, and it's the part that comes to a conclusion through reasoning and feeling.

The subconscious mind is the storehouse in which all mental impressions are stored. It houses your memory, your habits, moods, and all thought-imprints. Just because we don't always recall something doesn't mean we are unconscious of it. We just have stored it away into our subconscious. The subconscious is also the part that is connected to your Soul and the greater part of Universal consciousness. Our intuition, mental messages, and vibrations, our spiritual frequency, are all transmitted to you through your subconscious. That's why it is so important to listen to yourself. It is of utmost significance that you allow quiet time with yourself so you can hear these messages.

I hope this makes sense to you, as I want to be very scientific in what I am telling you. Make no mistake; there is only one mind, with two functions.

April 12

Excessive, overboard thinking is reflected in what we call obesity; too much emotions, too much drama, too much of everything. Low self-esteem, a constant beating of self, lots of critical thoughts towards self and others, and a general misunderstanding of cause and effect – thinking that food is cause - add to this excessive appearance.

What is too much thought?

The expression "excessive thoughts" means a going on and on about something rather than making an effort to solve the issue. Many times an excessive thinker cannot make up his/her mind about a subject. It is a sense of going overboard in everything they think and do. It's a mental hamster wheel.

All mental activities need to stay in balance. Exaggerations of taking their responsibilities and obligations too serious, over-planning, rigorous scheduling, too much repetition, and going overboard with everything, including eating - cause the widespread obesity issues in this country.

In some cases an excess of criticism toward others and self is present. Individuals with this character trait also react easily in a hurt or negative way and give too much thought to the unnecessary. Excess demands are being made upon self and others; it's an enlarged sense of what's important and they are making a big deal, or a "mountain" out of everything - literally.

Soft fat tissue can be contributed to a "baby" attitude; an immature and needy disposition. However, too much body fat can also be an inflated sense of ego. But the appearance would be a bit different. It will manifest in the torso area, above the abdomen, as a rounded protrusion, a hard belly. I'm sure you have seen it many times especially in middle aged 'pushy' men. They are 'puffed up' you might say.

Your only responsibility is the responsibility to yourself and your spiritual unfoldment. When this sense of conscientiousness and reliability is in balance you will naturally do the right thing for others. You also will naturally display a "normal" body weight.

April 13

Talking about weight issues...

Let's check in with our friend Ilene Waters

You remember her story and its effect called "obesity" - which her mental attitude had on her body. Since our introduction of the story of Ilene Waters, twenty years have passed.

"Pain is an extreme motivator. Emotional pain, physical pain ... it hurts like hell. As I closed my forties I began to experience more aches than pain but, every so often, acute pain would rear its ugly head and I would be no match for that kind of suffering. Time and time again I knew, just from a physical standpoint, that losing weight could only benefit me as the years passed by.

Again, as in previous decades, I made attempts at losing weight. Crash diets, commercial diets like Nutrisystem, Positive Changes, Weight Watchers, etc. I'd lose some, gain it back ... yo-yo syndrome time and time again.

Cut to my fiftieth birthday party. First dance of the night, partnered with my best friend's husband to get the groove started and BAM! Down I went! Seriously ... it was mortifying! A large woman going down isn't pretty to begin with - couple that visual with a totally unexpected give-way of the knee, and I was

139

embarrassed beyond! I had no idea what happened - my knee just suddenly gave way and I fell to the ground. Needless to say, no more dancing for me that night! I sat on the sidelines, knee elevated with an icepack on it, and I watched as everyone else had fun dancing and partying.

After a few months of more unstable mobility, and ultimately, excruciating pain one night that landed me in the emergency room, I had knee surgery for a torn ACL. It was painful, the recap time was long and, to this day, I have no feeling in my knee area and walk with a slight limp when fatigued. Finally - I was walking like my Mom. You know ... that old lady 'rock' from side to side when the gait is not normal anymore. Hard as I tried to walk 'normal,' those days are done. At fifty I was still fat but now physically challenged. Ugh.

My fifties have not been fabulous. They have been particularly trying, what with menopause and mortality looming like a finish line banner. I gained weight. I exercised less. I reached 250 at my highest. I'd look in the mirror and cringe. Who was that old fat sweaty lady anyways? My spirit felt defeated yet I would continually tell myself that one day I'd get motivated again to get SERIOUS about reclaiming my life.

2012. I turn fifty-five this August. I lost thirty pounds a couple years ago, but have gradually gained about twenty pounds back over the past three years. The weight gain scared me. Not only that, in January of this year something began to happen with my back and legs. Numbness. Pain so acute and debilitating that I literally could not sleep, focus, or sit for longer than a couple of hours. I can honestly say it hurt more than any pain I had felt to date. And it was doubly bad because I could not get a restful sleep for longer than a few hours and this went on for a couple months. I was emotionally drained, physically exhausted, and abused by a pain so intense I just wanted to medicate and sleep until it all went away. If someone told me I'd have to live the rest of my life feeling like this, I would ask for euthanasia. Seriously. I was too tired to fight.

Time and time again I have beat myself up because I've mantra-ed 'Enough is Enough' only to slowly lose steam and allow inconsistency to take the place of focus and follow-through; couple that with feelings of self-loathing, because I've labeled myself a 'failure' in this area and I almost feel sorry for myself. Notice I said 'almost.' The fact is, folks, that I always keep trying. And that continues to be my motivator - not one specific 'AHA' moment where my life turns around and I reach the rainbow of thinness. My life is a series of moments and, when I focus on self, when I commit to a goal and keep the forward momentum going, then I do move forward and I am proud of myself. My problem, as with most people, is falling off the wagon, not keeping focused, not being consistent, and not following through. It's a winding road, I know. I've walked a thousand miles and gone nowhere. But for right now, at this moment in time, right here, without looking back in regret or looking forward with fear, I am committed to being a healthier, thinner me."

What brought her to this point of sincerity, saying enough is enough after all that time of agony, and what are her goals?

I want to point out that Ilene has been a student of metaphysics for many years and that she has a very good understanding of the power of her thought and the Universal Law of Cause and Effect. The point here is that you can have a lot of theoretical understanding; however, it is the action – the activity of your right thought – that brings results. Your feelings and your honest sense of yourself is the savior. You can speak the words and know all the answers; nothing will change unless you do the work. We will continue this journey of self-improvement. You see – it is never too late. All that counts is what you believe today and what you are

141

willing to do, this very minute. You are "the change" in your life!

April 14

I am reading the full edition, yes, all 780 pages, of the Science of Mind. Here is a great quote from Ernest Holmes:

A headache is a mental knot that needs to be untied.

Suppressed emotions, focusing on dislikes rather than likes, stressed about anything and everything ... these are the mental knots that need untying!

April 15

Want. Want. Want. All we do is want more. Why not say: "Thank you Father, Universe, (or whatever your name for this Almighty Power is) I have everything I need!"

Don't forget about your gratitude! Today I will certainly focus on gratitude.

April 16

Healing thought:
No one can hurt or offend me unless I allow this emotion to arise within me. What does someone else's opinion matter? Is not what I think, feel, reason, and conclude, what matters in my world?

Today I will release all hurt feelings...
Why are you listening to other people's opinion?

April 17

Remember Lucas and Elma?

In the January chapter I told you about the homeless couple struggling to survive. I received the phone call from a dear friend last night. The baby was born a couple of weeks ago; a boy, born with a slight jaundice condition.

It's difficult to take this responsibility as a parent, but we have to realize that all inflictions, being it disease or imperfections, showing up in a newborn are the reflections of the parent's thoughts. At the time of the development in the womb and at birth, the thoughts of the baby are not developed and therefore cannot cause disease yet. The parent's thoughts and dispositions, unknowingly - as they are not fully aware of their own causativeness - are what cause the apparent imperfections. The word jaundice, per the dictionary, means a "prejudice or envy." In this case a clear prejudice or envious view toward life in general with much fear or anger present. Fortunately this is not a permanent condition and will clear up over time, especially when the child starts thinking and creating for itself, which starts approximately at age seven.

April 18

Always move forward, progress is a Law of Life. Your feet look forward for a reason!

One of my friends called me last night. Apparently her husband has had issues with his knees for some time.

Knee troubles

First of all let me tell you a little secret: Everything we manifest on the right side of our body has to do with your feelings and emotions. Everything that we manifest on the left side of the body has to do with our reasoning and understanding. This (manifesting on the left side of your body) means, that you know better, but are holding a certain wrong sense for a long period of time that wasn't "good enough" for your current state of unfoldment.

Most of my "stuff" shows up mostly on the left side of my body, because I generally "know" the truth but I don't always think the correct thoughts. My friend Karen for instance has mostly right side issues. She is a very emotional person and "feels" a lot.

The "legs" have to do with your locomotion or progress in unfoldment. Our feet look forward – symbolizing that we always have to move forward. The knees help us carry out this forward motion. When we are stuck in the past we are not moving forward as comfortably as we should.

Left knee: holding too much of the wrong thoughts, maybe too much self-condemnation. Not getting on with our progress, holding a lower standard of thoughts, or just trying to painfully force the forward movement in life.

Right knee: knowing what is the right thing to think, but not following through sufficiently. We might have some strong feelings about a policy at work or at home that we feel we had to 'yield' to.

My tip: Move forward in life easily, comfortably and without strain!

April 19

I talk a lot about right and healthy thinking. It's the basis of my teachings.

What is healthy thinking?

What do we mean when we talk about healthy thinking? Is it just our thoughts that need attention, are feelings involved … and what about emotions? What about our life styles, habits, and behavioral patterns?

Health starts with your overall view of life. Clean living like the avoidance of excess drinking, smoking, drugs, and choosing healthy foods are a given. That's your starting point. Balance.

Adhering to the Laws of this world is a necessity before you can hope to adhere to the Laws of the Universe. Healthy thoughts include thoughts of calm, peace, relaxation, and a generous all-inclusive sense of Love. Thoughts of courage, self-sufficiency and strength also fall into this category. Making an effort to always look at the bright side, acknowledging sickness as temporary and unreal, rather than permanent and real, is pertinent to healthy thinking. "I am well" is the daily mantra helping you to stay vital and well.

Make a list of thoughts that you think are healthy and make a list with the unhealthy ones so you can see where your improvement needs to take place. Is the stress you are feeling this morning healthy? Of course not! How can you de-stress yourself? How can you get back to the peaceful place in your mind that you are yearning for?

April 20

A conscious transition to the next dimension is definitely my goal in this lifetime. I'm done repeating my mistakes and having to do it all over again. What about you?

This post prompted this answers from a reader:

"Yes I agree but what must we do to not have to come back. I have been striving for this my entire life, well anyway in this lifetime."

What must we do to not have to come back to this plane?

I think we have to look at several aspects of our belief systems; and most of all we have to "understand" what is true and what is fiction. I believe we must know that all is mental in nature and not material, including our bodies. I am convinced that we must fully understand that all is good and we are to live our best possible sense of life. We have to focus on our unfoldment, rather than putting emphasis on the worldly aspects of life; and we have to be fully committed to the Truth and live according to Universal Law, which requires diligent study.

Now this doesn't sound so hard, or is it? Yes, of course it's not accomplished in a day, or a year, or a decade – but I also believe that if we at least have sincerely glimpsed at the Truth we will be able to move on and up the spiritual ladder, which is not to be mistaken with a chore or contest, but a natural unfoldment of your already perfect being.

Remember, "there are many mansions in my father's house" - and I for one would like to visit a different room at my next visit with Universal Consciousness!

April 21

Healing thought:
Your hands symbolize the ability to handle all things in the mental. Reach out and touch someone one with kindness, compassion, and love. Handle your affairs with self-respect and honesty. You will rest easy.

Today I will handle all things with care...

When I write the "healing thoughts" my intent is to show my readers and students the connection of their bodily functions/abilities to their mental functions/abilities. Every part of our body represents something in the mental. Throughout this book I will address and make note of my thoughts regarding many of the most common connections. This will help me to clarify for myself and hopefully will also be beneficial to you so you can get a good grasp of the meanings. So in this example, when an affliction manifests on your hand(s) it will nudge you to correct the way you handle things in your daily doings. It's fascinating! Watch it!

April 22

Here are some thoughts I had this morning on "our sense," which I chronicled in an article.

Our Sense

"It's a beautiful day today, here in Los Angeles. Yes - it's always wonderful to live in this vibrant city. It's a city full of creativity and possibilities. And don't let anyone tell you different, because it is your sense that dictates how you perceive anything, including so called 'places'. I can be anywhere in the world, and it will appear to me as a wonderful enjoyable location. Why?

Because we are taking our sense with us, our perception of things, feelings, and moods, and we see the world as we believe it to be. Isn't that wonderful? We have a choice. We can change our environment according to our beliefs and convictions. That is why our attitude towards everything is so important.

Let's talk about symbols of this visible life. What does the ocean represent, for instance, and its steady flow of ebb and tide? The waves coming ashore ever so gentle, yet powerful. Ever wondered what the ocean represents in the mental?

147

Well, it's a vast mass of unsolved thought, not yet purified. Not drinkable, and not usable unless it is purified or solved. Thoughts, or thought potential, have to be examined and cleansed, just like the Ocean water that has to be cleansed in order to be useful or drinkable.

The Earth symbolizes Understanding ... we stand on solid ground when we stand on the Earth - Understanding is solid and we have to stand firm with both feet on what we understand. We have to unfold more and more from within, so we understand more of the truth that is Universal.

All visible life, anything you can hear, see, touch, taste, and smell are symbols of the unseen. Our work is to look at the symbols and figure out their meaning so we can use them properly and to our advantage. We shall reason about what we see and find that everything is mental. Its origin is Universal Consciousness, which is mental in nature. We have, through our beliefs and convictions, made it look 'material,' or of material substance, in order to make it usable on this plane. The fact remains however: it is mental. Everything is mental in nature. It cannot be otherwise.

All creations started in the mind of someone first. It was an idea or a desire, and it became a reality through the individuals longing for the specific want. The desire was thought and reasoned about, and as it became a reality, an achievable goal in the individuals mind, it manifested into the visible realm. Remember, it has to be a solid conclusion in your mind first before it will manifest. This is how the process works.

Life is everywhere. Look at nature - even rocks, sand, and shells have life. Plants are also considered to be a lower form of life. We know that they do respond to our thoughts and our sense. It has been tested and proved. Yes, we could move mountains if we just would understand that even the biggest and most solid looking things are mere mental images, mind reflections. Think about it! I will say 'good by' for now, with a sincere wish of health, wealth, and happiness for you and everyone!"

April 23

Breaking the Cycle, article for Whole Person Magazine
("The undoing of happiness")

"Habits and behaviors are hard to break. Being taught since childhood that we have to confirm to certain standards has made us automatons rather than individuals. Parents and teachers, coaches, religious guides, and anyone that we've ever came into contact with have left an imprint on our subconscious mind. Deep down we have accepted the rules of society. We thought we were 'good' if we conformed to the mindsets of others. Some of us accepted that we were 'bad' and continued on this path, therefore proving the Law of Cause and Effect subconsciously.

In order to change your perception of who you are to who you want to be you must first create a clear picture of your ideal self. Then and only then can you slowly change your perception of yourself, hence your image and likeness.

Well, the truth is that we are naturally equipped to unfold from within and that all knowledge is already stored in this vast ocean of consciousness. We do not need the outside perceptions to show us the way. In a matter of fact these outside roadmaps all lead to the same place: misery, illness, unhappiness – an inharmonious life.

In society's view, a 'good' little girl must grow up to be sweet, nurturing, and loving. She must be there for the family 24/7, bare children and provide the husband with a good home. She must be the caretaker and the one

149

that holds the family unit together. Unfortunately, women also have to work fulltime and provide additional income to be able to pay bills and to live comfortably.

On the other hand, a 'good' little boy must grow up to be a strong man that can support the family; become the protector and a leader. He must be in charge at all times. You think this sounds like the old days? Think again. It is a stereotype still practiced in many homes. Yet in larger cities you can finally see a picture that is slowly changing. More shared responsibilities and a general acceptance of role reversal is taking the place of old and outgrown thought patterns. Maybe there is hope?

Pesky demands of our society also include the race for a career and always having to win and to be the best. This encourages competition and also may induce unneeded stress. The stresses of today's world have promoted alcoholism and addiction of any kind in order to cope. Your habits have strengthened over time. Your behaviors are the actions stemming from those gradually acquired habits. Repetition is the key.

Breaking a habit, or more than one habit, will require diligent work. Repetition, repetition, and repetition again is necessary to change your innermost thoughts and convictions. Your habits might be those of getting angry easily, yelling and using bad language. Maybe you are getting nervous at the first sign of trouble, you are over-eating, over-worked, constantly complaining, and overall project a sense of negativity. Are you in the habit of criticizing and judging others? Are you constantly tearing your fellow man down; does he/she not live up to your standards? Look in the mirror. Your self-image reflects what you see in others.
You are not alone; however, negativity creates illness and unpleasant experiences and who doesn't want to feel good, healthy, appreciated, and loved?

150

How to change your perception of who you are to who you want to be?

We certainly have a picture in mind of who and what we are. Maybe a distorted one, but nevertheless an image of who we represent. Our self-worth, self-esteem, self-love, accumulated beliefs during our upbringing, and other outside influences, including our inner belief system, surely shaped us.

So you think you know yourself pretty well? You are generally satisfied with your moods, mind sets, appearance and productivity, and you created a wonderful home for your family. Good for you!

What about you on the opposite spectrum? The one that feels he/she always gets the short end of the stick. There is always some roadblock and you just can't get a break. You live paycheck to paycheck and just can't get ahead. Would you like to live better? Of course!

Where and what you are in your life (believe it or not) is not due to outer circumstances, but it is solely the making of your own belief system and thought convictions. It is a complicated structure of accumulated impressions, teachings, mental habits, and most of all beliefs about your "self' over a long period of time. So let's reiterate that only you can create a new you; only you have the power to change.

Your first step is to know who and what you want to be. Honesty with self is required to accomplish this objective. This takes some diligent thought and sincere soul-searching. I'd say we can all agree that we certainly want health, wealth, and happiness, even though, health, wealth, and happiness might have many different meanings to each and every one of us.

So how can you break the cycle?

I would suggest the following five essential steps: Self-observance through honest soul-searching, establishing a new mind model of yourself through finding out who you really want to be staying focused and determined in changing your thought habits to a more positive outlook, not doubting that you can accomplish what you have set out to do and stay on course, and to love yourself and treat yourself as the wonderful spiritual being you are.

Once you have done this exercise you should able to see your life in a different more positive light."

April 24

Do you want to inspire others?

Your and my behavior should set the standard for right living in this world. We all should be examples of positive thinking, good clean living, and therefore teaching and inspiring others.

Higher thoughts on "The Purpose of Life"

When I ask people "What is the purpose of Life" or "What is your purpose in Life" I often receive a blank stare. Some say: "I haven't figured it out yet" or "I'm not sure." Some say their career or artistic endeavor to create is their purpose, and some feel that taking care of a loved one, raising children, or contributing to a charitable cause is their purpose.

I'm sure we all have a different sense and interpretation; however, the true purpose in Life is "to unfold from within and enjoy." This means that we are all already perfect and good, but have "forgotten" this wonderful state of being. Unfolding from within, learning more about ourselves, using our intelligence, and then enjoying this process is what we are meant to do.

Through our unfolding awareness and the recognition of the Allness of Good we are inching closer to the goal of God realization. This process will lead to utter bliss and enjoyment once we come to this self-realization.

So relax! Live and learn. See the beauty and be part of the ever unfolding cosmic consciousness; and most of all enjoy the ride!

April 25

Your mind has the capacity to reason (male element of mind) and feel (female element of mind). Both have to be in sink in order to produce a positive experience. So the question "How do you feel today?" should be carefully examined and answered honestly. Right feeling, or Love, is the Mother of all creation.

The battle of the mind

Mental activity, thinking, feeling, and reasoning is going on all the time. It is part of the mental process. The immature, indiscriminative mind asks a question to introspection when examining itself. There is a struggle between beliefs and ignorance and the internal existing knowledge. Consciously or not, you already know all there is to know. You know right from wrong. You just haven't brought it into your awareness at this point.

Materialism or belief in a solid existence will win at first since it seems real to the ignorant, not yet unfolded mind. We are still in the infancy state of being. This mental activity (thinking/reasoning), however, should be natural and unlabored - not strenuous and exhausting.

We have to discriminate between right and wrong. We have to control the inner power to resist temptation to believe everything that we perceive with our Earthly senses or were taught by our elders.

A calm mind can win against all wrong thoughts, beliefs, and bad habits by affirming the non-existence of them and the knowing that in reality all is already good. A sincere effort, however, to better yourself is absolutely necessary to win this battle. You have absolute control over your thoughts and emotions, and through the proper application of these activities you will shift your energy to the truth of being – which is the knowledge of "all is mental in nature."

The "Mahabharata," one of the two major Sanskrit epics of ancient India, describe the six main faults of the human ego: lust, anger, greed, mental darkness and confusion, pride, and envy. Those character traits are surely mental hell, right here and now. People on this Earth engaging in this type of thinking are condemned to experience the outcome of evil. When your thought is not pure, your life cannot be crystal clear.

In closing of this day I want to stress the fact that there is an essential unity to all religions. There is no difference in Truth. Truth can only be true.

April 26

Take the emotions out of your relationship and see if you still feel the same way toward your partner...

Reminiscing

Today, twenty years ago, I met a man that was to become my second husband five years later. Times had been tough after my divorce from the father of my son. All I had left was a suitcase full of clothes, an old Mercedes, and a six-year-old beautiful son. We had moved out from the family home in the hills into a duplex down deep into the city of Hollywood – glad to have a job as a hostess at a studio restaurant. The "fat" years seemed to be over, but I had to move on. The living conditions had become too much to bare and detrimental to my soul.

I am blessed to be strong enough to move on when it's time. I've never been fearful of the future and I am grateful for this gift.

I wrote this poem for my son shortly before we left home:

Little Boy Strong

Little boy
Conceived on Easter Sunday
Seven years ago
Born into a marriage which really never was
A mistake perhaps

They tried of course, for the child's sake -

Little boy strong
Big brown eyes
Waiting anxiously for the fight to stop
"No more yelling" he pleads
Clinging to his mother's shirt
Smiling at his parents, like it would make a difference

Little boy, little man
Only six, going on thirty
He is handling it all too well
We could learn something

And I hear his little feet running down the stairs
"I love you mommy!"
I love you too my son

I was determined to make this work; and I promised to make a good life for us. Today his father and I are friends and can laugh about our venture together.

However, not long thereafter, on a warm spring night in April of 1992 I looked across the room - I was working at a wrap party, – remember the show 'Cheers"? And there he was six foot three inches, big old hat on and a winning smile. He grinned and waved at me as to say 'hey, you found me!'

I saw him at the grocery store the following week, co-incidentally standing in line (remember there are no co-incidents) and we started talking about our kids and such. The rest is history and twenty years later, our two boys all grown and getting ready to start their own families, hair a little grayer these days, and maybe a few pounds heavier; but he still has the big inviting grin and he's still here. Bless him!

April 27

"Esta bien"

Before I forget, I have to tell you a little story about what happened a couple of weeks ago. I'm always listening to my animals, the splashing water of the fountains in my garden, and all other sounds of nature; especially early in the mornings during my writing hours.

One morning a new little bird shows up singing and chirping away happily. I stood still to enjoy his beautiful melody and he loudly exclaimed:

"Esta bien ... esta bien ... esta bien..."

How much better can life get when even little birds announce that

"All is good ... all is good ... all is good..."?

April 28

Are you attached to everything around you? Your house, your car, your family photos, and all of your

Earthly possessions? Or can you look at them as a temporary abode, a convenient means of transportation and fond memories? You cannot take any Earthly objects with you on your journey to your next state of being. You can only enjoy them here and now while practicing your higher consciousness.

Attachment

This is something I have been practicing for some time and I advise you to strive to perform all actions, physically and mentally, without attachment. What I mean is, do not attach yourself to things or the outcome of a specific desire. If you are doing your mental work correctly, you will manifest your outlined want, but look at it as a useful temporary and enjoyable situation. Don't think the things you manifest are of value. Only your creative power has value. Your creative power enables you to create, create, and create again.

However, if your results vary from your imagined vision, you either made a mistake in your thinking or outlining. It could be that the desire wasn't strong enough, or good enough, in which case it was a blessing to seemingly have "failed." When you are non-attached to the outcome you can move on to your next goal or wish without a sense of failure, anger, and disappointment or grief. You simply start your thinking, idealizing, and producing again.

Healing thought: "Every day is a new opportunity to correct your yesterday's thoughts. The true 'I' of me is ever unchanging. I am non-attached to any particular outcome. I am only expressing my specific thought at any time."

Ponder this concept!

April 29

My business partner and friend received the dreaded news: breast cancer

Reflections and a new beginning, her story in her words...

"Anyone who has ever been diagnosed with a serious or life threatening medical diagnose is familiar with the sinking feeling that sets in when being told the news. In an instant, life's stage looks different, it's a new scene, the background suddenly looks grey and dull and we don't appreciate the new part we are given in this play at all. We all know bad things happen to good people but for sure we don't expect them to happen to us, even though every third woman is diagnosed with breast cancer.

I wondered where the heck this came from, when there is no family history, when I have a reasonably healthy life style, when I am not overweight, when I try to eat healthy, don't smoke, and when I drink alcohol and exercise in moderation. Why?

Most likely for this group of women and patients there will never be an answer to the medical 'why', at least not yet. The simple answer is, 'It is what it is.'

But then, of course, there is the question of how much influence emotional stress may have had, and that I have had plenty of. Sixteen years of painful experiences resulting from parents not being able to resolve or at least work on their marriage and their serious personal issues with themselves and with their own parents, engaging the children in this growing family cancer, being blamed for the situation based on ridiculous and immature accusations and exposed to poisonous jealousy attacks, worrying about the mental state of either one of the parents, about one's own physical safety and that of the parents, all of which resulting in a family completely breaking apart and as a consequence the children, well into their adult years, relocating their lives and families to other countries and continents to escape the madness and to prevent themselves from drowning in the sea of hatred, negativity ,and bitterness. No need to mention the stress added from moving half way around the world and everything that comes along with it.

This ill family and my place in it has cost me a lot of energy in my life. My attempts to mend things and to reach out to a mother that considers me one of her enemies have gone nowhere; the seeds I planted seemingly did not fall on fertile soil and quite frankly, I got tired of my father using my ears as emotional trash cans. So after yet another drama took place, eighteen months ago, I promised myself to be done with this.

Now, I could blame all that for my breast cancer diagnose. I could, but I don't. It wouldn't fit into the picture I have of life, where everything happens for a reason and for sure it would be of no help in the healing process. Setting aside the past sixteen years, my parents actually did a pretty good job, I was cared for and very well raised and didn't lack of anything. Or did I?

On second thought, in my perception I did lack something. I missed love and affection from my parents. I really did. To this day I feel that way and I believe that it has influenced my personality and therefore my life tremendously. Does that make me a victim? I don't think so. I believe it is part of the journey, part of my own growing process and that of everyone in the family involved in this situation. There are no hard feelings and I am not holding anything against my mother or my father. It is also their journey.

How ironic, just when I was ready to let go and to not feel their pain as my personal pain anymore, the scary diagnose was delivered to me. Actually I consider myself very lucky as the cancer was detected at a very early stage. Surgery went well and so did radiation therapy. Because one of my favorite quotes is, 'If life gives you lemons, make lemonade,' I decided to distract myself from the invisible yet scary rays soon to come down on me and to 'make lemonade' during every treatment. Laying still under the machine and waiting for it to start, I imagined an invisible box and filled it with negative stuff that I wanted to get rid of inside of me: fear, anxiety, feelings of guilt, and doubt. When the machine finally started I imagined the rays transforming the bad stuff in the box into bright white light.

Oddly enough, after I announced the cancer diagnose and my upcoming surgery to the family, my mother began seeking contact again, sixteen years after she declared 'not having a daughter anymore.' Since that time we exchange e-mails every week and when reading her lines I somehow can't help but notice the lack of aggression and extreme negativity that used to be part of her. She even invited me to travel to Australia to meet at my brother's home. So I will be traveling soon, I have no idea what the outcome of this trip will be; it will be an adventure for sure. I am going without expectations, I do not wait for miracles, I go without resentments, and I am determined to let things fall into place. If nothing else, making peace would be more than anyone thought possible just a short time ago. Things happen for a reason and sometimes seeds take a long time to start sprouting."

Here is a real life example, happening all over the world every day. I can let you know as I am writing these pages that she has reconciled with her mother, she has enjoyed a wonderful time in Australia, and has invited her mother to stay with her in America for the past several months. I am also happy to announce that my friend recovered fully.

In my mind, the childhood drama, the not "letting go" of anger and resentment toward the mother, and the feelings of guilt and negativity all contributed to the cancer. It was eating her literally from the inside out. To achieve full health you must heal your mind, or the affliction will return.

April 30

Is this funny?

I've had a placeholder in the upcoming chapters for two months now wanting to write about something "funny." A story maybe, or anecdote, a hilarious joke, or just something that tickled my fancy and would have been of interest... I want this book to be uplifting and educational, but I also want it to be light-hearted and enjoyable to read. This life is not as serious as it seems at times.

So here I was in search of "funny" and nothing happened. Don't get me wrong, I smile and feel happy 99% of the time, but "funny?" I crack myself up when my mind plays those quick word games, I laugh at myself for being witty and easily entertained. But that qualifies for nerdy, not funny... I'm a comedian in my own eyes ... that's it.

So I went on the internet in my sincere quest for "funny" - and this is what I got. Lots of funny videos, pictures, games, funny stuff ... but searching and what I found was not fun!

Then I went to research the word in the dictionary, and it defined "funny" as "comical, funny person, attempting to amuse, facetious, peculiar, odd and just plain funny." I think my personality reflect all of those words at one time or another, at least in my mind - and that's what counts after all!

Chapter 5: All is Mental

May 1

May Memories

What does your country mean to you?

In 1953, the region of Salzburg, Austria, sent the first "letter of responsibility" to all citizens who turned twenty-one that year. It is called the "Jungbuergerbrief" and they have done so ever since. The word "Jungbuerger" translates into "Young Citizen." I think you will enjoy the translation and see the significance and importance of this document in a world that has lost a lot of its values.

"Dear Jungbuerger,

You have reached the legal age of twenty-one and therefore have earned the right to vote. With this responsibility you have the privilege, and it is your duty, to participate in the shaping of your future public life – which is also important for your personal fate.

Your successful participation in public life demands being responsible, and requires a good knowledge of the history of your region, state, and country. Since you are a citizen and this is your country, you are being asked to show also knowledge of the people of your homeland.

In this celebration of your 'coming of age,' you are herby accepted, and it is now up to you to handle your affairs after your own will and strength; acknowledge the duties of the communities, and with a sincere heart help the development of these communities.

Support and uphold the beliefs and customs of your forefathers, and stand up for the independence of your homeland, the region of Salzburg, and support the freedom of your country, Austria, in word and deed.

You promised to uphold and honor these rights and duties in these celebratory festivities, and with honor you declared your sincerity - and strengthened it with your handshake.

Oberalm, September 20, 1953

Maybe we should send a letter of responsibility to the young citizens of America on their twenty-first birthday?

May 2

Think about this idea: If you do not especially "like" or "dislike" anything, it will make everything evenly enjoyable.

"Who am I," "What am I" "Where am I," "Why am I"...

Those are some of the most important questions you can ask yourself. You will find the answer to these questions at the end of this chapter.

May 3

Don't worship your teacher; worship your progress in unfoldment. Accept guidance and appreciate the teacher's wisdom and insight, but always keep your eyes on the "pearl of great price" which is the Understanding of Truth.

It is really important that you do not put anyone on a pedestal. Many will follow a teacher, therapist, or preacher and after some time become dependent on their guidance and advice. They start to put this person above themselves, their friends, and family, and they worship this individual, breaking the Law of Individuality.

I fully recommend finding a teacher, therapist, or guide so you have structure and support. However, wisdom, love, and desire to know the Truth should be your motivators to follow the path to Understanding. And your focus should be on God, Goodness, and Universal Consciousness - the Almighty power that sustains all.

A good teacher will make sure that your focus will be directed to self-improvement, not worship of outside powers. He/she will point out the absolute control your thought has over your physical body and what tremendous miracles "love" can accomplish. So choose your guides wisely, diligently and with open eyes!

May 4

We still crave Earthly pleasures and that's totally OK in moderation. You should build your heaven on Earth, here and now; it's part of your journey. Where we fall short is in keeping the balance between desires for the flesh and desires for the spirit.

Did Ilene Waters stay on course with her weight loss?

How do I intend to do it? How will I stay on course with my weight loss?

"Well, first of all, I have a lifelong friend who has been my mentor and best buddy cheerleader for over thirty years. She believes in me and helps me to believe in myself. First and foremost, you (meaning 'me') have to have a deep seated conviction and desire to really want to accomplish your goal. Whatever your motivation is (and trust me, it's been both negative and positive in my lifetime) it must be coupled with passion - that driving force that keeps you on track, focused, and committed to self-realization minute by minute, day by day.

Every minute is a challenge with me. I have positive reinforcement posts all around my house. Each morning I say a prayer to myself that I will take care of ME first today, stay committed to a healthier and happier life, and that no one or no thing is more important than my good health or me living the best life I can live for myself. This little mantra in itself is very important. FOCUS ON SELF.

I cannot stress that enough. It's so essential. Secondly, I check back in all day with 'me.' I ask myself 'How am I doing? How am I feeling?' And if I'm not doing that great, then I try and change my thought or action to a better one. Seriously! I take a few deep breaths and just alter my energy in a more positive way. Keep self-love coming all day long. You'll never tire of it, even sitting at your desk for eight hours a day. Thirdly, write your thoughts down. Journal. Words. Thoughts. Expletives. Recipes. Goals. Weights. Stuff. Write it down and get it off your mind!

Your thoughts have no weight, yet they manifest as the heaviest weight of all on your body if you carry around all the wrong ones. By writing stuff down you free yourself. You get it out of your mind and onto paper, where you can visit it later and truly see it for what it is. Mostly negativity, I can assure you. By writing stuff down, your feelings take a form, and rather than having that negative mass display itself on your body, it's much better to have it scribbled out on paper where you can read it, analyze it, and finally toss it where it belongs. Yeah. Write STUFF down.

165

My goals are simple: Live a healthier life. This means losing weight. This also means becoming more self-aware as to the WHY I'm overweight and HOW do I start to actually reach my goals. I could say I'm a failure. Time and time again I derail myself from my charted course of becoming a success - of attaining and maintaining my goals. I can make a million excuses and beat myself up, but I know this just results in a negative self-fulfilling prophecy. If I keep trying and I make progress each time then I move my life forward in a positive way. That is what is important to me. I think reaching the 'big goal' kind of scares me. This knowledge in its own light is an important tool in helping me to keep on my positive path.

Why does actually attaining something I want scare or intimidate me? I've heard of people being 'scared of success,' but what does it mean? Each individual has to decide for themselves what it means for them. All my experiences have lead me to me. I'm an explorer and this is my journey. We are all explorers and we are all on our own individualized journeys. Just remember we are all in this together, as one collective team. For every thought or doubt I have had, I know someone else has most likely had the same thought and experienced the same doubt. This gives me hope. Hope that I can figure myself out. Hope that others can relate to me in a commonality that is called life. I've got my boots on. Let's start walking the talk."

What are your thoughts on her views and feelings?

May 5

Be even-minded, calm, and focused. Look at things from a distance, like an observer, rather than an emotionally attached person. It will put your experience in perspective.

After putting down my reading material this morning, I was looking up the word "renunciation" in order to understand the meaning of this often used expression, especially in Eastern religions. The dictionary describes the word as an act or instance of relinquishing, abandoning, repudiating, or sacrificing something.

I also read online this morning, researching the subject:

"True renunciation is an attitude of mind and way of life."

"Renunciation" from what?

What are we supposed to abandon or relinquish? Here are my conclusions:

First, we have to become aware of our spiritual self and our connection to the Universe, and understand what "renunciation" truly means in order to desire "renunciation."

Second, let's take a practical look at what we need to accomplish by "letting go." We have to set aside our excessive worldly desires and expectations to become free of so-called social bondage, which in turn will free us from fear and anxiety. We have to let go of our exaggerated ego, selfish motives, and overcome the attachment to sense-objects, also known as material stuff. All of this letting go includes excess of any kind, daily compulsive planning, over eating and drinking, addictions of any kind, unpleasant characteristics such as envy, jealousy, criticism, and any unhealthy habits in thought and action.

Third, by cleaning ourselves mentally, step by step, from the old habits (a lower sense) we are truly working towards the light. We can do this through the help of inspirational teachings or diligent self-education in spiritual matters.

May 6

It seems difficult to awaken from this power of illusion or cosmic hypnosis that our Earthly life presents to us. The direction of our consciousness has to be upwards, intentionally, looking to gain a better understanding of Truth.

Those who coast and are mentally lazy will reap the unpleasant rewards of staying in the same daily rut. The only way out is to clear your mind of this mental clutter and lift your thoughts to where they belong.

Thoughts on religion by Virgil von Bramlett:

Being Religious

"I have studied religion for forty decades, both Eastern and Western. It is, indeed, a fascinating and complex topic of study. The similarities between diverse religions are often quite fascinating.

Most recently I have been concentrating on the Early Christian Church, the development and transformation of Christianity during the first 500 years. My research through the years has proven to be very enlightening, if not a bit disturbing.

What I find disturbing is so many religions that are practiced today started with the Truth and devolved into institutions clouded by social, political and personal motives of those who made the teaching of the enlightened ones into massive organizations often devoted more to dogma and fear than enlightenment. I refer to the religions they promote as institutional religions.

Please do not misunderstand. I do not judge institutional religions to be either good or bad. They have a purpose, fulfill a need for many and often do good works. However, I find institutional religions to be very limited if one is seeking Truth and enlightenment.

I consider myself to be a very religious person on a spiritual path. However, my views, or my religion if you will, may not be traditional to any organized religion but rather an amalgamation of ideas or thoughts gleaned from my studies. These are the thoughts I have either tested and know to be true or sense they are Truth based on the 'sense of knowing' which each of us possesses when we think and feel with our real self, that part of us which is a part of the Universal God.

Religion, for me, is a spiritual path of continuous learning, testing what I have learned and striving for enlightenment. We are not physical beings living in a physical world. We are spiritual beings living in a third dimensional world comprised of energy forms which appear to be solid. Our soul, the part of us that is of and from the Universal God, is our true self.

We are all connected to, and a part of, the Universal God. We are all a part of Divine Intelligence. In fact, we are divine intelligence. I believe our ultimate mission on this beautiful planet is to recognize who we truly are and strive to reach the next level of spiritual existence.

Being religious is, in my opinion, a way of life. It is living, on a daily basis, that which you have learned to be Truth on your spiritual path. Personally, I begin ever day by giving thanks for what I have received and what I will receive. Since my thoughts and actions determine what comes my way, I am constantly mindful of 'right thinking' and my connection to all things living. I end my day by reviewing where I might have made choices more aligned with 'right thinking' and 'right action'. Each day is a new and wonderful experience of learning, understanding and trying to live the Truth. It is not enough to study and learn. One must live according to what they have learned. Actions often speak louder than words.

Well, enough about me. How about you? If you have finished reading this article, I believe you are most likely on a spiritual path. Your choices and actions will steer your course. Free Will is a powerful tool."

May 7

I am watching this little, brilliantly green humming bird bathing in my fountain. I've just watched God in action.

In the translation of the Bhagavad-Gita by Paramhansa Yogananda (edited by his disciple Swami Kriyananda) I found an interesting sentence that really spoke to me.

"The uppermost thought in a person's mind as he dies determines his next state of existence."

Now sit on this statement for a while! I know I will...

May 8

Relationships can be at times painful when one feels either disrespected or not loved enough. We have to remember that even though we promised to "cherish and love" we are still immature in our attempt to fulfill this promise. This lower sense of "personal" love will always be accompanied with attachments, expectations, and requests.

Say: Today I will give it my best and see my partner in a non-attached loving way. I will see him/her through the eyes of patience, kindness, and forgiveness. I will practice love.

Time to check in with our friend Sallie ... remember her relationship story?

"Dear Ulrike, I hope you are well. You said to let you know if I have any questions on my hiatus from class, and I do. I'm having a tough time with some of my husband's family members and I don't know what to do about it. I wish I could talk to you guys about it in class!

My sister-in-law gets drunk and messy almost every time we go out with them. Sometimes she gets belligerent, sometimes falls. We go out with them less and less, but he loves his brother, who I don't really care for either, so he wants to see them. I try not to talk to him too much about it because I don't want to put him in the middle, but sometimes I just complain about them.

My husband the caretaker of a very dysfunctional family and now that I'm here he is less so. They're probably a little resentful. And I'm getting resentful of his caretaking of them instead of us. My father-in-law always hits him up for money, and he often gives it to him which infuriates me because we are supposed to be saving for a new house.

Overall our relationship is good and things are well. There's just this recurring problem that is really starting to get to me. I thought u might have some perspective.

I really miss class!!"

How would you respond to this plea for help?

Unfortunately, we also "marry" the family of the new spouse. I know it's not always easy, but I think the key is to take "yourself" out of the picture and consider "yourself" as an "attached being." You are an individual and not in any way connected to anyone, unless you get involved in their affairs, and act as "part of" the other people. This is your choice.

171

What you can do - since you probably can't avoid the company of your husband's family at all times - you can show and feel compassion for the person that obviously has an alcohol problem.

When you start seeing the issues as an observer, you will feel less emotionally attached and release the need for judgment. Compassion for someone that obviously has a problem stemming from either severe insecurity, self-hatred, or other wrong dispositions will help you to put things into perspective. It will instill a sense of gratitude for your own life. And that is the correct thought you should be entertaining.

May 9

Intuition

How do we "know" in advance or/and perceive by intuition? What are the subtle triggers that pop up in our mind, telling us to either go for it or not? Why do we sometimes know the outcome of an upcoming event in advance? Why are some people more intuitive than others?

We all have the ability to "know" in advance. However, we do not always listen carefully. We drown out the signals with the business of the day. Running around fulfilling chores, paying attention to everything but what your subconscious mind is trying to convey to you, is how most of us spend our days.

In reality, instinctively we already possess and know everything there is to know. However, since most of us are not aware of this fact we are looking for the answers in all the wrong places. In an Earthly sense, all information is available to us, especially in this new world of technology. In a mental sense listen carefully to what your "gut" tells you and listen to the signs all

172

around you. You do know what's right for you, I promise!

May 10

We are indigenous to the region of the Universe – We are all One

I always love the research involved in writing an article about a certain assigned subject. The adjective indigenous is derived from the Latin etymology meaning "native" or "born within;" and from this standpoint we can say that any community might be called indigenous in reference to a particular region. Other meanings of the word are inherent, innate, original, first, or natural, which in my mind fully describes our true birthplace called universal Consciousness. Merriam-Webster Dictionary defines indigenous people as "a body of persons that are united by a common culture, tradition, or sense of kinship, which typically have common language, institutions, and beliefs." Doesn't this sound like "us" the searchers of light and truth?

We all stem from this same life source, originated in the Universal, mental realm - a true mental region. We are connected by similar thoughts and feelings, kind kinship and love, the love of service to others and a sincere spiritual tradition for self-unfoldment. We speak the common language of love.

What does it mean, "We are all one?" How can we connect through what I call the spider effect?

Think of a spider web. Isn't it fascinating? It can stretch, grow bigger and bigger, and it spreads until it entangles all. One little creature can create such a magnificent structure and have such an impact. Like the spider, we are all little creatures compared to the vastness of the Universe. But we all can create a giant web of goodness because we are all connected in the mental realm. We

173

all come from one source. This connection makes us all powerful.

Our ambition should be to be a spider in the World Wide Web. Not on a website online, but in using our ability of our thoughts webbing out into the Universe, connecting to all. Start thinking more all-inclusive thoughts, more Universal thoughts, and more all-loving and healing thoughts. Think of a bigger picture and don't stay in such a small vacuum called your personal sense.

Whatever beliefs are held strongly in mass consciousness will be reflected in the reality of this world, good or bad. If millions of people think the same way, or expect the same outcome, it will manifest. Again, the economy is a very good example. It reflects mass consciousness reacting to fear. You can also see this thought power in the creation of epidemics. In the extreme way this is how war happens.

On a positive level, as mass consciousness evolves, it shows the picture of better living, wealth, and prosperity in our world. The American people have long been known to have a prosperous attitude and a strong self-sense, which has been reflected in becoming one of the world's leading nations. The collective sense of America's population has made the USA what it is today.

We are in an age of great spiritual change

In this day and age people are awakening to the truth that the invisible cause and the visible effect is the result of their own right or wrong thought. They have come to the realization that the Universe is a mental rather than a physical, material state. As more and more people discover this truth, the reflection (your specific life experience and environment) will change to correspond to this newfound insight.

We have to start somewhere. This somewhere is our own right thinking and thereby creating our own right future. From there it is only a few steps to contributing to a greater picture. Don't underestimate collective consciousness. It is very powerful. It is a spider effect rippling out into the world. Yes, we can make a difference in this world, even though it still needs so much inspiration and healing.

Metaphysical education is becoming more and more important. We have to make sure that we include our brothers and sisters on this journey with us. We must not leave anyone behind. We cannot force them to do what we want them to but we can put the information and our knowledge out into the Universe. They will find this treasure when they are ready and prepared to take this journey on their own.

So be part of this phenomenon and spread the good word and let's use the tools given to us by the inventors of technology, who are certainly being creative sources of the Universe. It is exciting to become aware of more and more we didn't know before. We start seeing our mental growth and can enjoy the fruits as we go through this adventure. Our awareness constantly grows and changes; it evolves and gives us a sense of comfort, security, and peace of mind.

The willingness to embrace all aspects of life, being good or challenging, will further help and speed up your unfoldment. It is an ongoing series of action, never ending. You will take what you have developed and understood with you at the point of your passing to the next dimension. Do not forget this vital point. Remember, you have to start with YOU first. Entangle the world in love and happiness...

Lastly, remember these inspiring and powerful words:

"Imagine all the people living life in peace. You may say I'm a dreamer, but I'm not the only one. I hope someday you'll join us, and the world will be as one." (John Lennon)

May 11

Healing Thought:
Teeth represent the chewing over of ideas.
"Sinking your teeth into" something; a project, or
some new concept. They also illustrate your
patience of "thinking it over" in your mind. Make
sure your thoughts are properly "chewed over"
and beware of what's coming out of your mouth
(the spoken word) in order to avoid tooth aches.
Ill feelings and unkind words always will have an
ill effect.

Teeth and their purpose

Here is a personal issue I've been dealing with most of my life. Being raised in Austria in the '50s and '60s, dental care was barely heard of. You only went to the dentist when you were in pain. With little anesthesia used, going to the dentist was no picnic. By the time I came to America and discovered the benefits of proper dental care the damage was done.

Then I found out through my studies that even teeth could be healed and improved through the right mental attitude and the knowledge that all is mental in nature, including bones and teeth. Teeth are one of the "harder" things to heal mentally because they are seemingly made out of a "hard" substance. The more solid a bodily organ, body part, or material thing looks, the more difficult it is to acknowledge it for its real nature, namely its mentalness. The belief in materialism always keeps us in the dark. As I stated in the quote above, teeth represent the "chewing over of ideas," and we need to think carefully and with much reason about all we entertain in thought.

Going to the dentist should be manageable. When you have car trouble, you bring the car to your mechanic body shop in order to have it tuned up, inspected, and repaired if necessary. So it is with your body. It's a maintenance issue. Therefore, when I go to the dentist, I sit in the chair and start imagining the reality of my mental body. I close my eyes and feel the vibration of my internal energy. I envision myself as a being of Light, Spirit, and all sense of solidity dissolves. I am not a master of this practice yet, but I'm at a point that I can feel a difference in pain and discomfort. It's all about practice ... the only way you can better and heal yourself is by diligent practice. Try it!

May 12

I just love all dialog with my readers. The question of today was:

What is your general sense about Life, God, and the Universe? Tell me what you think about your overall beliefs ... or do you even think about these things?

Reader:

-I believe that I am co-creator of The Universe... I believe that love is the energetic glue that holds it all together.

-I believe we are all here to learn "lessons" and the biggest lesson is LOVE and how we treat each other. GOD is our "source" for learning all these lessons and the Universe provides all the necessary tools.

Me:
Yes, yes, and yes! All is Love, God, Spirit, Consciousness and Goodness. So we are this Love, God, Spirit ... in action - bettering ourselves each day when applied correctly.

Reader:
- Like plants, I am growing constantly ... sometimes it takes a while to see on the outside.

177

- I believe God is power and I'm plugged in like an electric cord to a socket. The Universe and the world around us is made of energy that we constantly borrow from and when we leave our physical bodies we give it back. Where does that consciousness go? Where was it before? I don't remember being born into this world and often wonder if I will remember it in the next one.

Me:
If you remember this life will depend on your understanding of the Truth at the time of your passing...

Same Reader:

- Does it make a difference if we understand now? And why at the passing point?

Me:
Because your highest thought at the passing point, even if you think you understand now, will be higher. We are always progressing and therefore the passing point will determine your next journey.

Love, love, love these conversations! Bring them on!

May 13

Are you hungry for more spiritual food? Or are you content with the daily fast-food you are providing for yourself? Start being a gourmet diner and feast from the delicatessens of true Spirit only. It is already waiting for you, ready to be served.

Personal sense and honesty

Our concept of your "Self" is our collection of our thoughts from childhood to now. It's our sense of our "Self" or what we believe our "Self" to be.

178

Contemplate the source of your consciousness. Focus on who you are (true spiritual self) rather than who you think you are (ego with a body). The world as you know it will change in many aspects if you see yourself as an observer rather than stuck in the midst of everyday life. Take a step back from your personal and emotional involvement. Problems will dissolve with this new awareness. The problems you encounter never have substance in the first place. Yes, I know they certainly seem real, but you made them up in your mind through incorrect thinking. These life issues are only a reflection of your beliefs and distorted concepts of self.

Your Consciousness will expand when you focus on self because it becomes your prime focal point. Take your attention away from the material world for a period of time and you will experience a shift in your awareness; you will realize that you are completely different from who you think you are. You are a Soul; a mental being, not a so-called human. You only bought into this story of humanity.

May 14

Healing thought:
A scar is a memory of a "hurt" in the mental. You don't have to hang onto and remember your pains and injuries. Forget the incident, and move on to more pleasant recollections. As your memory of the occurrence fades away, the visible scar will also vanish.

There are physical scars and there are mental scars. I truly believe that it is your mental scars that need to be healed first in order to prevent or heal any physical scars. Healing the mental scars will also make the physical scars disappear.

Mental scars start from the day you are born through wrong teachings and ignorance. We carry them throughout our lives and we hang on to them. Unless we

179

start to acknowledge the scares for what they are, heal them, and move on, healing will take a long time. However, there is a better world awaiting you - one without scares and pain, and it's right here and now!

May 15

Talking about mental scars, here is someone with an abundance of those dark memories.

Dexter's relapse

It took a lot longer than expected to get Dexter in mental and physical shape to enable him going back to work.

After making nice progress at first, and a seemingly slow but steady recovery, Dexter started to complain about other minor aches and pains, especially about being tired all the time. His drinking increased and even though you would never see any visible signs of abuse, his wife could tell. Still being on disability, he was sleeping most of the day without any desire to accomplish anything.

Depression at its best! The therapy sessions were excruciating as he didn't want to open up and share what was really going on in his mind. He didn't trust anyone with his true feelings, keeping them all bottled up. However, he continued to "talk a good game" with his friends and drinking buddies; all the while being frozen with fear of having to move on and live life. Being able to go back to work was one of those fears. After a six months hiatus he was just not able to adjust with the daily routine.

His anger issue and blaming others for his misery flared up again; reminiscing about the past and how much better the "good old days" were - it again was part of his daily disgruntled attitude. No surprise his hypertension and back issues continued. Where is his healing?

In the conversations with his wife he revealed that he always wanted more, mostly material goods, and he didn't see that he already had everything he needed. He possesses more than enough, a nice home, great cars, and a loving family. And even though he says he knows "he's blessed," his heart wants more and more, signs of a true addict. He feels empty and poor, the therapist called it a "donut hole" inside of him.

Finally, after several more sessions, he had understood the concept of thinking better thoughts and being more open to the idea of letting go. Once again, he promised to think about his issues honestly and apply what he had learned.

When he went back to work, the work environment that seemed so "unpleasant" greeted him with open arms and he came home feeling better. Each day improved and by the third day of work, he was asked to apply for a position that offered him higher pay. Excited and with a much better spirit he did just that. We will revisit him in a few months to see how it played out … and hopefully he keeps his new and improved attitude.

May 16

Healing thought:
Hoarding is a lack of knowing that the Universe is abundant and that you are part of this abundance. Fear of not having and clinging on to material possessions as the symbol of "having" shows that you believe in the possibility of "lack." Let go of material things, they mean nothing in the vast ocean of Universal Consciousness.

When you see people always wanting more and more "things" and nothing is enough you can surely tell that there is a lack of something within their Soul. This line of thinking triggered my desire to explore the thought of "hoarding."

What makes a person so desperate that they hold on to everything including what most of us call trash? Studies have shown that this type of behavior is prevalent in people over the age of forty and more so in men than in woman. It also shows that there is a connection to childhood abuse; proving traumatic events are positively correlated with the severity of hoarding.

The amassing of possessions, even if of no value, masks a greater problem of emotional imbalance; a hiding behind the mountains of trash (emotional problems), so to speak.

In the lesser offense of "wanting more and more" it also shows a fear of "not having." This fear of not having enough, or being able to lose your possessions, a wrong sense of materialism and what it means to you, a "doomsday is just around the corner" attitude, all contribute to wanting more. It's like a security blanket; you can hide behind your possessions. However, in reality, only your sense of abundance can save you from lack. It's your mental sense that governs your life, and your thoughts of wealth will bring fortitude into your experience.

Abundance is a mental state.

May 17

Giving and receiving are in equal relationship. When you start seeing that both are mental not material, you will experience abundance flowing in easily.

Let's talk about business!

I hear it all the time: "I'm financially challenged right now" and "I'm broke" or "I can't afford it." All the negative statements are readily at the tip of your tongue. As I said before, abundance is a mindset and your first affirmation should be "I have everything I need."

How do you create new business?

First, you have to outline the desired business in your mind and switch your mind-model from where you are to where you want to be. It takes a change of mental attitude, from lack of business to "I have plenty of customers." It takes a rigorous change of your word habits, thought habits, and your feelings of not having enough.

Good business is a fulltime commitment. When you are a business owner you are in it for good. See the words I'm using? It's all good, your business is good, your state of mind is good, your income is good ... good, good, good, and don't you forget it!

If you want your business to thrive, or your career to take off, you have to live it, breath it, and most of all "be" it. Only if you identify "being it" can you be successful. This also means that you better enjoy what you are doing or you will not experience the ultimate satisfaction.

Now the key is to know your "real business" – which is your business of self-discovery and self-unfoldment. Your first business in life is YOU. Do not forget this vital point. Make it your number one concern, work on your mental business, and your Earthly business will reflect this state of mind.

Be about the "father's business" as Jesus said, your spiritual business. Be busy with good and right thoughts. Conduct your Earthly business to the highest standards. Always remember that the best principles in business are to provide good quality, good service, value, making people feel good, honesty, integrity, sincerity, giving/ being generous and fair pricing – it all will come back to you a thousand-fold. With that attitude you cannot fail!

183

So remember, don't just focus on the big dollar signs at the end of your wish list. Focus on what good you can do for others. Will they like your services; will they enjoy your product? You bet they will!

May 18

In an article I wrote recently, I shared my thoughts on:

Your "higher good" - what is it?

We have to learn to use our inner energy in a positive way before we can hope to change our mental dispositions, personalities, and moods. To reach the "higher good" takes a rigorous mental housecleaning and an honest approach to allow yourself to open up to life.

Staying open when you meet new people, being neutral when encountering a new experience that you are unfamiliar with, and releasing blocked up mental energies are part of the process.

Blocking your inner energy makes you listless, fearful, and tired. To release those old mental blocks you need to allow yourself to take one last look at this past occurrence that caused this blockage, which was nothing than a ton of garbage that you allowed to affect you. Look at this past event, don't dwell on it, just observe it – and let go of the attachment, your sense of "it happened to me." Take yourself out of this self-inflicted bondage.

Say: "I am letting go, I do not want any memory of hurt, lack, and despair in my life. I want positive energy only. I am free."

What is this positive energy? Enthusiasm, love, vitality, vim and vigor, awe of life, are other names for this vital life   vibration.

"Looking forward to" a new day or new experience rather than dreading what's coming up. Thoughts of confidence will make you feel strong and vibrant. Open your eyes to the beauty of Nature and a sense of awe will rush through your body as a response to your mental openness.

Every thought you think sends out energy into the Universe. Some are strong and some are weak, but this vibration or energy will attract or reject the corresponding effect. Positive, energetic thoughts will produce positive and energetic vibrations and help you to open up your mental blockage. This positive force will lift your Spirit to where it belongs – Up!

I like to call our personal vision for our future "grounded dreams." They are dreams that have their basis in reality and are built on a solid foundation. Dreams will come true when built on solid understanding. Like a new house, the foundation has to be constructed on a rock, not on shift sand, in order to last for a lifetime.

Your "higher good," which is your understanding of truth with its corresponding brilliant effect, will be in reach once you have done your diligent exercise in opening up to Universal Goodness.

May 19

Daily corrections

Ask yourself: What is bothering me and why? What enrages me about a situation? What makes me fearful or uncomfortable? Go to the root feeling and dig it out from the deep within. This is your starting point necessary to healing.

Don't get lost in your problems. Some people seem to be followed by "bad luck," all sorts of issues hanging over their head and their experiences are mostly unpleasant. I doubt if they see that it's not about being

185

jinxed, cursed, or accident prone – but that it stems from their beliefs, actions, behaviors, and mental attitudes. It must be corrected in self.

May 20

Do you believe your problems are real? What is a better way of looking at them? Aren't they challenges to test your understanding, your moods, and your attitude toward all? Aren't they showing you where correction is needed?

I'm all about application. Application is the only key to a successful and fulfilled life. Looking at the daily challenges a little bit closer made me think. Why not embrace our problems - step back for a moment and see them for what they really are. This stepping back (or non-attachment) will allow us to emotionally distance ourselves.

Let's observe what has been going on in our experience and look for clues in our thinking. What have we been focusing on? Have we allowed ourselves to feel worried, uncertain, and stifled? Have we reacted to someone else's issues, instead of paying attention to our own good?

The next step is to let go of the fears and the imaginary mountain of problems will look like a mole hill instead and will become manageable. Allow your Self to open up and embrace the natural flow of the Universe to alleviate this mental blockage of fear.

May 21

What is inspiring?

Every day, in this Earthly life, there are ups and downs, deep emotional valleys, and steep mountains to overcome. We have not yet learned to travel the straight and narrow road of Understanding. We still coast and veer off the path we travel. A sudden change of attitude or a jump back into a dark habitual mood always deters us from moving toward the light.

It is this light, or moment of "seeing with the mental eye," that inspires us to keep moving and trying to get back on the road to eternal bliss again and again. This glimpse of the Truth that all is good and that we are part of this Universal Goodness with its wonderful effects is what keeps us going.

Inspiration comes in many forms. A wonderful reminder of a past experience, a certain smell reminding you of a pleasant encounter, the sound of a song that triggers loving feelings, looking at nature and its wondrous bounty, or the birth of a baby are just a few examples of new hope and a fresh want for living.

Knowing that God is close and ever present is all the inspiration I need to keep moving forward. Seeing the sunrise in the early morning hours reminds me that I have another chance to change my course and I will travel happily toward my ultimate goal, which is perfect Understanding of the Allness of Good.

May 22

Healing thought:
The word "Anemia" comes from the Greek meaning "without." A lack of love, a lack of purpose, too much focus on the negative and a sense of listlessness, manifests into "Anemia." To correct this condition, generate a great sense of interest in the good things of life, your true purpose, and circulate this loving interest throughout your being.

Inner energy

Have you ever noticed how exhausted you are after being very emotional, crying, fretting, worrying, being afraid and terrified – you spent your inner energy.

We are energy. We are vibration. We are beings of Light. We are mental beings.

Depression is a lack of energy. Not wanting to do anything, lacking positive vibration, and focusing on negativity and sadness is what causes this mental hell.

You've experienced dragging to work, having no energy, but as soon as you get home and there is an invite waiting for you to a concert of your favorite band your energy level changes immediately. In no time you are rejuvenated, dressed, and ready to go.

Do what you like and you will have all the energy in the world. This is the key to inner energy – always do and focus on what you like and follow your heart. You will burst at the brim with vitality and love for life!

May 23

Your voice in your head is constantly talking. Start listening to the excessive chatter and observe its mood. Is it positive, negative, or just going on and on about something? This voice is your reasoning ability. It will debate between the options you have. Start choosing the positive side only. You can train your "voice" to instantly seek the right and good side of all, but make sure your feelings are also in check.

May 24

More thoughts on Mental Healing

I have, and will, incorporate many healing thoughts throughout this book. As I said in my first book *"Better Living...Because You Can!,"""* all sickness is caused by our own wrong thought. This statement is not to be taken as criticism. It is just a statement of Truth. This "mental" healing cannot be accomplished in a day or two; only through diligent analysis, study of self, and a willingness to change one's dispositions and beliefs can it be achieved.

There is nothing mysterious about mental healing. It only means that you have to correct all of the wrong thoughts and concepts you have been holding for a long time and replace them with true and good thoughts. The healing will take place naturally after you have cleaned up your mental household.

Once your Consciousness has acknowledged and accepted the fact that all is purely mental it will not look outside of itself for healing. Material medicine will be seen as a human crutch, helping the ones that have not yet grasp these facts.

May 25

Healing thoughts:
The "belief" in the reality of allergies plays a major role in this discomfort. However, all allergies are caused in the mental, by being too sensitive, too easily hurt, or taking offense quickly. It is an over-sensitivity to emotional excitement, or an aversion to a specific idea in mind. Stop reacting and let go of your "touchy" sense. Start thinking from the basis that "all is good" and "all is mental'."

Sometimes when I post the "Healing Thoughts," I frequently cause a commotion; but we would not experience progress if we would only state what is already known. In order to discover the new and improved, we must ask questions and search for answers and we must state the Truth as we know it.

Reader:

"I want to ask you about the allergies... Seriously, I am allergic to medicine... I was also told I would die, because of a few insects... I do not see it as being weak mentally, it is a real problem... Explain how children have allergies? I never knew I was allergic to anything! I do mean to be respectful; this is just a simple question.

Me:

"Hi Tracy, I am happy to answer your questions. You are most likely allergic because of belief. We happen to belief what doctors, parents, and teachers taught us since the day we were born. Much of the illnesses are manifested through this solid belief. However, since you are Spirit, a mental being, you cannot be hurt by insects, pollen, or animal hair, etc. When people stop being over-sensitive and easily hurt they will be relieved from certain allergies. I had one to "dust" and cleared it up many years ago. Children pick up the sense of their parents. You will see this problem in children living in a household that is very emotional. Let me know if this cleared it up a bit?"

Well, this lady didn't like to hear what I had to say. She became slightly agitated – you could even feel it through the pages of the e-mails - and said that she never listened to doctors, teachers, or parents growing up. When I pointed out that she subconsciously was maybe listening to TV commercials about medications and allergies she also denied watching TV ... really?

190

She proved my point. She was so touchy, defensive, and emotional that I was surprised she didn't break out in hives right then and there...

I told her that it was OK to stick to her opinion and that brainstorming was a good thing for all concerned, bringing new ideas into the light. She took a moment and then apologized, saying that she was grateful that I didn't get offended.

Lesson: Don't take everything so personal. An opinion is just an opinion. We are here to find the truth...

May 26

Observe yourself. Are you constantly complaining about something? Is there always something just not good enough; an irritation just around the corner? Who do you think causes your unpleasant experiences? Take a good look in the mirror ... there you are! Stop and promise yourself that from today on you will see perfection only; and you will think the best possible thoughts exclusively.

Going back to the basics

When we are absorbed in the study of Life we sometimes forget about the basics. What are the basics?

Looking for the good in life, thinking an abundance of positive and loving thoughts, and treating everyone we come into contact with kindly and respectfully. With the ups and downs we experience in life, we can either grow and expand or we can shut down and close ourselves off. We can become more afraid and shut down completely. It really depends on how we view our life. Wouldn't you rather open yourself up to more goodness and more love even though you might have to work out a few kinks along the way?

191

Clamming down with fear, expecting the worst in every situation will suck all the joy out of you. Change is good. It opens you up. Newness is good. It gives you inspiration. Unpleasant experiences are good - really? you say... Yes, really! They show you where correction is needed. All is good.

Fearful people like to control their situations and environments to make sure their fear is under control. Opening yourself up without knowing what's around the corner takes courage.

How do you overcome fear?

Start with the lesser fears, called worries, first. Write down all that you worry about. Reason about your concerns and disturbances: Do you really have to worry about every single one of them? When you get in the habit of not worrying so much your fears will lessen. You will start being more open and courageous. Fear is nothing but a bully of the unknown. Let the light of reason shine and be assured that the more you expand and grow, the more you understand the truth of being, the lesser your fears will become. Fear will no longer have a grip on you; it will dissolve to its native nothingness.

May 27

Healing Thought:
Migraines, an extreme and painful disorder (of thought), appears more commonly in people that are considered "perfectionists." Contributing factors are severe frustration about the job or relationships, ambitious character traits that want to achieve but have reached a stumbling block, tension and rigidness in thought, and a feeling of not being "approved of." Remember, letting go of this exaggerated attitude will relieve this tightness and dissolve the migraines. You are loved.

We all agree that headaches occur many times when we are stressed out about something. Uptightness and worry will also lead to this discomfort. Can we also agree that a sense of frustration, a strong feeling of not being "approved of," tension at the workplace, and a sense of hurry are contributing factors?

Headaches and how do pills affect you?

How does an aspirin know to affect your head and not to your toes? How does any medicine know what to do? Have you ever thought about this?

Your mind is the only medium that knows and can think. Everything else is just effect of your minds activity, which is your thought. You believe that the aspirin will go to your head and heal it – and so it is. Doctors and scientists have imbued their healing thoughts into this medication, the pharmacists have put their healing thoughts into this pill and you have absolute faith that it will work according to this belief.

Voila!

May 28

Facial expression research

I thought it was interesting to find out that we are born with these facial expressions: happiness, sadness, fear, anger, disgust, and surprise.

Even a blind child will express similar features, never having seen someone else's face. The face as a whole expresses much of the moods and thoughts you are thinking. To take this idea a little further, looking at it from a mental standpoint, I will add that in the study of Eschatology, the Walter Method, it was discovered that each facial feature represents a specific virtue and character trait. When you are trained you can diagnose

193

this specific disposition and character trait of the individual.

May 29

Your true purpose of upward progress, when achieved, will free you from karmic bondage.

A lot has been talked about karma and its effects. In simple words: "Don't do anything to anyone unless you want to experience the same thing." If you want to move upward you have to behave from a higher perspective. If you want to experience a happy life you have to give and exude the sense of love and happiness. Karma is the Law of Attraction.

How many times can I say: Let's be good!

May 30

Question from a reader:

"What do I say to someone that will be transitioning to the other side? Or what can I say to their spouse? I am so at a loss for words..."

My response:

"I would tell him/her that they are loved and that they had a purpose on this Earth. But there is more love waiting for them, and that they can do more good on the other side now. Also tell him/her that they will always be in your heart. Same goes for the spouse. I think when one knows that a greater purpose is awaiting them, the transition will be easier."

Most of us are taking the path of delusion and mortality. Let's understand that Universal Consciousness pervades the entire Universe. It is the substance, spirit, and all creation stems from this substance. As all manifestations are of spirit or mental substance, they

194

only appear to us as material in order to serve a purpose here in this state of being. We are also this spirit-substance and therefore this delusion of mortality has to cease. We have to wake up to the truth of everlasting life, preferably before we are on our so-called "death bed."

May 31

What is Spirit? Spirit is the substance underlying all creation, individualized as Souls. Consciousness is your awareness - and your thoughts are the activity of your Consciousness. Got it?

Early in the chapter I asked you this question. Did you think about it?

"Who am I," "What am I," "Where am I," "Why am I..."

Those are the most important questions of your life. If you once understand the answers to those questions you are truly blessed, you are ready to move on.

I am who I think I am
I am what I think I am
I am where I think I am
I am because "I am"

Everything rests within you. Your perception of the self makes you who and what you are on this plane. However, in reality, you are a perfect Soul, Spirit. You are a mental being of spirit substance. You are always where your mind is and you "are," exist, because you are a part of Universal Consciousness. You are aware of your being.

You are God-consciousness itself... You just don't know it yet.

Chapter 6: Journey of a Lifetime

June 1

Don't forget a sense of humor when searching for the Truth. Truth includes a light heart and loving silliness. Playfulness and a good-natured attitude will lead to more joy!

Let's start this month with something fun!

I love colors - the wide range of shades of color, musical notes, mathematical numbers, and the abundance of flowers, animals, and so forth are all examples of the limitlessness of the Universe. Let's explore some of the meanings and effects colors have on us.

The sun, the symbol of energy and love, with its life-giving warmth and its bright yellow or orange glow, invigorates us. It is a well-established fact that regions with a lack of sunlight have a higher depression and suicide rate. Looking at the sun's light releases endorphins, which are known to stimulate good feelings in the brain. Light, bright colors tend to make you feel terrific and lighter. "Light" is always associated with the positive and "dark" with negative emotions and moods. You have heard the expression "he/she is a dark person."

Here are some interesting, known, fun facts I found in my research:

Red stimulates your emotions and passions. This powerful color is intense and makes you feel excited. Red is the warmest of all colors and is most often chosen by extroverts and one of the top picks of males. In China, red is the color of prosperity and joy. On the negative side, red can mean hot temper or anger. "I saw red when I heard this" or "He makes me see red" are common expressions.

Red and yellow have been known to stimulate appetite. Yellow is also the highest attention getting color due to its high reflection of light. Why do you think the colors of McDonald's are Red and Yellow? Orange means vitality. People who like orange are usually thoughtful and sincere. I thought orange would also show playfulness - but no mention of this thought found.

Yellow symbolizes wisdom, joy, and happiness. People of high intellect tend to favor yellow. Like the energy of a bright sunny day, yellow brings clarity and awareness. The shade of yellow determines its effect: Yellow-green can mean deceit and creates a disoriented feeling. Orange-yellow imparts a sense of establishment. Clean, light yellow clears the mind, making it active and alert.

The color Blue, studies show, is preferred by men (most likely right after red?). It stimulates calmness, serenity, and tranquility. People seem to be more productive in blue rooms. Looking around me, I realize that my office and writing space is painted a light blue and a pretty aqua. Blue is an orderly color - but it can also be related to sadness. Remember the phrases "I'm having the blues," "I'm blue without you" or "Blue Monday?"

Blue has also been found to be the least appetizing color; there are not many blue food items. Blueberries … what else? The color aqua is associated with emotional healing and protection. Light blue is accredited with health, healing, tranquility, understanding, and softness.

Purple is the color of good judgment and is the color of people seeking spiritual fulfillment. It is said if you surround yourself with purple you will have peace of mind. Purple is a good color to use in meditation. It is the color most favored by artists. Purple has been used to symbolize magic and mystery as well as royalty.

Green is the color of nature. It symbolizes growth, harmony, freshness, and fertility and is also the "lucky" color. Green is favored by well-balanced people and symbolizes the master healer and the life force. It was believed green was healing for the eyes. Old drawings show that Egyptians wore green eyeliner. Studies show you should eat raw green foods for good health.

Abundance and health also fall under the color green, with olive green being the traditional color of peace.

Brown is the color of the Earth and is associated with the material side of life. Brown is a mixture of red, blue, and yellow and can be a stabilizing color. Brown gives a feeling of solidity and allows one to stay in the background, unnoticed. Some shades of brown create a warm, comfortable feeling of wholesomeness, naturalness, and dependability.

Gray is the color of sorrow. People who favor gray can be loners or narrow-minded. Native Americans associate gray with friendship. Gray is the symbol for security, responsibility, conservative practicality, maturity, and dependability.

Think about other examples that show how colors are used in language: "Do you have a green thumb?" "Once in a blue moon" and "You look red-hot tonight"- quite interesting isn't it?

June 2

Sabrina says "Hello"

I said it before and I say it again, my middle name is Dr. Doolittle and I speak Bird, Cat, and Dog quite fluently.

The last few months, my cat which is going on sixteen, has a new word. Frequently, during my morning writing hours, I hear her calling me in a deep and clear "hello." She is looking for me, hollering out the back patio doors as I am busy in my office. "Hello?" "Hello?" again and again, until I step outside the office and yell back ..."I'm here, Sabrina - come over here." And even though she is deaf, she then slowly strides into my office and comfortably curls up under my desk. I hope the neighbors think she's a human being; she surely sounds like one.

June 3

Healing thought:
The liver is the largest internal organ in your body, showing you the importance of this virtue. Use your patience correctly. Do not be patient with the wrong and stay in unpleasant situations or "put up" with something that you know isn't good for you and all concerned. To use patience correctly means to allow the Universe to do its perfect work. Not to hurry and worry, not wanting more and more right now, and it means to know that "all is already good." No need to push and shove. All you want and need will show itself in its good time. If you can understand this point of view, you are on the way to use your patience wisely.

Julie, a reader, asked the following questions:

"In the past few months I have been having problems with pain in my feet (non-diabetic neuropathy) and lately with my teeth. While I know some things about some ailments, I cannot figure out the neuropathy or teeth, which I am having taking care of on Thursday. They tell me that the neuropathy will become progressively worse (not a good feeling) and I want to stop it ASAP. Can you tell me anything? I would be much appreciative. Also, I have liver disease and while I have grown used to it I would like to stop it as well."

I responded after much careful thought:

"Hi Julie, thank you for writing! Here are some thoughts about your ailments. Since I don't know you personally, and don't have a full picture of your diagnosis, I will keep my points regarding your issues somewhat general. Hopefully it will give you food for thought. Remember that all illness can be healed in mind, through thought-correction. The doctor's diagnosis stating "things will get worse" is only a belief and an opinion. Unfortunately health opinions are easily accepted in our minds. So stay strong and know that you, your mind, is the most powerful tool you have to overcome anything. Your condition will only get worse if your thoughts continue to be fearful or get worse.

Feet: Feet symbolize/represent in the mental your progress and ability to go forward in unfoldment. The ground/Earth symbolizes Understanding. So your feet have to stand on firm ground (on Understanding), and you must stand on your own feet and progress soundly. Step by step. Don't rush your unfoldment.

I looked up the word neuropathy. It is described as pain, tingling, numbness, nerve, and tissue damage. Pain is always a sign fear is present. The nerves symbolize your being connected to all senses, touchiness. So think about your unfoldment and progress in unfoldment. Do you need to take things a bit more slowly and step by step? Are there any hurt feelings present?

To give you more insight in some of your other issues, here is a healing thought I posted a few weeks ago

200

(thought listed on May 11th of the 'All is mental' chapter. Teeth represent the chewing over of ideas in the mental. I'm not sure what exactly your problem with your teeth consists of (brittle, decay, gums?) but it seems to connect with your liver which symbolizes 'patience.' The chewing over of ideas requires patience.

Liver disease: The liver represents patience and it is the largest organ in your body, which shows you how important patience is! Remember the scriptures: "Let patience do her perfect work, that ye may be perfect and entire, wanting nothing."

It also separates the bile, which represents your hateful, bitter thoughts from your loving thoughts. Patience holds to the good and removes the wrong. There is a difference between impatience and not using patience properly. For example, putting up with something that is not good is not patience. Maybe you are "putting up with"
something (a family issue maybe) that is using up all of your patience? See, only you can know what your deepest thoughts are. So take these examples and think about them carefully..."

Part of my journey of writing this book is the documentation and sharing of the more detailed explanations about certain illnesses and diseases. The mind is a powerful tool and has total control over your well-being and life experiences. The sooner you realize this Truth, the better you will adjust. You and I, and most of this world's inhabitants, have a long road in front of us. We, the Souls that are actively searching, barely scratched the surface of Understanding.

June 4

Healing thought:
The cause of arthritis can be found in individuals that hold resentments for a very long time. The individual believes that he/she is justified to feel

that way because they are convinced that they have been treated unfairly; or they are of the opinion that they are "right." There might be an accompanying sense of guilt and anger present thinking that injustice had been done to them. The remedy is clear. Forgive and forget, let go of all sense of resentment and anger. Is this the pain and suffering you experience and endure worth hanging on? Why not correct this wrong thinking and feeling? Forgive and forget, forgive and forget...

There is much to talk about resentment and thinking that you are "in the right" no matter what. Feeling that you have been persecuted or unjustly accused of something is another mistake. Are the judgment calls of others really that important to you? Do you believe that in the big picture of the Universe, someone else's opinion really has an impact? I don't think so. Stop focusing in those small irritating issues, you know better by now!

June 5

Focus, focus, focus - we are too easily deterred from our goals. Outline your desires, set your goals high, and go for it without fear and doubt.

Ilene Waters continued to focus on her goals. She has lost thirty pounds so far and has a big smile on her face. I asked her in class last week: "Why should the readers believe your story? Really, why?"

Why?

"Why should this time be any different, you may be asking yourselves... How is she gonna make it work, i.e. 'really work,' this time? Well, here are some clues as to why I think I'm gonna make it this time. I've spent the greater part of my life being a second-hand girl. This time I am determined to be consistent in putting myself and my needs and my focus on myself first and foremost.

I know that I'm the best cheerleader on the planet for everyone else. If I put my positive energy into myself, my goals, my life - and then I will reach my goals. I may realize some of my own dreams. That excites me. That motivates me. The possibility of succeeding is exhilarating. However, none of this means anything if I don't have a real exacting plan. So here it is, folks, and it's simple. I will write down five goals that I want to reach each week. Every morning I will read aloud those five goals and recommit to myself. During the course of the day I will check in with myself mentally and see if I'm holding true to course. If not, I will not feel guilty or call myself a loser. Instead, I will stop any negative thinking. Focus only on the positive and stay the course. At night before I go to bed I will again read my goal list for the week. I will again reaffirm my commitment to self. I will write one sentence each day about how I feel I did. This will help me track how I'm really feeling about things. I've come to realize that in order to realize your dreams you must live a successive and successful series of moments. Live in the present.

I've lived most of my life beating myself up. My personal problem is that I live on the extreme spectrum. I perceive myself as either 100% in or 100% not in. The problem has been, in the past, that if I don't stick to a diet or life style 100% perfectly, then somehow I've failed. Forget the fact that maybe I've done even 50% ok, or even 10% ok…. My feeling has been if I could not do it the 'right' way … expecting 100% and sticking perfectly to how I think it should go, then I have failed. I have let myself down. So I sabotage myself and just say 'screw it. I've failed. I'm just going to revert to my old ways.' Of course, this kind of faulty logic makes it really easy to develop a yo-yo mentality.

Well, I have come to learn that I really do need to recognize that learning to live healthier and losing the weight is just a minute part of my entire life experience. The weight is part of my parcel, and I've got many other parts working in conjunction with it on many different levels to make me the individual I am. My weight is not who I am, what defines me as a person. Inside this shell casing is an amazing woman with wonderful qualities and attributes. Self-Love, not self-loathing is the way to really be successful in this lifetime."

June 6

Fear and Hate are the lowest vibrations in the Universe. They are the opposites of Universal Intelligence and Universal Love.

Just a gentle reminder for the day: Fear and hate are the lowest vibrations in the Universe. Fear, worry, doubt, and hate are the culprits you need to work on first. It's easier to let go of hate. Do you really, really hate, or is it just a bad word habit? "I hate this outfit" or "I hate this new hair style" ... really? Why use such a strong word?

You can start using the word dislike and soften the blow. Then you will start seeing that there is nothing to even dislike on this wonderful planet. Start loving everything and slowly you will also gain a sense of love for people. All people that is. Loving people requires a bit more openness, forgiveness, and a general sense of embracing the Allness of Good.

Getting rid of fear is a bit more challenging. It requires getting rid of ignorance, erring supposition, erring beliefs, and longstanding habits. It's mental housecleaning galore. You will need to focus on each and every fear; and with diligence and an honest approach you will be able to see that there is really nothing to fear. Let's keep talking about how to conquer all fears as we go along.

June 7

What about newborns? Why are they born with birth defects?

Question from a reader:

"I have read and heard a bit about the influence of thoughts on our health. It makes 'sense.' Years of anger and fear has to take a toll on the body since our thoughts create our reality. However, when a child only a few years old develops a life threatening disease, the negative thoughts equaling the disease factor does not seem to apply. Instead, I would suggest there is a karmic factor involved. The child, actually the essence who is really the child made a decision when he was in his non- physical form to enter into this world to help another learn important lessons in their spiritual path. When you have a moment, please give me your thoughts."

My Answer:

"I have heard this karmic view before, and do not disagree with this viewpoint; however, I tend to believe that the child rather carries the burden of the parents' thoughts. For instance, after conception every thought of the mother affects the unborn child. I did a lot of work with this idea when I was pregnant with my son and it seemed to work perfectly. Not only was he a healthy ten-pound baby, he had no afflictions at all, no crying, no colicky behavior, and turned out to be extremely intelligent. I'm not just saying this because I am his mother.

As the child grows, they of course start thinking for themselves and at about the age of twelve you "lose" them to their own thoughts and beliefs. Unfortunately, school, friends, and all other outside influences have its toll. That's around the time when my son started to have a cold here and there, allergies started to manifest (due to his father's constant telling him about his own allergies) and so on. I know it's a rather harsh idea to accept, that I can severely handicap my child in the womb by being careless in thought, but it makes a lot of sense.

Did you know that the gender of the baby is determined by the parent's thoughts also? When more "`feeling'" is present at the point of conception, it will produce a female child. When the sense reason/or knowing is stronger in the mentality it will produce a male child. I've watched this for many years. Planned babies are many times males, females are the unplanned or surprises, or are conceived by very emotional couples. Watch it. I'm not negating the concept of some karmic debt, but I do think this theory is at least 90% of the cause."

June 8

Appreciation is the starting point of abundance. Start being grateful for what you already have and deeply feel this sense of thankfulness. This is the foundation to a more abundant life.

It's time to think about abundance again...

I hear you - there are still too many people who struggle in their daily lives. There is never enough income to cover the outgo or there is just enough. Poverty levels are humongous all over the world, but today I'm only talking about you, the reader who had enough money to buy this book. You are probably in good financial shape.

What about the middle class, and let's be specific here. You are not poor, so you have some sense of abundance but you are not rich, so you lack wealth consciousness. You feel that you get so-so compensated for your work, and have enough income to pay the bills. However, you would like to have more. More of what?

A vacation in a faraway country, a new car or bigger house? What does wealth mean to you and is it really all about money? Let's look at it from a mental standpoint, which is the correct way to achieve happiness. What would make you happy? Wouldn't you prefer your children's health and welfare over money? What about a good relationship with your spouse and loyal friends? What about your own health and peace of mind? Isn't that a much more important way of looking at what makes you happy?

Abundance means many things: An abundance of love and kindness, sufficient time to yourself to do the things you enjoy, or constant good feelings - these are the riches of mind that put you in tune with the mentalness of all. Now it's time to appreciate those feelings. Sit down and really be grateful for all you have NOW. This is the starting point of abundance, including financial freedom.

Once you experience this good feeling of being satisfied with what you already call yours, you can move on to more abundance. Money is a natural outflow of your sense of "having." When you see yourself as "having" you will automatically attract all that you want, because now you have become one with the sense of abundance, which means you are "being" it.

Always expect money to come in easily. I always say to my husband: "Let me find some money" or "I know it's in the mail," or my favorite "I can feel a big chunk of money coming my way." See, feeling it is the key. Remember "feeling" is the mother element of creation. Thinking about money and abundance is fine and dandy, but you also have to feel it - believe it - and expect it. Money will be circulating freely in your experience when you acknowledge that it is your right to be wealthy. There is nothing bad about money. You deserve it. You deserve as much as you want. The question is: Will you continue to put your spiritual wealth above all Earthly wealth. I would strongly advise you to do so!

June 9

Bear no ill-will toward anyone. Be even-tempered, kind and forgiving, and let go of the "it's all about me" syndrome.

Life's truth is it's not all about you. Only in your mind is it "all about you" because all you can do is to sense your "Self." Let me explain:

Every thought you think comes from your consciousness and subconscious. Thoughts, your reason, and your feelings are the activity of your Soul. So everything you think and you're convinced of, with a deep feeling of the thought being true, is what composes you. This formula comprises your innermost essence.

June 10

Constant bodily aches show a tendency to repress your feelings - being sore about things and situations, rather than dealing with them and practicing forgiveness. Maybe you are aching about something within yourself. Get busy correcting this sense of mental ache and replace it with a sense of peace, comfort, love, and have mercy on yourself and others.

Dig deep down into the innermost chambers of your Soul and set yourself free!

June 11

When looking for Truth it doesn't matter who wrote it, said it, or taught it. Truth is Truth. Embrace it when you find it. How do you know it's the Truth? Does it feel right, loving, uplifting, spiritual, true, pure, honest, good, and good for all concerned?

Always make sure that your motives fit within this category!

June 12

Let go of the linear concept of life. Allow three-dimensional ideas to enter your mind and explore them. Play the 'what if' game, but make sure you don't wander off into left field. 'What if' will allow your creativity to unfold.

What if...?

Just finished off a book called "Dreaming Worlds Awake" this morning from a writer's friend of mine; Esme Ellis from Bath, England. It contains quite an interesting concept and features many out-of-the-box thoughts to ponder. One phrase especially reminded me of a topic I wanted to write about. "Let go of the linear concept of life;" the linear, straight forward, one-dimensional, and somewhat boring life.

Ask yourself "what if" I would pursue another career, "what if" I would travel more, "what if" I would take up yoga, meditation, or a work-out-class, "what if" I would move to another state, "what if" ... and envision those ideas as vividly as you can. It will get your creative thinking juiced up. The linear concept of life consists of basic cultural expectancies, social formulas, family traditions, birth – youth – school - adult – work – retirement – old age – death. You get the picture.

But three-dimensional, out-of-the-box thinking is an outlining of desires in your mind, which at the time might look non-realistic. For whatever reason you might think that you're not able to achieve these goals. But when you start to create any want in your mind and dare to think outside of the box, and are not taking "no" for an answer, you will soon see that life becomes more colorful and interesting. This mental practice will make your imagination flourish. Be creative!

209

June 13

Push your imagination; push your boundaries and capabilities. Allow your creativity to shine from within.

Another writer's friend of mine put me in contact with the editor of "Women Writers, Women Books" and I was asked to write an article. Not a self-promotional piece, but a story of my becoming a writer. What made me travel this path in a thousand words or less? Here it is.

Journey of a Lifetime

"How did all this happen? When did I decide to become a writer in this world of many? Should I call myself a teacher instead of a writer?

Looking back, it was meant to be. Born in a small town in Austria, I always felt displaced. From early childhood on I remember being the "different kid" that stood out. Not in a rebellious way, just more creative and inquisitive to the standards of my village. Somewhere around the age of twelve I knew I wanted to be a singer, and the dream of traveling foreign countries and meeting exciting people held a grip on me.

On the midnight train heading to Vienna I started the journey and teamed up with a Top Forty band playing in a somewhat seedy nightclub. This union lead to living my dream: Germany, Switzerland, England – working as a singer in hotels and bars, all the while moving on to bigger cities – moving on up!

After a concert I attended in London, a friend pointed out that I should visit Hollywood, California – "You'll fit right in," he exclaimed, and even though I wasn't sure about this new idea I was willing to give it a try.

Mentally this move produced a shift in my consciousness that proved to be the biggest step I would make. Everything fell into place with astonishing ease. No doubt, I was home. Thirty years later I am still in California, in the same spot: physically but not mentally.

Shortly after this life-changing move I found a job working as a waitress at a Hollywood nightclub. Seemingly out of the blue, I was asked by another waitress if I thought "Jesus was suffering on the cross." At the time I only had read a few New Age articles and wasn't well versed in all of the topics. I, however, believed that Jesus was a man that had true Understanding, and with this Understanding he surely was only showing his disciples the power he had over his life and death. "No," I said, "I don't think Jesus suffered. I think he knew exactly what he was doing. He was absolutely aware of this demonstration, and he chose it as a way to prove that 'life lives.' Death is nothing but a big bully and unreal; imagination at its best."

This dialogue proved to be the pivotal starting point of my awakening.

This new journey of soul searching and truth finding was exhilarating. I read everything I could get my hands on. I joined a metaphysical class and tested everything I learned. I experienced faith, hope, amazement, and wonder. I had to learn the English language basically from scratch, and I did this through reading book after book after book.

After five years of intensive study and application of what I learned, I began to teach metaphysics to a few students and I loved it. We are all teachers and students of life and this was a wonderful way to grow and learn. As this desire developed further, I reached back to my "other" love - writing. I started a book many years ago about my travels in Germany. I had written many poems, but I had also made a promise to myself that "one day I would actually publish a book."

211

Little did I know that it would take another thirty years to make this dream come true. Life happened with the usual ups and downs, but I never veered off the path for long. I knew deep down in the innermost chambers of my Soul that I meant to write, teach, and spread the Truth of Being. I embraced the Universe and all New Age teachings. I drank from the Eastern philosophies and feasted on many wonderful teachings of the West and East alike. The idea of a better Universe, and a "We are all One" concept was engrained in my being. However, even though this journey proved to be exhilarating I was still waiting "until the time was right" to dedicate my life to my passion. Why?

At that time leaving the corporate world seemed impossible, too many bills to pay, and too many expectations of this Earthly life... What would it take for me to make the transformation?

Early 2011 the change came unexpectedly and fast. I was laid off from my job of almost twenty years. Even though I was surprised, I really wasn't. I had known for some time that I was mentally through with this type of work. I was longing to fulfill my dream, I could taste it, feel it and I knew that it was only a matter of time. And here it was. The Universe had made the decision for me; had helped me to get where I wanted to be all along. "Thank you Universe," I mumbled as I took my last paycheck and trotted home. "Thank you!"

It took no time to get that pencil sharpened and the ideas started to flow effortlessly. "Someone" was constantly whispering in my ear - my own "knowing" took charge. My goal was to write about my knowledge of the workings of the mind and I wanted to share all the goodness it had brought into my life.

Today, I feel that I am a messenger of Truth and that it is my duty to help others. My first book "Better

Living...Because You Can!" was finished in eight months and affirms my beliefs of unity and goodness for all.

And lastly, even though it seems that I have accomplished everything I set out to do, I know in my heart of hearts: The Journey of a Lifetime has only just begun!'

June 14

Rejection stings in many ways. This wrong feeling goes back to the basic wrong idea that something outside of yourself can affect you. No one can cause anything for you, no one can affect you unless you allow it, and no one's opinion is important to your unfoldment. The old saying that "if one door closes another one opens" is a fact and should always linger in your mind. There are limitless other opportunities waiting for you. Do not get discouraged, ever!

Rejection

Not sure why, but I woke up thinking about rejection. Maybe it's because I am thinking about submitting several articles to different online publications. Not just the one mentioned before, which was gracefully accepted. But we all experience rejection during our lifetime many times, in many different ways.

How do you cope with the feeling of "not being good enough" for whatever you are being rejected? Maybe it was the new job you wanted so badly, maybe your boyfriend, or worse - spouse, decided to look for another partner. Or simply some idea you submitted for consideration was disregarded. Someone had the power to refuse your want. What did it mean to you?

213

Does anyone really have power over you?

Change can be exciting or terrifying - it depends on how you look at it. Positive change always means growth, rejection or not, in one area or another. Growth keeps you active and sparks a fire needed to keep you moving and yearning for more. It keeps you interested in life which in turn makes you love life even more. And it will give you the resilience needed to keep going no matter what others will say or do. It will give you the strength to carry out your vision and stay on track - always moving towards your goals.

So remember, if anyone rejects you or your work, don't take it personal; see it for what it is: nothing more than someone else's opinion. And that's OK. We all have our opinions, hopefully kind and loving ones, and we all have to reject others/or their work at one time or another. Just be kind and think before you do it. Love should always be the motivator.

June 15

How do you solve your personal problems? Acknowledge them, reason about them, handle them or just hide? Any situation can be handled by you if you are willing to take the time and apply careful, right, and positive thoughts. As a matter of fact, it takes a lot of energy to stay negative. So why not turn it around and turn each challenge into an opportunity to grow and evolve?

What disturbs me? Having cleaned my mental household many times, I am wondering what is still hiding in the dark corners of my mind. What situations make me uncomfortable and why? What kind of issues did I shove under the rug? Who do I still need to forgive?

Life is always presenting people and situations to us that not only stimulate growth within us but also show us where correction is needed. There is a reason for every person we meet; for every experience we have. Our feeling of happiness or sorrow is the outcome of our dispositions, our pent-up anxieties or carefree attitude. Happiness comes from inner contentment, sorrow from fear. Looking deep within your Soul can be painful. There are hidden secrets that none of us want to address. It hurts too much. However, unless we get the courage to face our true Self we cannot be healed.

Are you scared to relive some of the experiences that you prefer not talking about? Why beat yourself up? It's passed, it happened, and you have learned from it. You are a better person for it. Nothing to fret about, nothing to fear!

June 16

Money, money, money... Ever thought what money represents in the mental? It's a convenient means of exchange; nothing more, nothing less. Our wealth does not depend on money; it depends on our understanding of Truth and the meaning of wealth consciousness. What does "wealth consciousness" mean to you?

How to preserve good habits

A list of good habits (not character traits) includes timeliness, being courteous, politeness, cleanliness, being tidy, organized, practical, dependable, health conscious by taking care of your body, eating healthy, and so on. Are you in the habit of naturally acting this way on a daily basis? You don't have to consciously think about it, you just are?

Wealth consciousness, for example, is a good habit. It's a habit of feeling prosperous. It means that you are constantly in a state of wealth. Not just money. A wealth of good thoughts, imbued with love and kindness, a feeling of "having it all," a knowing of "you are abundantly supplied with everything you need" and an enormous sense of gratefulness is what's needed. You are in a state of prosperity, mentally and therefore physically. You are the cause of your riches. In order to preserve your good habits you have to apply them daily not once in a while but every minute of your waking hours. You are your habits.

June 17

Healing Thought:
Your aching joints represent a general lack of harmonious thoughts. Ask yourself: "Am I feeling out of joint about a situation or incident?" Soreness and stiffness in the joints also reflect a stiff and rigid attitude, maybe erring self-justification. There is no stiffness in Intelligence. Harmony requires a fluid, relaxed, and easy mental disposition. Don't accept stiffness, be willing to change!

Harmony

Harmony is the principle quality underlying all life (William W. Walter). Think about this statement. It means that any non-harmonious thoughts are without merit. What are harmonious thoughts? Make a list, and review with the full chapter later in August.

June 18

Love

Feel love, not emotions. What most of us experience is not true love or unconditional love. Rather, it is a mixed and wild ride of emotions, untamed to say the least. Today, love seems to have strings attached at all times. I love you, if... I love you, but... I love you, because...

Love encompasses all and everyone; the lame, the blind, the less fortunate, the decrepit, the ugly, even the dishonest and crooked ones. It does not differentiate, as

Love is the mother of all creation. Our mother, Love, of whom we are born of, loves her children without discrimination.

June 19

Creativity

"Being creative" - words used frequently and carelessly. What does being creative mean? Most people associate creativity with daily activities. Let's say designing clothing, planning events, painting, and any type of artistic work, writing, music, and all pursuits that are connected to free spirited individual expression.

But, "creating" means so much more. You are the creator of your destiny. Ever really thought about that? You not only create every moment of your life, but you can also alter your life experiences at will. That's how powerful you are. That's how genius you are and that's the responsibility given to you by the Almighty Universal Power. You are the creator in your Universe.

Pause! Think! Explore! Create!

June 20

Healing Thought:
The lungs represent our ability to take in new ideas, inspiration, comfort and hope, which is necessary for our continuity. We breathe from the essential, 'air' - which symbolizes Spirit. Air is ever present, and like the wind unseen. When lung or breathing problems show up in your experience, remember, we are Spirit and we have to supply ourselves with all the inspiration, newness, fresh concepts and lively ideas we can envision. Always inspire from the good, perfect and spiritual.

Spirit - the essential

Air, the symbol of Spirit, encompasses all. We are surrounded by air and cannot live without breathing in this pure substance. We cannot "be" without this essential element. We need inspiration, hope, comfort, vision, creativity, and new idea s- and this "taking in," or breathing, is natural and automatic. We do not need to force our breath, it just is. If we do not exhale the old, outgrown thoughts and habits, we will be stifled and our health will reflect this disposition. When we breathe in the "past" instead of the "new" we are also holding ourselves back. We need to have fresh thoughts in order to keep our lungs healthy.

June 21

As Summer Approaches ... Thoughts about the cycle of Life

As the season changes once again and summer approaches, I can't help but think of the cycle of Life. I'm cheerfully looking at my garden through my large office patio doors. Tomatoes, jalapenos, and zucchini planted firmly in the ground ready to sprout; small buds appearing with the promise of a delicious meal. Oh, how I enjoy seeing this growth, the unfoldment of nature - reflecting the workings of mind.

Everything you see is a visible expression of your Consciousness; a mirror image of your innermost soul substance. "Thought in action," you might say, acting out your own personal movie. However, in your life's play you are the writer, director, and actor. You are in charge.

Looking back at winter, the dormant or reflective time, has passed. A new awakening is in the air. Winter represents a resting period in the mental, a timeout in order to allow rejuvenation shown forth in nature.

Renewal, revitalization, refueling of Spirit, and getting ready for the abundant explosion of more Life!

Reminiscing about the gentle awakening of spring; representing the infancy state of Consciousness with its germs sprouting eagerly, unfolding tiny flora and curiously peeking out of mother Earth's fertile ground. Still small, yet powerful seeds of Life are always pushing upwards towards the light - just like our Soul wants to push upwards towards God's glory. The gentle warmth of spring embalms our Spirit and gives renewed hope to a new day.

And here we are approaching the full splendor of summer. We embrace the life sustaining light and warmth of the sun. We fully absorb this invigorating force and feel the growth our Spirits have achieved.

Youth with its unlimited strength and fearlessness! The "summer of your mind" is the time to reason and to make sound choices, the time to pave your path. Enjoyment of the moment so desperately yearned for; this is the season to define who you are and to choose the road you will travel.

What does the fall season represent? Autumn reflects "maturity of the mind," fruition, fruit at its best! At last we have come to an understanding of our true purpose in Life. We have reached yet another stage in our unfolding process. This season is the culminating mental state that defines who we are at this moment in time.

And so we can rest once again! Namaste**

June 22

Negativity, per the dictionary: "A quality characterized by a person who is habitually skeptical, has a tendency to deny, oppose, or resist suggestions or commands" – is life denying.

Positivity, per the dictionary: "A quality characterized by a person who is displaying certainty, acceptance, affirmation, positive answers, confidence, and positive criticism" - is life giving.

My thoughts on Negative versus Positive vibrations

The immature mind gives a lot of attention to the negative rather than to the positive. This immaturity allows us to focus on what's wrong and digs itself deeper and deeper into a muddy hole of discontent and complaint. As it spirals down it absorbs the energy of negativity and feeds on itself until we hit rock bottom; and be certain - we will. There is nothing good in looking for the negative, it only leads to misery. "Poor me," we think, and that adds to the devastation as we acknowledge ourselves as a victim. We are not a victim, we are the victor! We hold the power of change in our hands. So why not use this power for a delightful invigorating experience, full of love and harmony.

I am certain that we all know the difference between right and wrong, good or bad, negative or positive. Let's not deny our pessimistic traits – let us affront them and say: "I will never think this way again!" And mean it. Practice it. Live by our word. Any 'wrong' is only an absence of "right." It is corrected by supplying right and good thoughts about the subject. And we are in control of our thoughts. We cannot allow inferior thoughts to enter our mind. I know I will spend time on the corrections necessary. Step by step, I will conquer even the most stubborn dispositions.

June 23

Watch your inner melodrama, it's like a movie. Be the observer, stay out of it- don't get lost in it. Just observe. By getting involved in your own movie you allow yourself to become emotional and fuzzy. Only detachment will keep your mind clear.

Have you been to the movies lately?

June 24

Why do we think about ourselves so much?

Why is it always "me," "I" and "my?"

Because all I and you can ever experience is our "sense of" ourselves and our "sense of" others. There is nothing or no one in your world but you. This is not an egotistical statement, it just is. There is nothing wrong with this sense, as long as you keep it good, right, loving, and pure. If you have mastered this perfect sensing you will live in eternal bliss. This sense will elevate you to a higher state of being.

Here is also where the "getting involved" in your life's movie starts and ends. Your movie - you being the writer, director, editor and actor – is your sense of your world. Since, as I pointed out, you are also the director of your drama and emotionally connected to this creation of yours, it's best to step back and look through a lens, and be an observer. You cannot just be the actor.

Stepping back and looking at the screen will give you a perspective of the scene changes necessary. You then can call "cut" in true Hollywood fashion. You can edit your movie to your liking and you can repeat the scenes if necessary. As the principal editor make sure you like your film from beginning to end.

June 25

Life is good, that's the bottom line. If you doubt this Truth at any time, remember that it is up to you to bring this Goodness into existence.

I've said this in my last book *"Better Living...Because You Can!"* and I'm saying it again: If each and every one of us would be doing and acting good, and would spread this goodness to our friends and family and everyone we come in contact with, the world would be a perfect place. The spider effect would tie us all together. We wouldn't have to worry about other countries, poverty and disease. This world would be a perfect web of helping each other and lifting each other's spirit. You would return to become a self-contained entity of positive energy, constantly exuding this vibrancy into the Universe. Just imagine that! What a wonderful thought!

June 26

It takes courage and strength to deal with your everyday challenges. It takes wisdom and right reason to handle daily encounters appropriately. It takes kindness and love to deal with "others." It takes persistence and endurance to finish these tests. You can easily overcome your challenges - which are opportunities to learn - because you already possess Courage, Strength, Wisdom, Right Reason, Kindness, Love, Persistence and Endurance.

How do you solve your personal problems?

Do you freeze, or hide? Do you try to protect yourself, attack or go into war mode? Are you justifying living with your problems because you don't know how to fix them? Is it too painful to deal with them and therefor you would rather "put up" with them? What is your first knee-jerk reaction when a challenge arises?

Or on the positive side, do you embrace the situation because you know it's only a pointer to a needed correction? Do you look at what's good about the occurrence first, knowing that you can easily rectify the situation? It's important to see your specific mode or habit of action when confronted.

June 27

A problem is only a challenge waiting to be solved.

Where do we begin to fix our problems? My quest for enlightenment and helping others to do the same includes the question: "Where do we begin?"

The goal of reaching perfect understanding is quite a lofty one and requires a firm commitment. Many people, being busy with their daily doings, do not see how it is possible to spend the time necessary to such a commitment. Will small steps of betterment make a difference? You bet! Any step toward a calmer, more spiritual life will make a difference. In my case, all I do is think about the next step of betterment. I give thought to each little detail, correcting them as I go along. I love to read and study. I embrace the comfort of knowing that my actively searching for the Truth will bring the betterment I desire. Imagine being in a state of harmony all the time! Nothing can bother you, no one affects you, everything always turns out perfectly and any situation you experience is loving and fulfilling.

Let's confess, we can't even imagine this state of complete bliss. We can only envision a degree of such heavenly sensations because in our life, no matter how good it is, there is always turbulence or another challenge. This is what this life is about: A series of learning curves, one test after another.

June 28

Yoga - more than a stretch

There is yoga and then there is yoga. Per my research in several publications, yoga is a physical, mental, and spiritual discipline originating in ancient India and found in Buddhism, Hinduism, Jainism, and Sikhism.

Yoga is a Sanskrit word and literally means to join, to unite, or to attach. Someone who practices yoga or follows the yoga philosophy with a high level of commitment is called a yogi or yogini. Classical yoga was used as a system of contemplation with the aim of uniting the human spirit with the "Supreme Being."

Hatha yoga and Raja yoga are the two more common forms of yoga in the Western world and focus on the physical culture. Both of these are commonly referred to as Sadanga yoga. They mainly focus on postures, with Raja emphasizing on getting the body ready for prolonged meditation. Traditional Hatha yoga is a holistic yogic path, including disciplines, postures, purification procedures, gestures, breathing, and meditation. The Hatha yoga predominantly practiced in the West consists of mostly physical exercises. It is also recognized as a stress-reducing practice.

Kundalini yoga is a physical, mental, and spiritual discipline for developing strength, awareness, character, and consciousness. Practitioners call Kundalini yoga the yoga of awareness because it focuses primarily on practices that expand sensory awareness and intuition in order to raise individual consciousness and merge it with the Infinite consciousness of God Brahman. Considered an advanced form of yoga and meditation, its purpose is to cultivate the creative spiritual potential of a human to uphold values, speak truth, and focus on the compassion and consciousness needed to serve and heal others.

Kriya Yoga is described by its practitioners as the ancient Yoga system revived in modern times by Mahavatar Babaji through his disciple Lahiri Mahasaya. This is one of the highest developed forms of meditation and communion with God. Paramhansa Yogananda's book *Autobiography of a Yogi* made this practice popular in the West in the early 1900ss. The system consists of a number of levels of Pranayama based on techniques that are intended to rapidly accelerate spiritual development and engender a profound state of tranquility and God-communion. Needless to say – it's not for beginners; don't try this at home without a Guru.

June 29

My Guruji

Here is my own story of Yoga. A brand new experience, yet so familiar. How could I have lived for so many years without the connection? Why did I find my Guru so late in life? You'd think after all this time of searching he would have found me earlier; but then maybe the time wasn't right. There is always the mental readiness that is necessary to move upward, and it took diligent research, study, and commitment to come this far.

My dear friend Virgil had asked me many times about my thoughts on reincarnation and other related topics. I wasn't particularly interested - yet. And so I told him that there were many other subjects to explore before worrying about the coming back to this Earth. He didn't let up and I finally gave in. I started to research, all the while having the idea of "why would we have to come back here to this simple plane?" in the back of my mind.

This digging '"into" not only my Soul, but also into historic writings and ancient wisdom, suddenly came to an unexpected event. On the sixtieth anniversary date of the death, or better called "transition" of Paramhansa Yogananda, I had an epiphany. Reading up on his life and teachings I found a curious coincident. We not only shared a birthday exactly sixty years apart, but I also "found" him at my age of fifty-nine, which was his age when he made his conscious transition. Coincident you might say? Remember there are no coincidences. That day I also discovered a photograph that was inserted in a book that I bought for my research. I held the picture in my hand and it spoke to me. No words necessary. The

225

connection was so profound that instant tears were running down my cheeks.

From that moment on I knew for sure that life is relived and relived until we get it right; reincarnating over and over again until we have paid our karmic debt. "There are many mansions in my father's house" as Jesus pointed out, there are many dimensions of Life and we will experience them all, step by step. There are still many questions that need answers, but I can be assured that my Guruji will feed that information to me as I am open and ready to receive.

June 30

OM or AUM is cosmic vibration, which is the sound of energy of the Universe. Universal energy is what all so-called material substance is made out of. We, our Souls, are also Universal energy.

With this additional new found devoutness I went on to ask for more guidance from the eternal Spirit and was led to the earlier mentioned forms of yoga. I am not one to exercise and never had an interest in any sports but casual swimming. However, yoga sounded more along my lines as it was supposed to include a spiritual component, but again, the postures and exercises seemed strenuous and boring to me. Little did I know that there was much more to it and after reading *Autobiography of a Yogi* I realized that certain yoga practices are studied in private and are not accessible to just anyone that wants a new toy.

Shortly after my newly established interest a lady friend of mine asked me to a get-together to tell me about her new Life Coaching venture, and scheduled a meeting at a nearby yoga center after her class. I happily agreed as I wanted to investigate this place for some time. Turns out that this school wasn't a modern Sadanga yoga center but taught Kundalini which features a more spiritual and healing approach as mentioned above. The teachers are committed yogis and yoginis with long histories of dedication to this practice.

Within a couple of weeks I enrolled and I was mentally ready to receive the first class. Physical pain aside (certainly not due to the exercises but to my inexperience), this was one of the most wonderful encounters in my life. The sounds of OM and the intense fire breath of the students in the rhythm of HAR and the bows to SAT NAM lifted the entire frequency in the room within minutes. Yogini Tej, with her great sense of humor and compassion, was leading us from simple exercises to a more intense meditation, accompanied by beautiful inspirational music. The voices in the room sounded angelic and I was seeing the white light with my Guruji's face smiling and keeping me going. HAR, HAR, HAR ... louder, louder, louder - pounding the floor in the lotus position.

SAT NAM – hmmm – internal silence.

Chapter 7 Mind Seeds

July 1

In the science of metaphysics the principle is strongly held before the student that to work scientifically he must have ever in mind the reality of good and the unreality of evil.
(Excerpt from 'The Allness of Good' by William W. Walter)

Feelings gone wrong

Some people think that over-sensitivities are feelings. Pure Love is the only true feeling. Unfortunately most feelings felt are wrong and detrimental to our Soul. They add to the already present negativity, as most go immediately to the "glass half empty" rather than the "glass half full." Why is that? Let's explore.

Feeling unloved, lonely, not good enough, helpless, insecure, embarrassed, discouraged, overwhelmed, anxious, powerless, victimized, fearful, panicked, tired and worn out, unwell and sickly, weak, distraught, jealous, envious, hateful, poor or lacking, never having enough, and less than, (shall I go on?) are just starting points of a more complex and intricate mental framework. Take a look at each of the above words and their meanings and add the corrective affirmation.

Feelings are not as easily corrected as our thoughts. Thoughts and feelings are two different "things."

Thoughts pertain to our reasoning ability. Feelings are emotions, sense, which are established starting in early childhood. Anyone making a sincere effort to better themselves, and with a reasonable amount of willingness to reason correctly, will agree to what is right and what is wrong thinking.

But "feeling" is a whole other matter in itself. We feel intuitively without thought. We go right to a certain emotion established over a long period of time. A certain occasion will trigger a feeling within you, liking it or not.

Practice to "feel yourself," your body and your vibration, and do this mentally without touch. Close your eyes in a quiet environment and just lie there comfortably and feel. When your thoughts start racing and jumping to all kinds of other subjects, pull yourself back and center on the feeling part of you; experience "feeling." With honesty and sincerity, go to the root problem. It will "feel" like a battle, but like all "fights" of life you can win. Let's be more specific and address each and every one of these culprits.

July 2

There are many lonely people in this world. They might have family and friends, they might be surrounded by people, but their hearts are lonesome. A feeling of emptiness permeates their being. If you are one of those people remember that you have your Self, your most important treasure. When you once realize the completeness of your Soul you will no longer feel lost. You will be whole again.

Unloved, lonely, jealous, and envious

We all want to be loved; it's one of our basic desires. However, we can't feel this love until we love ourselves. I think most people understand this concept. Self-love, as simple as it sounds, is not practiced by many. Rather a self-loathing takes place deep within the psyche, blaming yourself for all kinds of things gone wrong. You think you are not good enough, smart enough, strong enough, and you make mistakes. Read my lips: Everyone makes mistakes. Mistakes are good, they make you learn and rethink your actions. They are here to show you a better way of living.

So you look at others and their lives. Feelings of jealousy and envy creep up in your mind. Why are they better off? Why can't I have what they have? Well, you can! Jealousy and envy are ugly dispositions. Be happy for everyone and their fortunes. They have earned it and they deserve it. If you feel any differently, remember, they are also creators of their lives and obviously are doing something right in order to have received this abundance. Think about it, and thank the Universe for what you have right now.

July 3

When feeling tired use appreciation for a quick pick me up. Focusing on all the good things in your life will certainly wash away fatigue and listlessness.

Unwell, sickly, tired, worn out, and weak

Most sickness stems from the ignorant belief that ill health is something physical. It is not. It is a reflection (knowingly or not) of the unhealthy mental state of the affected individual.

Feeling healthy is the natural state of life. It is our nature to be well; anything else is our lack of a sense of good feelings. It is an absence of healthy thoughts.

We always try to avoid pain; physically and mentally. Pain is temporary and passes if you pay attention to the cause, which is mental. Observe your inner pain, not just the physical discomfort and the shift in your energy flow. Don't be afraid. With proper mental care and self-love you will certainly, and quickly, be sucked into a vortex of good feelings.

July 4

Fearful, panicked, and distraught

Face your life's situation without fear. Relax and allow the blocked energy inside you to surface to the top. Experience the pain, or tumult, you are feeling at the moment. Stay with it and allow it to pass.

I had my own experience with fear in July of 2001 – here is my story:

Memories of fear - the 4th of July 2001

My husband had never been to Austria. The kids were grown and on their own and we finally decided to take a trip back to see family members. I was excited to show him my home town. Just picturesque this time of year and we certainly were enjoying good food, drink, and laughter.

Time past quickly and soon enough we were back on the plane to Los Angeles. As everyone knows this is a long, long journey – thirteen hours without touching the ground. I'm one of those people that can't sleep on the plane; my neurotic sense of control compels me to fly the aircraft in case of emergency.

So here we were, cramped in the seats of American Airlines, tired and waiting to reach our destiny, with a couple of hours to go. Suddenly we saw four men of Middle Eastern descend roaming the aisles. Our seats were toward the back of the plane, right in front of an emergency exit.

Mind you, 9/11 had not happened yet, and race or skin color was not an issue at the time. We only noticed them because they kept walking up and down the gangway several times always staring and glaring. After a few minutes three of them disappeared, the fourth stepping behind us, discretely trying to open the exit door. I nudged my husband and we both observed the man testing the flap. My stomach was in a knot. I waved at the stewardess and explained my concern. She sat down for a few minutes allowing her to observe the actions of the man. She agreed with my uneasiness and asked him to please stop. He frowned at her and moved to the other side of the plane, pushing the opposite door. The Stewardess again gave him a warning, and he left.

As everyone knows 9/11 happened two months later and after hearing the devastating news it all made sense. I'm not sure how many planes were tested this way by terrorists, but I knew that we had been blessed. Safely we landed.
I never flew again. It's been eleven years and thinking about it still makes me wonder what "if"?

All of this talk about affirmations and right thinking is great and beneficial. But when you are in the midst of terror and something occurs that evokes a huge amount of fear in you, all of the knowledge and right reason goes right out the window. All your good intentions disappear.

However, when you are ready to conquer a fearful disposition the sign will appear, and so it happened that I am challenged to work out this sense of anxiety this very year. My son is getting married. Out of all places they chose Washington, DC as their home base and I am pressed to fly into this city with the greatest threat potential of all. This is how life and the Universe work. Face your fears, affront them, reason them out, and conquer them, or you will be pushed into a situation that will test you even worse.

Dealing with your fears is very important, and I am in general very good in all other aspects of life. I am courageous and not fearful at all. Before this incident I had been traveling all over the world and loved to fly.

I want to allow myself to fly again.

July 5

Realize the completeness of your Soul and you will no longer feel lost.

Helpless, victimized, overwhelmed, anxious and discouraged

The excessive chatter in your mind needs to be stopped. No wonder you are feeling overwhelmed when all you hear is negative messages. Everywhere you look there are victims of crime, and helplessness is portrayed as if it would deserve a medal of honor. When you buy into this picture of despair you feel discouraged and say, "well, I guess this is life - I have to live with it."

Anxiety is a widespread dis-easiness in this country. You feel unable to control your life, you feel helpless to affect a change, and you feel overwhelmed with the tasks at hand. There is always too much to accomplish. Not enough money to pay the bills and restraints in all areas are looming over your head. Take a deep breath, step back, and take the position of the observer. You do not have to live in a world of woes; you can create your own loving and happy place.

Now repeat: "I am the cause of all that befalls me every day of my life. No one has power over my experiences. I have all the time in the world and I will manage each task step by step. I am well, I am good, I am talented, I am safe!"

July 6

It's time to heal, time to grow spiritually so you can understand your true heritage, and it's time to love.

Poor, lacking, never having enough and less than powerless

Many times with my students, if it's not one thing, it's another. One problem is solved and the next one is already waiting at their door. The outside occurrence of the issue, even though it looks that way, is not the problem. The underlying issue stems from the thoughts and beliefs about the problem; this is the culprit and cause. It is apparent that the student didn't apply the correct application and is experiencing his/her beliefs.

This is a whole different way of looking at it, isn't it?

If any country on this Earth can claim "unlimited possibilities" it's the US. With all the options given to us it takes some time to separate the right from wrong. But in the end this diligent thinking process is worth it. The freedom and creativity allowed makes up for the often mistaken materialistic views. We just have to be careful not to fall into the "bigger is better" trap. Because of this general acceptance of "everything is possible" the spiritual awakening in this country is far more advanced than in most other regions. Let us keep working on raising this positive energy level as much as we can.

You are not lacking; it's your sense of abundance that is lacking. You are not poor, or less than; you are abundantly provided with everything you need by this generous and limitless power of the Universe. This is the correct thought to hold in mind. Cement it in your mind: "I am wealth, health, and happiness."

July 7

Catching up on Friendships

Someone on my Facebook page posted the question: Does marriage still hold importance in the 21st century? Well, let me tell you one of my example stories:

My childhood friend

We were only fifteen when my best friend and I went to a soccer game in the small village we grew up in. My dad was a soccer coach, and like most Europeans, all males tended to be heavily involved in sports, especially soccer.

That particular day my friend met this young man that became the love of her life. He was twenty-five at the time, and as she found out later, already engaged. He didn't seem to be concerned about his commitment to his fiancé as he laid his eyes on her, and so they started to talk and giggle. That very same year Ulli had to start working as an apprentice. Going into the workforce at fifteen was common back in the days. With little job opportunities she started to work for the largest company in the area which produced auto parts. Her lover also worked for this business and so they had an easy way of dating and deceiving his fiancé.

The affair went on over a couple of years and her beloved boyfriend got married. Not to her but to his fiancé, fathering two children and building his family. No one could convince Ulli to end this relationship even though her heart must have been breaking many times. Her youth and innocence believed his lies and pretentions. As she matured she tried to sever her ties to this man that only had his own selfish welfare and satisfaction in mind. However, the bond she established so young in her life was a tough one to shatter.

I remember vividly one day when she came to visit me in the US, she bought several high-priced sports equipment items for her married boyfriend so she could surprise and please him. I asked her outright when he would finally leave his family and commit to her, knowing very well that this was a farfetched question. "Only a couple more years," she said, "as soon as the kids are grown!" Oh, delusion - mother of all miseries!

When her man reached retirement age and left the company, the regular visits lessened, but she held on to whatever time and affection he still gave her.

Ulli retired early, about five years ago. Having worked her whole life in the same company, she had accrued enough benefits to live a comfortable lifestyle. But he had vanished and ended the relationship staying with his family - as everyone could see - but poor, blind Ulli.

Forty years had gone by, a lifetime of hopes and dreams. She never had children or her own family, living through her brother and his family gregariously. I thought of her today as it is her birthday, and I wish her more love and happiness than she ever can imagine.

So to the question: Does marriage still hold importance in the 21st century?

I would opt to say yes. It is important. Not just from a legal standpoint, but from a sincere, loving, and committed attitude that shows your honest intent of doing the right thing. I'm not judging the people that have both come to the agreement to stay in a union that is not bound by matrimony, if it was both of their wishes, or people that decide not to marry at all. Everyone has a choice. However, I hope that one day all people, including same sex couples, do have the right to experience this ultimate state of Earthly union, if they wish to do so.

July 8

Spiritual transformation might be subtle but certain.

My friend Ilene Waters continues her battle with her weight

"Everything in its own good time." That's always on the back of my mind these days. Every day is a struggle for me, sometimes more so than others. I wake up with the best intentions, I will write in my little journal about focusing on myself and recommitting to my goals, the main one which is weight loss and being healthier.

And yet, every second there can be a twist and turn in the road that I allow to steer me off course - a little here a little there - and before you know it, I'm dead in the water again; a duck going round and round in a pool. Why is that, I keep wondering?

Everybody has their own story - that goes without saying. How I've dealt with much of my emotional garbage has involved excess in some way or another. Early on it was food, who was and remains, my best friend. Food doesn't judge, turn on you, and desert you - although I've deserted it quite often! It doesn't yell at you, restrict you, or beckon you in other evil ways. It also doesn't give you praise, make up for abandonment, shield you from harshness and protect you from evil. Food is food, people. You eat it for nourishment and enjoyment. Nothing more, nothing less, I know that, and yet, I've equated it over and over again with the lacks in my life: Love, comfort, happiness, relationships and fulfillment.

When I am thinking rightly and good, there's no way they can infiltrate my mental fortress. When I revert to negative thoughts and let my mental defenses down, they stand: ready to move in, beat the shit out of

237

me, and take a non-righteous stand for evil. Again, I am my own mental command post for all my troops - good and evil. How many multiple personalities can I have to allow such double-mindedness? As many as I allow myself! Because at all times I am in control of every thought I think every second of my life. Commander in Chief of a million mental thought soldiers."

Remember, the above story is written by someone that has struggled with excess weight all of her life, and her thoughts about food and weight are still in an immature state and therefore she is still struggling with the same issues over and over again. Weight loss should be about health and not about fitting into a size prescribed by society. We all have different bodies, fitting our mental journey.

July 9

Don't see others as "less than" yourself. They might appear to be "less" talented, "less" quickly to act or understand, "less" tolerant or "less" gifted - but by judging others you are taking away from your own good. They are not "less" - they are as perfect as you are. They are just on a different level of unfoldment or frequency - working on their own issues and challenges. So be compassionate and focus on your Self.

July 10

Your Soul is the unbroken connection to the Almighty universal source

How to attract good Souls

Let's get away from the idea that Souls are "people.". The word "people" is described in the Merriam-Webster dictionary as "human beings making up a group," "the mass of a community," "a body of persons that are united by a common culture," and so on. All of those expressions imbue a material sense. Calling someone a human being also does not imply a connection with his/her natural God state. It projects a sense of an Earthly, vulnerable, and corrupt creature.

The real you is your Soul, not your body. You are not a human being. You are a mental being. When you once realize your divine heritage you will only attract good Souls, other wonderful mental beings, clothed in this Earthly human body. Of course there is one other requirement: Well, you have to be good yourself first. Good attracts good, that's a law of life.

July 11

There is a wonderful little tale, with great impact, in the book *Karma and Reincarnation* by Paramhansa Yogananda, available at Crystal Clarity Publishing. It's called the "Magic Carrot" and in essence tells the story of an Indian woman that never did anything good. She was pure evil.

The Magic Carrot

"The Indian woman became more and more wicked as time passed, and at the time of her death she was thrust into Hades. The Angel of Death was hearing her complaints and the awful loud noises this woman was making, and asked her to please remember one good thing she had done in her life. After thinking about it she told him that once, having a bunch of carrots for a meal, she found one with a worm inside and gave it to a hungry person. She told the beggar to only eat the good part of the carrot and to not kill the worm.

The Angel of Death said to the wicked woman: 'That will do', and quickly made the carrot appear. Then he told her to hold onto the carrot as good as she could; and promised that the carrot would get her into paradise.

As she was ascending to heaven another sinner grabbed onto her leg, and another, and another. As the woman saw that many others would benefit by holding onto her leg she got so angry that she tried to kick off the sinners. In the attempt to not allow anyone to be saved with her, she let go of the carrot."

You can imagine what happened next. She spiraled down even further into the most unimaginable hell. Remember, even the smallest good deed or kind act will contribute to your salvation. Every tiny contribution you can make will be counted by the unalterable Law of Attraction or the Law of Cause and Effect. As Goodness is all there is, nothing less is acceptable in this lifetime, or in the next and the next.

July 12

Every man's world picture is and always remains a construct of his mind, and cannot be proved to have any other existence. (Erwin Schrödinger)

There is only so many ways of saying this. You create and perceive your world, and it is always unique and very specific to your own ideas and vision. Your world only exists within you and not outside of you, or in anyone's mind. They, so-called other people, have to deal with their own worlds; one by one.

July 13

The negative is really a positive when you see it as a learning tool.

Eventually, as we unfold and gain an understanding of truth, negativity will not show up in our experience anymore, for the simple fact that our sense of "negative" will have changed. When we stop to recognize the so-called "bad" it will disappear as it is not real in the first place.

July 14

Your Soul reflects the image and likeness of God, or Universal substance; and this almighty substance does not age. It is timeless, eternal, limitless, and perfect. And so are you!

Dexter's midlife crisis

I was checking in with Dexter to wish him a happy birthday and to see how he was doing. He made mention about his "midlife crisis" and I thought, interesting... What does the phrase "midlife crisis" really mean?

The basic idea behind any drama or unpleasant experience is fear. In the so-called "midlife crisis," it's a specific fear of having "missed out" on things that one wanted to experience or achieve. The attitude of "it's too late now," "I'm too old," "I can't anymore," all brings out tremendous anxiety and regret. Pity, guilt, and a desperate attempt to make up for lost time, and a rush to experience any and everything that wasn't accomplished sets in. All of this of course goes against nature and the natural flow of life's plan.

You are where you are in your life for a reason. You haven't lost anything. Life is eternal and you will get your chance to experience everything there is. Maybe not in the way you imagine, but in ways that are far better than you could ever dream of.

I know, it seems your body isn't quite functioning the way it used to. But it's our belief system that dictates the decay of the physical body. Your mind cannot decay or get old. Your physical state is only the reflection of your personal perception. Age, just like any other human suffering, is merely a sign of human belief and ignorance.

241

July 15

Prayer of Saint Francis of Assisi

Lord, make me an instrument of your peace.
Where there is hatred, let me sow love;
Where there is injury, pardon;
Where there is doubt, faith;
Where there is despair, hope;
Where there is darkness, light;
And where there is sadness, joy.

O Divine Master, grant that I may not so much seek
To be consoled as to console;
To be understood as to understand;
To be loved as to love.
For it is in giving that we receive;
It is in pardoning that we are pardoned;
And it is in dying that we are born to eternal life. Amen

July 16

A shift of consciousness to a higher dimension is inevitable, because progress is a law of life.

There are many online magazines and blog sites with an abundance of New Age writers. The site I frequent often, a magazine I write for, addresses many different metaphysical topics and is also a forum for networking and getting your name out there into cyberspace.

As I mentioned before, it's a very popular site and I love to write. In these articles I express my true viewpoints of the understanding I have gained so far. I'm sticking to my message, keeping it real. Without being disrespectful, I really don't care if all readers "get it" or not at this point. Truth cannot be masked to please. That is also the reason why I wrote another book called *The Seeds Will Sprout Somewhere*.

Esme's story

"I like what you say about not caring if they get it or not - the seeds will sprout somewhere. So positive and good. Kuthumi always says the same."

Esme is a sincere believer in channeling and says she has contacted the ancient master Kuthumi many times through a study group she frequents in the US.

"I'm about to listen to a recent Awakening Zone, blog radio of Marisa channeling him and answering questions online. The sound quality is awful, but I heard half yesterday and will go back to the rest now. It was live on June 10th from Colorado, but she was in Sydney at the time and Joep Claasens, her "compare/interviewer," was in Colorado.

"Enjoy," I tell her, awaiting her detailed report of the call. With excitement in her voice, I received this e-mail shortly after.

Esme:

"And would you believe it! Kuthumi was saying exactly the words that you spoke earlier, 'Don't bother if they don't get it. The seeds will sprout somewhere,' as I tuned in. Those exact words!!!! And he smiled back at me, as I gulped and smiled at him. And then he said, 'Yes, I'm with you - any of you, whenever you want me to be.'"

The moral of the story? Don't force or impose your believes onto anyone. Each and every Soul will be ready when their time comes. All we can be are instruments of the Universe and spread the good seeds, no matter how small, because ... "the seeds will sprout somewhere!"

July 17

"If you want to learn something, read about it.
If you want to understand something, write about it.
If you want to master something, teach it."
(Yogi Bhajan)

July 18

Gratitude and its role in the creation process

What is gratitude's role in the creation process, you ask?
Gratitude is a feeling that results from honest
appreciation. Appreciation of the life you already have.
It is a knowing that you are blessed no matter what the
circumstances are in your current life. The surest way to
a better life is through gratitude and an appreciation of
even the smallest things. I would suggest to pay
attention to your thoughts first thing in the morning and
to observe what comes to mind.

Are you waking up smiling, ready to enjoy a day at
work, ready to stroll through a park, jog at the beach, or
meet a friend for lunch? Are you ready to embrace your
children and your spouse or significant other? Are you
prepared to love and act kindly? Are you excited to see
a new day and look forward to new adventures? Are you
ready to learn?

Or, are you unhappy and resentful the minute you open
your eyes? Are you miserable already, even though you
haven't put on your clothes yet? Do you dread going to
work or resent not having a job to go to, spending the
day with an elderly family member? Are you still upset
over a meaningless argument from the night before? Are
you bored and don't know what to do with yourself
today or any day?

Wake up every morning "giving thanks" and end the day with a "grateful heart"

Give thanks for the blessings you have received and for the blessings that are coming your way today and every day. Saying "thank you" to the Universe with sincere appreciation puts you instantly into a positive frame of mind. Gratefulness will catapult you to a higher frequency and will trigger loving thoughts naturally.

Even while sleeping, your subconscious is working, digesting and systematizing your day's experiences and impressions. It will register the mood encountered while dozing off. Going to sleep with a grateful heart will let you rest a lot better than a worried and disturbed mind. Say "thank you" to the Universe or source of all being before you drift away. Know the next day will be even better and greater and you will be closer to your goal of happiness.

What to watch for

Watch yourself during the day and listen to your inner dialogue. Do you easily get discouraged or angry? Does your temper rise quickly? What triggers your mood to change?

On a mental level, give thanks to the fact that in reality your consciousness knows all there is to know. You have only forgotten who you really are and you are in the process of remembering your true nature. You, not being fully aware of this fact, are on your way to unfold this knowledge from within.

No matter your present circumstances, acknowledge and be grateful that you are not a helpless human being, struggling to survive. You, at this point of your unfoldment, know that you can change your situation according to your sense about the situation.

You are made of Universal substance: Wisdom, Goodness, and Intelligence. Your true nature is mental in origin.

It is your Soul that does the living, not your body. Your body is the visible expression of your Soul. So be grateful for the body you have and treat it with respect and kindness. It is the only body you have here on this plane and it should be treasured.

What about the unpleasant experiences? Should you be grateful for those? It's easy to be thankful for good things, but what about things and situations that "look" bad? Like anything else, it gets easier with practice, and it will keep your focus on what's right rather than on what's wrong. A seemingly bad situation is only another opportunity for you to make a change in your life. Jolt down a list of big and little things that warrant appreciation every day. Putting it on paper will put it in perspective and you will see the importance of appreciation.

The "black hole"

"What is going on inside me?" is a good question to ask yourself when you feel angry or lonely or just plain miserable. Do you wonder why you feel the way you feel? Is it a habit? What triggers it, and what makes you tick?

At one time or another, we have all experienced that vicious cycle between habitual wrong thoughts and raw emotions. They feed each other, and the downward spiral begins. I call it the "black hole."

You can feel the "black hole" coming on when all of a sudden your mood changes. Something triggers you to jump back to an old hurt or disappointment, jealousy, or resentment. You're not quite sure what made you think of this occurrence, but suddenly and unwittingly you experience this knot in your stomach and you mire in

246

negative emotions. You recall instantaneously the negative emotions this incident had at the time.

Continuously dwelling on the wrong situation or person feeds energy into the emotion, which in turn energizes the wrong thought pattern. As I said, it's a vicious cycle. Stop these feelings when you feel them coming on. Believe it or not, bad experiences are really good. They are a lesson; they are what you need to progress at the time. They are blessings.

How do you turn the black hole into a radiant circle of light?

We turn the black hole upside down by refusing to fall into it. You have a choice: You can either continue to dwell on the past and the thoughts that led up to your mood, or you can say "No, I will not think such wrong thoughts again." You can acknowledge the situation, feelings, and emotions for what they are, or you can continue to suffer. It is up to you.

How grateful we should be to be able to switch unpleasant things around. We only have to change our view of the situation. Each experience helps to complete the puzzle if Life is to be complete. Each challenge that is solved by you is necessary to make you whole. So the black hole exists to point out areas in your thinking that are still dark and unresolved. Allow your radiant circle of light to illuminate your being!

July 19

Talk about metaphysical diagnosis

In the next few days I want to address several more common illnesses and the connection of your thoughts to these manifestations. As I said before, all illness is only the reflection of your sick or wrong thinking. Ignorant of this fact or not, you will always get what you think in the exact proportion to your convictions. Each

247

organ in your body reflects a quality in thought. Every inch of your physical appearance is a symbol of something in the mental. To learn about the corresponding manifestations is lifesaving.

Please do not try this without a teacher or sufficient study. This cannot be learned in a day or two. It takes serious commitment and understanding of the Law of Cause and Effect. However, if you are genuine in your desire and apply the principles with an honest heart you will be rewarded with health and happiness.

July 20

Healing Thought:
Bronchitis reflects an extreme disharmony within the family. Since it's mostly a chronic disposition it shows that the in-harmony has been going on for a while. Especially small children, which always think it's "their fault," react to their parents fighting and inharmonious behavior. In adults it also reflects a want for change or being in control, but with the stifling feeling of "I can't." They are holding on to this powerless thought and are "hacking away" at it. A home should be loving and kind. Give it your best effort to create a pleasant environment and don't subject your children to this unnecessary stress.

Let me tell you a short story of my childhood

The earliest memories of my childhood evolve around bronchitis. As far as I can think back it was my constant companion, and what stuck with me the most was that I had it for years and years. I remember the days vividly when my mother would come to my bedside and put hot grilled onions on my chest, then believed to have healing powers. I was sent to a high-altitude summer camp in the mountains with pristine Alpine air which was believed to relieve the respiratory system so I could breathe easier. I was advised to sit in the sun or go swimming without a shirt so it could shine its healing rays on my chest.

I was told later that my sickness started when I was three years old and continued heavily until I was six. It took several more years to completely heal, but as I grew up I seemed to grow "out of it." Little did I know that my parents, who constantly fought, were getting a divorce at the onset of my bronchitis and remarried each other three years later. They never made it and eventually divorced again when I was fifteen. However, by then I was pretty grown up, very head strong, and left home to follow my own dreams and goals.

How do you deal with your feelings towards your parents if you had a difficult childhood? How do you not carry the baggage of disharmony and hatred when all you learned is by the elder's poor example?

First of all - forgiveness; they didn't know better at the time. Even beatings, verbal abuse, and neglect can be forgiven once you are an adult. It might take some time and rigorous soul searching, but it can be done. I am living proof of it.

The final healing that needs to occur after you have made peace with yourself is to break the wheel of Karma. Do not repeat the mistakes of your parents on your children. Make sure that you are not treating your kids the way you've been treated. Repeating the ignorant mistakes of your parents would be a great sin.

July 21

Healing Thought:
A "sore throat," a somewhat common occurrence, can be accredited to a feeling of anger and other negative feelings going unexpressed. The throat is your symbol of your ability "to put up with" or "swallow." You should "put up with" or "swallow" only the good, lovely, pleasant and right ideas.

Keep that in mind next time you are tempted to get angry over something unimportant or lesser than perfection.

What is "hard to swallow?"

Look around you. What is going on in your immediate life? Are you listening to others behaving a way that doesn't agree with your morals and beliefs? Would you like to speak up, but you feel it's better to go with the flow? Are you in an office environment that tends to gossip and complain about everything and everyone? Are you mad at your spouse because he/she is constantly trying to tell you what to do but you decided to "keep the peace"?

There are all kinds of situations that warrant your "standing your ground" in a loving way of course. Don't just "swallow" what you really want to say. It will manifest in a sore throat as it will picture forth your painful, sore thoughts about your feelings towards others. Think about and correct this inactive, passive behavior.

July 22

Healing Thought:
Ulcers are (even per the medical book) due to worrying, pressure at work or home, and stress. Let's take this explanation a little further. What about frustration about not having things go the way you want, a feeling of anxiety that you are not good enough, and too much to bear in general. People with ulcers are usually highly emotional, tense, and nervous. They not only worry about the outcome of a situation, they also try to force it, causing constant pressure upon themselves and disappointment. Stop - this unhealthy behavior will literally make your stomach walls bleed.

Life is good; it is meant to be enjoyed and lived calmly. All good things will be done in due time. There is nothing to worry about; what's the worst that can happen? Ask yourself this question when you fret over some insignificant issue.

July 23

Healing thought:
When your thoughts are bitter and hard, over a long period of time, you will manifest a disposition called "gallstones." Feeling condemned, criticized, and reacting with a harsh, stern, and unforgiving attitude makes things worse. Apply all the calm, forgiving, and tolerant thoughts you can muster up. Let go of the bitterness in your heart, and your spirit, and practice love.

So here is a disposition that takes a long time to manifest. Lots of bitter thoughts, a hard attitude toward something that happened in the past, and a determined sense of "not letting go" all contribute to this painful illness.

Is it really worth it? Do you not want to forgive? Why? Do you think you are in the right and that it was unfair? Even if you are in the right, does it really matter to a degree that you risk your health, your happiness, and your life?

Really?

July 24

Your aches and pains are the reflection of your painful thoughts from past thinking. Make sure your "now" thoughts are full of love, appreciation, and free of fear, so you don't have to experience the same agony and discomforts tomorrow.

The positive side of all the above is that it can be avoided by you. It cannot be stated often enough that you are in charge of your thoughts. You are in control of your feelings and emotions.

Let me tell you the truth about right thinking. It's not a quick fix or easily obtained. It's not a magic wand that you wave and all life experiences are all of a sudden healed and wonderful. No, it's a step by step, every minute of your life commitment; a sincere want to be better, think better, do better, and a fulltime job. Do not take this lightly. Crave it, and then honestly look at every area of your life, every thought you think and action you take – and only then have you begun to move in the right direction.

The rewards are peace and a calmness you have never known. A lightness and grace in your heart that goes beyond all of your past experiences. I can't describe it in a few words; you will have to encounter this bliss yourself. It's time to heal and live.

July 25

What else will make you feel better?

Maybe it's yoga, prayer, or exercise. Maybe it's a walk in nature or visiting a peaceful place. Maybe it is a bowl of ice cream you want. Maybe it's all of them.

You can also focus on forgiving any old grudges you are holding against someone. You can slow down, giving yourself permission to rest. You can stop worrying so much and obtain a more easy-going attitude, let go of the constant "hurry" mode and clear your calendar of all the unnecessary "business" posted by you, for you.

You know in your heart what would make you feel better. But for once don't focus on the materialistic gifts you want, thinking that they will fulfill your emotional needs. Focus on the true gifts of the Universe; your self-worth, self-love and your Spirit. Pamper your Soul!

July 26

This is what makes my mission so wonderful – this is what I posted this morning:

Everyone's goal is happiness. No matter what the desire is in your heart, you ultimately yearn for happiness. What are you going to do today that makes you happy?

And here is one of the answers from a reader:

"Spend the day in the knowledge that I found the courage to leave an abusive job behind and within three days found a position that offers full benefits, a caring management staff, and advancement opportunity. I took the plunge last weekend and quit, and the Universe filled the void with blessings and abundance! I am so excited with this new opportunity and grateful for the lessons I learned from this recent past experience. Life is truly good and I am loved and blessed! Thank you for these wonderful words of encouragement post every single day. You have no idea how many rough days you have helped me get through with these postings. By focusing on gratitude and positive feelings, I finally found the nerve to walk out and trust that the Universe had my back and something better waiting in the wings. And so it was!"

July 27

Planting new seeds of lovely and good thoughts in your mind will bring you the blossoms and blessings you are yearning for.

Mind seeds
Article at the Los Angeles Examiner

In the mental, the Law of Cause and Effect is always in operation. There is no such thing as getting away with wrongdoing, wrong acting, or even wrong thinking in this world of Universal Consciousness. This Law is fair and just, and cannot be altered. It just is.

Many call this law Karma, but whatever your name for "it" is, you should be aware of the consequences you will experience if you do not adhere to its rules. This is not meant to be a warning; It is only a statement of Truth.

In this age of awakening, with a huge shift being on the horizon of cosmic consciousness, and all true "thinkers" being on the brim of emerging awareness, the involvement of each and every one of us needs to be assured and certain.

Your thoughts are blossoms of the mind. Some unattended notions will come quickly and wilt away. Some are nurtured and cared for; seeds put in fertile soil. The purpose of flowers is to bloom beautifully for your enjoyment, and even after they are spent, reaching full fruition, they turn into more seeds, ready to produce more beauty. So it is with your thoughts.

A steady focus on your thought patterns and habits will assure that you are on the right path, paving your road with a sturdy surface and not walking on quick sand.

Seeds produce more after their own kind – just like your good thoughts produce more good thoughts. See, everything is mental. There is nothing that is made of matter; nothing on this plane is solid. It is only our dream-vision that makes it so. A movie, your particular motion picture of life – you made what you see and experience. You are the writer, director, actor, editor and watcher of the screen play you are putting on, right here and right now, on this Earth.

This is only the beginning. A mortal dream, lived, to help you grow and learn, and to unfold your understanding of the workings of your mind.

July 28

Judging by appearances

What is a judgment and what is a true statement? Could we say that a judgment is what you assume, whereas a statement is based on truth? Could it be that a judgment tends to be more negative and a statement more a positive fact?

Reader:

"I think the only truth we have is for ourselves. Any statement made about anyone else has a touch of assumption and judgment considering we don't know the entirety of their belief systems."

Reader:

"I agree with Renee. What we believe is true is only true for us based on our past experiences, upbringing, world view, etc. A statement that qualifies is by definition a judgment. We tend to think of 'judgment' as something negative, but a judgment is basically an opinion. An opinion hopefully based on fact and evidence, but even facts can be relative according to interpretation. I think the key to preventing a statement from becoming a judgment is to simply begin with saying, "In my opinion..." or "As I understand the situation..." We are, in that manner, acknowledging that what we are saying is the truth according to our own beliefs and perspectives. How many of us can truly say that we really *KNOW* with absolute certainty?"

Give this conversation some thought and write down what you think. Putting it on paper will make you be more precise.

July 29

Healing Thought:
The blood symbolizes "love" in the mental. Anemia is a longstanding sense of a cold mental attitude. There is too much focus on the negative instead of the positive; coupled with feelings of "I'm not good enough" and "I'm not worthy." Those individuals don't love themselves enough. This absence of loving feelings in their daily doings result in a lack of joy, vitality, and a sense of listlessness.

Love the good you already have and imbue more loving thoughts into your daily life. Know that all is good. Love is the mother element of Universal substance.

What is a cold mental attitude? I'm not talking about detachment. Detachment from things is necessary as you go further and further along towards your spiritual unfoldment. However, it requires love at all times which also is not to be mistaken with a personal sense of love. It is an all-inclusive sense of love, not a "pick and choose" kind of love. A cold mental attitude would be a sense of "not loving life" enough, always finding fault with what's going on in your life and/or the people around you.

When you feel that you or someone else is not good enough, you are projecting a downgraded or lesser sense of love. Blood, the reflection of Love flowing through our whole body, shows that we cannot live without this sense of love. So your blood has to be kept pure; it cannot be contaminated without dire consequences.

Keep your thinking pure and good at all times. This is a tall order, I know, but in the end your efforts will be well worth it.

July 30

Healing Thought:
Where does "fatigue" come from? Why are you feeling burned out and tired all the time? Maybe you are feeling bored or are doing things you don't want to; you are unhappy at your job or in your relationship. Or are you simply not liking your place in life?

All of those mental dispositions are a way of resisting life rather than embracing it. Start by appreciating what you have rather than complaining about the situation. Get going and do the things you love. See the beauty and the good in everything and soon you will be inspired again. Inspiration is the key to feeling full of vim and vigor, which in turn annihilates fatigue.

You inspire from within - look deep inside of yourself and you will find all the inspiration you need. Don't give up so easily. Your purpose in life is to enjoy - enjoying what? Well, all the good you are creating. This is the circle of life.

July 31

Healing Thought:
Did you know that "snoring" also has a meaning in the mental? It reflects a "not letting go" of old patterns or a refusal to change. A feeling of pressure and a heavy sense about your daily experiences will make you think you have too much on your mind. You are not clearing out your detailed thoughts of the day.

Do not allow the sense of things to pile up just because you don't want to adjust and accept the new. Reason what's true about life. Handle details one at a time and go with the flow; change is good!

One of your first exercises you will have to practice as part of your mental housecleaning is to let go of the old habits and concepts you have set up for yourself. Clear out your cobwebs and you soon will be able to breathe easier and sleep in comfort and peace.

Chapter 8: Harmony

August 1

Allow yourself to flow with Life's current, not against it

Changes

Embracing "change" is not everyone's cup of tea. I, for one, love change. It is exciting, exhilarating, and makes me feel alive. When I am stuck for too long in a rut I get restless, always looking for growth and newness. I don't look for excitement; really, it's not that I need additional adrenalin. No, I honestly can say I am a natural high-speed mental racer. I am going down the spiritual highway in a steady pace - sometimes on auto-pilot because I trained myself to make right thinking, and the awareness of my Universal connection to the All-power, God, my life goal.

The month of July had many wonderful opportunities and door openings in store for my business and my Self. I reconnected with an old study-buddy of mine who is a video producer and, like myself, has worked for a major studio for many years.

I've been thinking of producing a video similar in concept to "The Secret," imbued with my teachings for a few years now. It was on the back burner, my bucket list, but it was definitely a future goal. I had to publish several books first, build an audience, and establish my credibility as a writer. Things were going great and most of the above had been accomplished.

And then, a few weeks ago, I stumbled upon this class mate of metaphysics online. Checking his profile I saw that he no longer worked at the movie studio as I remembered and he had started his own video production company. I wrote him a quick note that read: "Hi, we should produce an inspirational video together." Within twenty minutes he replied, saying: "Yes, we should. I've wanted to produce a video just like 'The Secret' for six years."
Coincidence? Of course not!

For several years now, without knowing of each other's vision, we had the same dream - the dream of producing an inspirational video; a tool for people helping them to learn about the workings of the mind.

"The Secret" by Rhonda Byrnes did a wonderful job in presenting the Truth of the Law of Attraction to the masses. However, it is time to get a bit more into the "nitty gritty" and also show the relationship your mind has to all health related issues in a more detailed and powerful way. Affirmations are wonderful, but as I said before, it will not do anything for you if you do not know HOW to apply these Truths. We will certainly focus on the step by step process of "how to" heal and to become more abundant and happy for the rest of your life.

August 2

Spread your wings and fly

How to become successful? Achieving goals requires a focused and determined mindset. Focus and knowing "what you want to be" at a young age is not what we call common. Many young people drift without a specific aim in life. You can achieve anything you set your mind to, just "...because you can!"

This is a great example of a young entrepreneur that has vision and determination acting on his dream ever so diligently.

Berny's story

While Berny's mother was busy carving replica cars out of cake for her artistic cake orders, three-year-old Berny kept himself busy in the back of her cake shop with paper. By simply folding the sheets and connecting the pieces with tons of staples, he created the most amazing 3-D vehicles, cars, tractors, and boats.

His parents told me that Berny's first word he spoke was "tractor," due to the many and extended trips he took to the Austrian countryside together with his grandmother. Engine powered vehicles have always fascinated him but his true passion, from a very early age on, was anything "remote controlled." Countless remote control cars and trucks were his and as he got older his toys also became more sophisticated and, needless to say, more expensive. Soon though his focus shifted to planes and helicopters and his talent in handling remote controls became more and more obvious.

While attending high school in the United States he dreamed of designing and inventing cars that were able to take off; private car-micro planes. After graduating from aviation college in Los Angeles, Berny's certificate as FAA-approved airframe technician landed him a temporary job with a special effect company which eventually led to what he does now.

Currently, at the young age of twenty-two, he is company co-owner of Aerial Film FX, specializing in aerial videos taken with remote camera attached helicopters and works with real estate agents, special event companies, wineries and vineyards, and movie production companies. Berny is truly an inspiring young man!

August 3

Your heart needs happiness

Taking care of self physically and mentally should be your number one priority every day of your life. Unless you are happy and healthy you cannot be of any benefit to others, including to your family. A happy and healthy "you" is what contributes the most value to this world of challenges.

Reader:

"Hi, I had four bypass surgeries, had a few complications but turned out ok. Then, I had a total knee replacement. I worked in a flexed position for some time and since then I have had severe pain in my right lumbar area when I bend and twist to the left. I had some tests done several days ago and now find that I have another situation with my body that needs attention and further study. A CT scan revealed that I have atherosclerosis of my aorta. No idea from the report of how bad it is but this can progress to an aneurism and possible rupture. Now, I am calling my cardiologist in the am to see him to find out how serious this is or if it is just something to watch."

So here is a very nice seventy-four year old male with a great attitude and lots of health issues. Let me give you some thoughts on his woes, looking at it from a mental/metaphysical standpoint.

Anytime there is trouble with the heart

The heart represents self-sufficiency. It is your ability to cope with your life; the heartbeat of your life, ever pumping blood (the symbol of love) through your arteries. You must maintain "thoughts of life" and feel fully self-sufficient to maintain a healthy heart. Repeat: "I love my Life and I am self-sufficient."

262

Knee replacement

Knees, as part of your legs (which represent locomotion or progress in the mental) are helping you in moving forward. Knowing what is the right thing to do but not following through sufficiently begs the question: Are you utilizing what you know? Are you holding onto too much wrong or negative thought? Are you walking smoothly through life, or with painful feelings in every step you take?

When you barge ahead in life, rather than moving forward in an orderly manner, you are straining your sense of spiritual growth. You are painfully trying to force your progress. This ailment can also involve some degree of self-condemnation or holding a "lowering" thought about self. Don't have a sense of restriction. Allow the Universe to do its perfect work, and keep your eye on the prize, which is perfect Understanding and Happiness.

Pain in lumbar area

Suppressed ill feelings, riding over something you don't want to think about. Therefore you are feeling "crossed" up. You are trying to think better about your situation, but don't quite get it right. You must change the underlying concept and think right about it. Pain always has a good amount of fear attached.

Atherosclerosis of aorta:

Many times this stems from a sense that the individual had it "hard in life," "hard to cope with," "difficult experiences," "hard to take," and so on. Make sure you keep your interest in the good and continue to see only lovely things. Know that you can handle anything that comes along your way. You are powerful and perfect, right now. Fear of any illness intensifies the symptoms. Say aloud: "I am well, I am perfect, I am health, I am safe."

August 4

There is no question about this: Health is our biggest treasure

"Good thoughts" manifest into a healthy body (the body being the reflection of those good thoughts), and "right thoughts" manifest, or reflect, in abundance, i.e. money. It is important to know that all illness and disease many times stem from the belief in the reality of these dispositions, as well as the mistaken idea of heredity. Therefore, so-called "good people" can also be sick. (People ask me all the time, and say they can't understand, that if good thoughts produce health, why "good" people get sick.)

Here are some examples of the difference between right thoughts and good thoughts:

Good thoughts are loving thoughts, caring and kind thoughts, giving selflessly, honesty, helpfulness, and so on. Right thoughts are: "I am a mental being," "I am connected to the Universal source/God," "my thoughts are creative," "I am self-sufficient," "I am wealth," and so on.

Do you see the difference?

This is very important for you to know, because you can be the nicest, best, most giving person on the planet and still be without abundance. You'll be healthy but poor. Or you can think correctly about abundance but you carry character traits like resentment and envy. You will be wealthy but sick. There should be a balance; naturally you deserve health and wealth.

Good thoughts come from the heart, your loving feelings - right thoughts come from understanding the Truth!

August 5

True relationships are unselfish and kind. They are supportive, loving and all-inclusive. Yet they are non-attached. Yes, this sounds like a conundrum – but can you see how vital it is to be emotionally non-attached to the other person? Attachment only creates selfishness, expectations, and jealousy. Can you love without attachment? Think about it.

When I see a small child I always remember the beautiful way Paramhansa Yogananda expressed his view of children:

'They are little God-Souls emerging...'

Remember, you are a full-grown "God-Soul." Isn't that wonderful?

August 6

Unfortunately, we, the adult "God-Souls" are sometimes stuck on our own opinions and ideas, right or wrong.

You can take many symptoms literally like "constipation." You are stuck on an old idea and don't want to let go. The digestive system, which is processing your thoughts and reflects your reasoning ability, sorts the right ideas from the wrong. It eliminates what is not needed in the mental. So your daily "output" should be natural and easy, eliminating the unnecessary.

Don't hold onto thoughts and ideas that are no longer needed. Don't be stubborn and inflexible, and unwilling to release old emotions. You will not solve your problems by holding on to them. Life is all about going with the flow, Life is fluid.

As you are working on correcting your feelings and dispositions, you might find the changes more difficult

265

than expected. Don't give up. You accumulated your habits over a long period of time. It will take time to unravel the emotions.

There are many layers of unresolved thought issues. Keep digging and reasoning, and soon you will see the progress of your labor. It only takes fifty-one percent to tip the scale to a more positive experience.

August 7

The Universe is fluid

This statement took me a while to fully understand. We are so wrapped up and afraid at times that we cannot let go of our preconceived notions and opinions. We tend to have a certain idea or picture in mind that we pursue with stubbornness and inflexibility. Let's always remember that the Universe knows best.

If something doesn't go our way immediately and seems to point us in a different direction we shouldn't fight it. We need to give it a good and sincere look, consider what would happen if we would follow the "new path," and then make a wise and informed decision. Patience.

August 8

Healing Thought:
Are you experiencing stiffness, a tenseness of the joints and muscles? The stiffness can result from a mental stubbornness or false pride. It can be an inability to give, an inflexible attitude, rigid feelings, and opinions. Feeling pulled in different directions, under tension and stress, will also make your muscles tense.

Soreness reflects erring self-justification, which causes one to be unforgiving. The area of your body where your discomfort appears will show you the area of error. If it is from your belief in matter, remember: It's not necessary to be stiff after a work-out or strenuous work.

Repeat: I can easily change my attitude. Life is not stiff, it is fluid. There is no stiffness in Intelligence. Life is perfect and good.

Sometimes I get some very interesting comments, and I'm using the word "interesting" very lightly:

Reader:

"OK, I get your point. But that's only for MINOR stiffness. If you are experiencing pain and stiffness, go check with your doctor first before assuming that it is due to the things mentioned above. I had joint pain, muscle stiffness, weakness and a general overall tired feeling for a few weeks. It turned out to be rheumatic fever and I should have gone to the doctor much sooner."

My answer:

"I always recommend going to a doctor for diagnosis. Most of us have not mastered the science of metaphysical diagnosis and healing. My comments are meant to be looked at as an additional tool for wellness and improved health. This change of thought pattern will be helpful to supplement your healing process."

Different Reader:

"And with a good common sense of proper diet that helps too. I do think we need to change the words a little on the affirmation. Instead of reading 'no' or 'not' because these are negative words and the Universe doesn't understand those words it should say something to this effect: life is relaxed, it is fluid. There is relaxation in the universe. What do you think?"

My answer:

"Yes - good point, but please remember that the stiffness stems from a rigid mental attitude and 'relaxation' might not be enough to heal this disposition. A total shift of your thought patterns to a more fluid, accepting, loving, and all-embracing mind set will be very beneficial. Thank you to all of you for your thoughtful input! Have a wonderful Sunday!"

August 9

Since this reader brought out the condition called "Rheumatic fever," let's take a look at the mental cause of this illness.

Rheumatic fever

The medical field explains it broadly as an inflammation of the connective tissue structures of the body, especially the muscles and joints. The most dangerous part (per our medical professionals) is that this illness can also affect the heart tissues.

Looking at it from a metaphysical standpoint, this is a sign of a lot of anger. For instance, if the individual feels unable to express his/her true feelings and is holding them in for too long, he/she will build up this rage.

In some cases the person doesn't want to listen to what others have to say or ignore their opinions even though they want to help, because these individuals developed rebellious feelings with an underlying stubborn attitude. A fever always includes fear and a "heated" mentality.

Anytime there is "inflammation" present you can be sure that your sense of calmness and peace has been disturbed. Your inflamed thoughts play a severe role.

August 10

We all have to deal with the subject of elder care at one point in our lives.

With Love & Grace
By Karen I. Kritzer

"I'm not exactly sure when I started to assume the role as my mother's caregiver. It's been a gradual transitioning - more of a natural selection, you might say, seeing as how I've always assumed the role of 'caretaker' in our family for the most part of my adult life.

Maybe it comes from being the middle child - maybe it happened because of all the dysfunction in our family growing up - I'm not sure when I started wearing these shoes, and perhaps I've had them in my closet all along, just in different sizes as I've grown up. But here I am, and I'm wearing them and I will tell you this: Caring for an elder parent or family member is a gift. Others may readily say it's a curse, but for me, and my situation, it is indeed a gift.

I think I was the obvious choice because I never married, nor had children. I am also the only one in my family to graduate from college, which, again, sometimes led my family members to give me the title as 'most responsible' of the bunch. But in my heart, I know I chose this role and would not have it any other way. Trust me, it's not easy by any means. Being a caretaker has etched away periods of my own life that I can never take back. It has meant every other weekend going to my Mom's house and assisting her with maintaining her house, her chores, her finances - everything her husband did prior to being diagnosed with Alzheimer's some eight years ago.

When he was first diagnosed and my Mom had to start handling the finances and the actual running of the house, she was petrified. She had a third grade education and he was a Doctor of Internal Medicine, so she was overwhelmed by it all. I stepped in and started to assist her. She was grateful and relieved, and also knew she could trust me 100%. Trust is everything as we grow older I am learning. Trust in self and trust in others.

As my stepfather's health deteriorated and we moved him into a skilled nursing facility, I helped alleviate my Mom's burden and stress by doing more and more for her wherever I could. I'm running errands, schedule repairs on her fifty year old house, finances, etc. and, most importantly, I am providing companionship to a woman who had never lived alone in her life. Her own Mother (my grandmother) was fourteen when she gave birth to my Mom, and they had been like sisters. My Mom was an only child so she grew up depending upon my Grandma for guidance for everything.

Thank goodness my Mom is still fairly young - 78 - and is physically in pretty decent shape and also has her wits about her. I have noticed some changes in the past few years since my stepfather died. She feels even more scared of the future and talks more of her own mortality. She is also extremely fearful that she will develop Alzheimer's or dementia, due mostly, I think, from my stepfather having it and dying as a result.

There are some weekends when I'd like to take care of my own life - just deal with my own personal stuff, and I feel a little resentful that my time is not my own as much as I'd like it to be. But as quickly as that ire sets in, it dissipates with the knowledge that one day my Mom will not be here to call me. And in that instant, I do not feel like a caretaker. I feel like a very blessed daughter to have such an awesome Mom - one who has been there for me some fifty-four plus years, through the good and not so good times.

Life, I am coming to realize, is sometimes about balance, but mainly it's about love. The future will come, that is certain. But for this moment, I will take the now and continue to be the best daughter I can be. And always, always, I will take care of my Mom with the same love and grace she has shown to me."

August 11

Remember that your past difficulties did not come to crush you, but to strengthen your determination to use your limitless divine powers to succeed. (The wisdom of Paramhansa Yogananda.)

I've been meaning to write about "harmony" for a while now. Finally, yesterday, I did.

Harmony – the mental meaning

Out of curiosity I looked up the word "harmony" in the dictionary, Wikipedia, and researched online to see if other people wrote articles about "harmony;" and I'm not talking about singing. Basically, all I found was nothing. Sad but true, "harmony" - a mental state of being - isn't discussed very much in our society, even though it is identical to "happiness," which all mankind strive for.

"Harmony is the principle underlying all life"

Think about this statement. The Universe is working perfectly and harmoniously at all times. The planets are moving flawlessly, the plant life grows and flourishes without our help, babies are born every second, and life in general keeps flowing per the great plan of Universal Consciousness. When left alone and undisturbed, life lives and progresses picture-perfect.

The quote, however, also means that any non-harmonious thought is without merit. Webster-Merriam describes the word harmony as "internal calm:

271

tranquility," which unfortunately was the only description that can be used to explain the mental sense of the word "harmony." All other examples were related to music or art. Are we really so absorbed with our material sense of things that we haven't even thought about the true meaning of simple yet powerful words like "harmony?"

What are harmonious thoughts?

Ease, calm, comfort, in sync with nature, in tune with love, pleasant visions, inspiration, relaxed, and a healthy outlook in life to name a few. Harmony does not allow any disturbance whatsoever. It is "internal calm," a genuine knowing that all is good, that you are indestructible, and that you are in charge of your life. "You are the arbiter of your own faith," as declared by many of the metaphysical writers around the early 1900s.

Are you setting time aside for your daily thought exercises?

I hear most people say "I'm just too busy with my daily work, or chores," "I just don't have the energy at the end of the day" and so on. They move on with the same routine rather taking the unpleasant experiences from their in-harmonious thinking and acting. They don't want to think about "working" on their own self-development and growth. It feels like just another "thing to do." Have you any idea on how much better your life would be if you would just spend fifteen minutes a day to contemplate the Truths of life?

How does in-harmony affect your body?

This disturbed mindset influences your overall health in many ways. Hurry, worry contribute to tenseness in the neck areas, stomach troubles, and of course many accidents happen while rushing, or being absorbed in your own nervous energy.

As someone who has observed mental healing for many, many years, I can attest to the fact that the bone structure of the body represents this mental "harmony." When you experience aching bones, or even worse broken bones, you can be sure that your mental "harmony" was disturbed or broken.

Start looking at your mental "harmony," your loving thoughts for life itself, and learn how to better your daily experience by the simple mantra: "Harmony is the principle underlying all life."

August 12

Associate with joyful minds and leave the pessimists behind

Some people are always looking at the negative side of everything. They immediately jump to the "I told you so" and expect the worst at all times. What a miserable way of living! What is it that makes them so afraid on a daily basis? "Experience" they say, it happened before. Do they know that they cause everything that befalls them every day of their lives? So who is to blame?

Are we willing to give it another chance with the innocence of a child and the heart of a true believer, showing faith in the Allness of Good?

August 13

I don't regret the past, I don't worry about the future; I am only interested in today.

Today is a new day, and I will do my best to make it as harmonious and loving as I possibly can. I am in charge of my experience and I choose to be happy.

August 14

God is my idea of myself.

I have to deal with day to day issues just like you. But my life has improved dramatically since I started to search for the Truth. Every bit of correct information has helped me to understand more and more of Universal Law. It is a work in progress.

I ask myself every day: "Was this really the highest thought I could think?" or "Was this outpouring of emotions really necessary?" and "How can I improve my thoughts and correct my feelings even more?"

There are many good and earnest people today, spreading the truth, or at least making an effort to be part of this Universal shift to a better mass Consciousness. They inherently know that it is good and right, and necessary. They are not teachers or preachers, but it makes them feel good, it gives them purpose. It is a natural part of their being. You too can make a difference. You can be an inspiration. You can be part of this "uplifting" the world needs. As I said in my book *"Better Living...Because You Can!"*:

Let your star shine bright! Shed off all limitations, doubt and fear. Enter the realm of all possibilities. This is your true state, your spiritual heritage. Embrace this birthright and love with all of your heart.

So be that light, let it come out and shine. Teach the ones that want to learn and listen. Truth and Love equals Godliness.

August 15

Spice up your life with some fresh, new ideas. Why be stuck with the old and outgrown? You have

imagination, you have desire and you have the power to create!

We have to always remind ourselves of what is true. We also have to remind people who are in close contact with us. It is a matter of retraining our previously poorly conditioned minds to stop seeing the wrong in this world. Why not look for new and fresh ideas that will bring some different, original, and innovative concepts into your experience? You might learn something new!

August 16

Partners in life are meant to balance, complement each other's character traits, teach, and support. Cherish and love the true spirit, not the superficial.

Allow the other to be "themselves" rather than control every move and decision. Freedom is the right for all, including your spouse or partner!

August 17

Get out of your comfort zone. Experience something new. Freshness invigorates Life!

Me

This little word: "Me"- what impact! "Me," "I," "My," "Mine," - designates all I ever will be, and all I ever will know. It is my sense of my perception of me and my world.

Ulrike was the name given to me at birth by my parents. I was named after a calf, raised on the farm where my mother grew up; she found it cute. Interestingly enough my nickname "Uschi" (sounded "oo-shee") means "Cow" in Japanese and it translates into "Happy" in Kundalini. The Cow represents "Patience" – a patient and happy cow, I like it!

275

This name was the first ego ID established for me. It made me someone, in their eyes, a person - it established "who" I was.

I am Ulrike.

The important words in this sentence, I am Ulrike, are the words "I Am." I am alive, I exist, I am spirit, I am conscious, I am aware, and I am Life itself.

Sit still for a minute and think about YOU. Say: "I Am" and feel your aliveness. Feel yourself think. Know that you are conscious. Being - nothing else matters; at least not at this moment.

August 18

Resolve painful memories. They are nothing but residue of a past life.

Prejudice

I'll never forget the lady from my hometown that lost her daughter to her own prejudice. She lived in a little town in a rural area of Austria. Here is how the story began:

Many years ago the miniseries "Roots" was also released in Austria in the late '70s and translated into German. This woman loved the show and especially was fond of one of the main characters, "Kunta Kinte," played by LeVar Burton. She told her daughter how wonderful he was, and how good looking, and shared her fascination regularly.

A few years later, after her daughter Anna had left to live in the United States and settled comfortably, she told her mother that she had met LeVar at a function and shared that he was very nice and cordial.

Time went on and Anna met a man and they fell in love. He was African American and Anna told her mother that she and the young man were going to be married. Her mother was outraged. She said that it was wrong to marry someone from a different race. Anna reminded her of her infatuation with Kunta Kinte, but the mother didn't want to hear of it. She said that as long as she was with this man she didn't want to speak to her again. Anna, hurt, but a forgiving spirit, said "If she'd know better, she'd do better" and went on to marry her love. Her mother didn't talk to her for over fifteen years!

Many years later, Anna is still married and in love with her husband. The mother missed out on so much. She has no communication with her grandchildren, and even though she started to write letters and calls once in a while, Anna does not have the desire to visit her.

What a loss of life and love!

See, prejudice does not only breed in multi-racial countries like the United States. There are pockets of unspeakable discrimination everywhere. Ignorance and fear are the culprits.

I can only speak for myself and therefore share my personal experiences with an honest heart. When I would visit my home town, I was called "the American", not necessarily a flattering thing in the days. I happened to be proud of my new country, so it didn't hurt. I had found what I was looking for, but it took courage.

You have to be all-inclusive. You cannot love someone because of his or her race or status and not the other because they are born into a different culture.

I am not sure why we are born into a certain family. But since there is a reason for everything in this life, I know there must be a reason for your birth circumstance. I felt, since I was a small child, that I was displaced. I didn't fit in. My parents appeared so different. My goals, wants, expectations of life varied so greatly from theirs. There must have been a reason. I am still working on finding out the connection to this conundrum.

I am a child of the Universe, part of life's expression, I know that. However, the reasons behind certain circumstances I'm still trying to clarify.

August 19

Worry is a mental poison. It robs you of the calm mind necessary for your progress in unfoldment.

Have you ever realized how much harm "worry" can cause? Stop the unnecessary worry-chatter of your mind!

August 20

Your vision will become clear only when you look into your heart. Who looks outside ... dreams, who looks inside ... awakens.
(Carl Jung)

Last night I had an interesting experience

I will try to explain this revelation on this piece of paper in simple words.

I was home alone; my husband had driven to Orange County and I went to bed early. I didn't want to watch any TV, which I usually do very sparingly anyways, and just laid there in the dusk thinking of how to increase the intensity of meditation, my path and studies, and I was in a very calm state of mind. After some time of quiet contemplation, I noticed that my husband, who was helping a friend, a fellow electrician at a church conversion, wasn't home yet. It was getting very late.

I tried to call him to see what his time of arrival was. He didn't answer the phone and I started to worry. I tried to

278

call again and my worry increased. And so it went. As time passed, nearing midnight, I became agitated as I was concerned that maybe he went out drinking with the boys after the job. This visual, plus many exaggerated assumptions of danger while driving drunk, triggered this unpleasant knot in my stomach.

Mind you, I very rarely have any kind of negative emotions – I am a pretty steady Soul. So I did what I do best and I started to reason with myself, affirming that all was good and nothing bad had happened. I continued for some time and I felt that my reason took over and I knew in my heart that this was the correct application.

However, my feelings, my emotions, did not want to adhere to what I knew was the Truth. And for the first time I felt the separation of the two, called "feeling" and "reason." I knew that reason must control feeling in order to discriminate properly and I also knew that a new perspective of awareness had just opened in my mind.

At this point the sense of 'feeling' was totally standing on its own. I was the outsider looking in. I was the 'reasoner' at this moment starring at this 'madness' of feelings gone wrong, but I knew that I could win the battle and bring my natural loving, and good, feeling back into my mind.

Most of us automatically jump and answer to our feelings without proper reason. That's why we have so much painful suffering. We are not aware what tremendous part "feeling" plays in our daily lives. To "be" means to feel, sense, live – but it has to be governed by your true reason, the savior of all. Watch it next time you start to worry about something; even a small concern can trigger a slew of feelings and unleash years of piled up frustrations, anger, and resentments.

What an awakening!

August 21

I have the most fascinating task to perform. I am engaged in the business of lifting myself from ignorance to understanding and enlightenment. (The Wisdom of Paramhansa Yogananda)

This is how I feel every morning, day and night. Good or bad, each experience contributes to my, and in your case "your," awakening.

August 22

Facial features

The face reflects your character, and as they say, the eyes are the windows to your Soul.

When studying someone's face, you can see the hardships and pains, the joys and the excitements of their past life written on it. There are wrinkles and lines, different sizes and shapes of your nose, eyes, lips, and the overall facial features, like jaw and brows, etc.; all of them showing your characteristics and longtime moods.

You've seen people with their mouths pointing down, looking like a constant frown. You have seen deep wrinkles between the eyebrows from constant worries. You've seen empty eyes on individuals that have lost their purpose in life.

But what about the shifty eyes that look like a fox ready to steal his prey? What about the bulging nose that looks imposing and ready to bully you? What about the eyebrows that are pointing upward in constant disbelieve and doubt?

Extremely deep wrinkles show an over-emotional character, so if you don't want those lines in your face, make sure your emotions are in check. If you don't want a lip looking miserable by pointing down, make sure you are smiling a lot. If you want happy eyes make sure that they twinkle with joy.

August 23

Character symbols on the body

The body also has certain clues pertaining to people's character. Here are just a few.

A hard and protruding belly, especially on men, shows that they are in the habit of pushing others around. You can observe that on older people that have habitually pushed their "weight" around. Excessive "soft" weight (obesity) also can show the individuals "baby-like" attitude. A poor me, take care of me, syndrome you might say.

On the opposite side, a meager, skinny, almost anorexic body frame will show a mentality that "deprives" itself of all the joys in life. They are extremely controlled and do not enjoy certain aspects of their daily lives. The list goes on and on. I'm sure we'll address some more later as the year goes on.

August 24

You cannot sit idle and expect things to change, nor can you do the same thing over and over again expecting a different result. Unless you start right now by changing your part of the world, it will appear the same to you. Yes, you must be the change that you want your mental mirror to reflect back to you.

This is a reminder that you must walk the walk and you must act on your desires if you want results. I know so many people that have the best intentions. However, as soon they are going back to their daily rut, all good intentions are quickly forgotten. They moan and groan, complain about their woes constantly, but do not listen to reason or good advice. Many times I have to step back and allow them to handle their business the way they think life is handing it to them. It is not my business to correct them. Trust me, I am tempted!

August 25

Why are we talking about our problems all the time? What does hearing ourselves speak out loud do to our thought habits? Does it intensify the feeling of being right? Or are we reaching out for help? Focusing on the negative is an addictive and destructive habit. Talk about what's good in your life, the joys and upsides, rather than the daily frustrations.

Not only are the good intentions forgotten quickly, we are also constantly reinforcing our troubles by talking about them. Why would we torture ourselves by reliving the unpleasant situations by verbalizing them aloud? Let's make the promise of watching our speech, word habits, and daily communications to ensure we are only allowing positive language in our vocabulary.

August 26

It is your choice. You are free to choose and think anything you so desire. So choose wisely!

Frustrations

Why do we get so frustrated? What is it that triggers that feeling in your stomach and that onset of rage? Being out of control about a situation is the main culprit. Let me tell you about my recent experience, when my mantra: "Learn a new thing every day" took on a different meaning.

I decided to change my TV, phone, and internet provider. The ad of a bundle deal looked promising. Great price, good service, and an upgrade to all three items lured me to pick up the phone and call the company. The sales person talked fast and upbeat, made me laugh at times, and I thought how easy this all would be. Voila!

Not so fast, the inner voice whispered, you have to sit around for the installation, make sure the billings are correct and so on. Little did I know what was yet to come.

As soon as I had agreed to the plan I found out that the "bundle" wasn't really a bundle. It actually involved another company and that all aspects of the internet/phone would be handled by them. The original bundle was only for the TV. OK. No problem.

I can't even write the whole story without taking up the rest of this book, and so I will tell you in short. There were about six appointments, each scheduled for a minimum of four to eight hours. Each day I waited patiently for a technician. Every time I seemed to be the last customer scheduled at the end of the day. Several of the technicians wanted to finish the day and go home rather than finishing the job at my house, and so they casually said: "sorry, this can't be done" and left. Each time I had to call both companies, being put on hold and talking to computers that repeated themselves and do not allow you to speak directly to a customer representative unless you've heard the whole spiel again and again.

This went on for three weeks. My patience had worn very thin, and I asked myself "Why?" Why am I attracting this situation? What is it that I have to learn from it? This hasn't happened to me in a long time, I never have issues like this. My life is smooth and comfortable, flowing like a pleasant stream. Did I become too complacent? Did I need to test myself to stay polite in spite of the despondent situation?

I had my spouts with some of the customer care specialists, as they are called, but I also made a point to let them know that I knew it wasn't their fault. That I appreciated their help and that I was sure all would be fine in the end. And so it was.

August 27

Let no one see you hurt or angry. You can be firm and honest, but do not react to others in an unkind or confrontational way. Stay composed and reasonable, stay away from personal opinions and, most of all, mind your own business. We all have plenty of work to do with our own business; there is no need to get involved in anyone else's!

Mind your own business...

Remember my comment a few days ago about being tempted to tell people what to do?

Sometimes we don't even realize that we stuck our nose in someone else's business. We think we are helping and being supportive. I wrote the above quote over a year ago but today I had to swallow a bit of my own advice.

A dear friend of mine, hard worker and all, has a business that she has had for several years and struggles like everyone else these days. Special events suffered greatly in the recession out of obvious reasons. Who wants to pay for a party when there isn't even enough money for the regular bills? I know of many event companies that had to rethink their strategies and several of them closed their doors for good.

My friend was hanging in there, making due with smaller jobs. Having a good name in the business and being reliable, providing good product and service all helped her to survive. However, she never has been a great promoter of her services; as a matter of fact, she is rather shy.

A few weeks ago I hired her to work for a friend of mine who hosted an event at her house. All went well and I thought how pleasant it was to work with someone that I've known for a long time. This particular work sparked pleasant memories of my old job, due to familiarity you might say. I'm not in that business anymore, but as a writer I spend my time mostly in solitude, so the change of pace was welcome.

In the past year and a half I learned a lot about social media and marketing. I developed websites, videos, and dug into what was necessary in an age that depends on technology, especially in communications.

Looking at her business (yes, you heard right - "her" business, not mine) I offered her to help with the social media aspect. I created a promo video, had a friend write an article for a newspaper, revamped her Facebook page and spent many hours in research and brainstorming. All went well and looked great until a few friends of her started to make comments about the new posts and ridiculed her knowing that she was not the executer of the posts. I didn't hear the exact remarks but, being shy and introverted as she is, she withdrew immediately and asked me to stop working on her site.

Now this should not have bothered me, but it did. At first thought I was miffed about the "friends" that didn't have anything better to do than to make fun of her trying to improve her business. "They are not paying her bills," I thought. I had spent many hours on this project and I really enjoyed it.

It took a couple of minutes and I heard myself say clearly: "That's why you have to stay out of other people's business. Even though she seemed happy and pleased, you weren't hired to do this job. You offered to help for free, thinking she needs you and your talents. Stay out of it."

The wise choice would have been to stick my nose into my own business, and keep working on what I am supposed to do; which is unfolding my own understanding of the truth and spreading the seeds of kindness and love (which by the way is what I thought I was doing!).

August 28

Look deep within your Soul. Ask yourself, "What is my purpose and what is my goal in life," and then listen carefully. Your quest will be answered because it all stems from within.
Soul searching

Part of this book's purpose is to show you how to manifest your desires and the practical application of right thought. As I usually am in the habit of manifesting what I want rather quickly, some of my methods might be helpful to you.

I spent the weekend really thinking about the last couple of weeks and the apparent unsmooth happenings and an additional interesting "flash in the past" that happened this Friday really made me aware of the shift that had occurred.

Even though I'm not really looking for a job (I'm busy enough as a writer) I sent my resume out into cyberspace. I wanted to see what would happen. It was a test to find out what the Universe would bring back to me. How would it answer my call? I didn't expect many offers as my former job is a rare profession, especially in this world of Hollywood. Maybe I wanted to see if I was still needed, oh little ego-self!

However, a couple of days later, I got a call from a well-known company in town. They were looking for exactly the person that was described in my resume. I chuckled. Fortunately, I am no longer the person described in this resume and therefore it wasn't necessary for me to accept this offer. The test, however, had worked perfectly.

At this time in my life I am fully aware that my path has with absolute certainty shifted to a different frequency. I also realize that all of the small and irritating occurrences happened because I was looking outside of myself for answers. I was testing myself; I had to make one last and final choice: Leave my past behind, separate myself from what "has happened" and only look at today and the wonderful future ahead.

I came to the conclusion not to "reach back" to anyone, constantly trying to stay in touch with "others." It was up to "them" to reach out to me if they wanted to join my journey. I had changed so drastically that most of my former acquaintances couldn't understand who I was now. I don't think anyone realized this shift consciously, but they faded away - slowly and steadily, moving on with their own life into their own direction.

I am looking forward to meeting new Souls, special people that are on the same frequency and have the same vision.

August 29

Taking friends with you...

In my current life there are a few special people. Most of the people that I've met were short term acquaintances, coming and going. Some of them are very happy people but many of them live in a negative world. When I decided to leave negativity behind, a shift occurred not only within me but also with the people that I was communing with.

As I said, like most people I tried to reconnect to old friends and acquaintances after leaving my job, but it all seemed to stall and no one responded. It was obvious: I moved out and on to a new frequency. There is a good reason why the people have drifted away. We live in different dimensions, even on this plane, and we have let go and allow them to continue their own journey, where and whatever that might be.

Awakening and shift always brings new people into your experience. You don't need the old and outgrown anymore; it's time to move on. I'm not saying that those individuals are lesser; I'm just saying that they are on a different path. It's a path that is right for them.

The old saying, "when one door closes another one opens," is true, and so it is with friends. The ones that have outlived their usefulness or purpose in our lives are gone. New friends who will contribute to what you need right now and benefit your vision or purpose will appear. When the old life is "dying" a new one emerges. This new life being born, while still on this planet, will be a step up towards my goal.

My advice is to choose carefully who you are in contact with. Love everyone, but only allow the positive thinkers into your immediate mental household.

August 30

Without aim in life, we drift and wander. We must have focus and determination; we must know what we want. Expectancy and desire must become one.

Focus

Earlier in this chapter I've told you about the Mind Seeds TV project "The Seeds Will Sprout Somewhere: and how it all started.

Within this month we have finished our entire website, social media, and set up our combined goals. We have produced several introductory videos. The main objective of course is to make a film. We established the creative outline and have begun to write the script. We meet regularly and are truly enjoying the process. This shows you that when things are right and for the good of all concerned, when your desire is clear and your focus is strong, nothing can stop you. Your world is yours to create. My world consists of writing, teaching, and producing more good. What a wonderful way to live and enjoy!

August 31

True Patience

Last but not least, to end the month of August, I want to address the quality called "patience."

Patience is not putting up with something you don't like because you think you should. It is not the inactivity of mind that makes you stop reaching for your goals and wait for the day when the time is right.

Patience is the knowing that all is good in this wonderful Universe of ours and the ultimate trust in the workings of your mind. When you know that you can achieve and manifest all of your desires with your right thought, and then – patiently – allow the Universe to do its perfect work, then, and only then, have you grasped the meaning of patience.

Chapter 9: Visions and Dreams

September 1

Go on a mental diet and abstain from hurry, worry, and fear. Take in only the pure and the calm and be confident that the power of the Universe supports you - as it is within.

Nervousness stems from an uneasy mind that lacks self-confidence, unfounded fear, or a guilty conscience. The individual constantly thinks that he/she has something to worry about or has done something wrong. Maybe they want to live up to someone else's expectations and feel unworthy or lesser than.

We only have to live up to our own expectation. When we do the best we can and we act loving and kind, we don't have to please anyone. So calm yourself and know that all is good!

September 2

Just as the seeds in the ground bring forth fruit after its kind, your thoughts will do the same. Alike things will spring forth. The gardener knows what he/she planted and can expect to harvest what was sown. You are the gardener of your life. Plant only the right seeds (thoughts) and water (nurture) them plentiful.

September 3

Goodness always returns to the sender

A friend of mine has one of the most kind and generous dispositions. She is always helpful and takes care of the needs of her family and friends, sometimes to a fault. However, I've been watching her life over many years now and I can truly say that she is a fine example of the above statement.

Her inert goodness and temperament has always returned to her. Even though living a simple life, she receives everything she needs through her right thought and loving attitude.

Last week her boss invited her for a birthday dinner and at the end of the night handed her a plane ticket to Paris, the city she loves to visit most, for no particular reason. This is how right thought works. Your desires will be met by the Universe through channels coming from any direction. Just know that you can fulfill your dreams and desires by being and acting good, by giving and therefore receiving, and by the power of your own right thought.

September 4

Right thinking is a science. It can be proven.

Right thinking has nothing to do with wishing, hoping, or having faith. It is pure and simple an act of understanding the workings of the mind and diligent effort on our part to follow the Laws of the Universe. It is a science. It takes commitment, the want to be better, and the determination of proving to ourselves that anything we desire can be manifested. Remember the word "right" in your thinking. Desires must be for your good and the good of all concerned. Those are the rules.

September 5

When you forgive (you are giving from yourself) and forget (you will get back your peace of mind) you are returning to your natural state, called Harmony.

Where is Dexter?

Love does many things. Used in yourself it makes you strong, caring, loving, self-confident, self-sufficient, and self-supporting. Love used with others makes you kind, generous, and most of all forgiving.

Dexter had his ups and downs since we last reported his progress. His health issues are mostly under control. He still experiences an occasional pain from his stubborn and critical disposition, but on the overall he has done much better.

"Forgive and forget" is a very difficult concept for Dexter as it is for most people. Emotions always get in the way. He takes things very personally. He feels easily attacked and is suspicious by nature. Not "true" nature, which is perfect and good, but in his thought habits and character. But he is making progress and is consciously striving to better himself. Acknowledging the issues within self wins half the battle.

September 6

Love is a certain sweetness of emotion.
(Sadhguru Jaggi Vasudev)

This sentence describes the word love perfectly. Love is not what we think it is. Our perception of love is emotion. This is where we get tangled up, suffer, and turn love into hate if we don't receive what we think we should get out of love.

As long as we think that love has to do with the way we feel, calling it a "sweetness of emotion" is absolutely appropriate; a wonderful way of describing this intense feeling.

However, in the truest sense, Love has nothing to do with emotion. It is the mother of all creation. Love is simple and pure. Love is God and God is Love.

September 7

You are made of Universal substance: Wisdom, Goodness, and Intelligence. You are wise, so draw from this wisdom - you are good, so be good - and you are intelligent, so act intelligently. Your true nature is mental in origin.

This cannot be stated often enough. Can you grasp the importance of this statement? Can you even glimpse at the meaning? We are mental in nature; there is nothing material about us or our body. You are wisdom. You already know everything there is to know. So draw from it. You are Goodness. Your natural state of being is good and no evil in this world can harm you. As a matter of fact, evil is only a manmade illusion. You are Intelligence. Intelligence contains all there is. For Intelligence to lack something would mean it is not intelligent, therefore you are health, wealth, and happiness.

September 8

You are the only one that can root for yourself. Others can be supportive and stand by you in hard times, but your true '"rooting" and "cheering" comes from an inner, sincere desire to be the best you can be.

Rooting for yourself

"Hi again, it's me – Ilene Waters, giving you a quick update on my weight loss...

It's Labor Day and I just got home from the gym; first time since last week, second time in almost seven or so months. Main reason why I haven't gone until now is lower back and disc issues, but even if I didn't have those, I'm sure I could have come up with plenty of reasons why not to go on a regular basis for such a long while. I was thinking about Labor Day as I was driving back from the gym, and I was thinking about the labor one puts into their own life. I am still on this journey to continue to lose weight and figure out what my 'weighty' issues are, and it occurred to me that Labor Day should be every day, at least mentally.

Labor implies, to most, a physicality of some sort. 'Doing labor' - hard work with some kind of compensation as reward; 'Well,' I was thinking to myself, 'Who deserves the most labor intensive focus in their lives?' And I realized that each of us is deserving of our own mental labor to fully unfold ourselves and be the best individual we can be.

As you know, I started this year out with a desire to lose weight and reach certain goals by certain time frames. Yes, I have lost some weight, but have I achieved my goals as I intended? Nope. Do I continue to beat myself up for straying off the path? Sometimes. Do I get angry at myself for acting this way? Of course. But I don't give up. I won't, not this time in my life. This past week I celebrated my fifty-fifth birthday; I celebrated for a few days. So I gained a couple pounds, lost a couple pounds, and am once again reigning in my focus to start another downward weight spiral. I'm rooting for myself. I always do. I can never give up on myself, because then what purpose would I have in my life if I threw in the towel."

September 9

Let's take a different view on the idea "Angels."

**Where angels fly
a fresh look at the phenomenon**
(Awareness Magazine)

In my research about angels I've come across some pretty incredible places, one of them a small store in Ventura called "Things from Heaven." This place is amazingly spiritual and has seen many miracles. The prayer notes posted all over the store are a living testament.

"We did not intend to open an angel store," says owner Keith Richardson. "We had something between a thrift store and an antique store in mind back in 1995 when we opened. Back then my wife Francesca began having reoccurring dreams about seeing angels in the sky looking down upon her. One night she had a different dream. A friend, who had died the year before in a car accident, came to her with a golden bound book. When he opened it to show Francesca its contents, Francesca found that the book was about angels and how they relate to the lives of people."

Another recorded miracle to emerge from the store is wood carver Bill Jeralds, who after a near death experience, lost his long-term and short-term memory. He received a gift from heaven - the ability to carve without prior experience. Miraculously, after being given a scroll-saw by a friend, he started to produce the most beautiful angels out of mere plywood.

In 2009, Bishop Donald Jolly Gabriel from Orange County, California became so impressed by Bill's art that he commissioned one for his friend Pope Benedict XVI. Bill became the first artist in the history of Ventura County to have a piece of art in the Vatican.

295

The word "angel" means "messenger" in Hebrew and Greek, and you might say that angels come in many forms. It could be a mysterious stranger being there at the right time, or a courageous animal protecting you from harm – and most of all human beings who selflessly assist others.

Angels can come to us in dreams in tough times when we cry for help or when we gratefully count our blessings. But however and whenever they appear, they bring both comfort and life-affirming hope. Interestingly enough, 90% of Americans say they pray for their health, their families, and for their prosperity.

However, today, I want to talk about a different meaning of the phenomenon called "angels."

Have you ever thought of angels, not as some heavenly messengers totally out of reach for a mortal being, but as the embodiment of your own good and right thoughts?

When you think of angels as your own good and right thoughts, you will realize that you can substitute the word "angel" with "my own right thought" and see that it's one and the same. Let me give you some examples. As they say, "the proof is in the pudding…"

Angels, we are told, are messengers from God coming down from the heavens. If you understand God correctly – and know that this God is the Universal All-Power, Intelligence, Wisdom, now and forever – then you, being his child, must also be part of this All-power. You, having glimpsed at the Truth, will now understand that your own right thought is part of and stems from, this supremacy. So yes, angels, or your right thoughts, come from God or the Almighty.

New Thought, sometimes known as Higher Thought, promotes the ideas that "Infinite Intelligence" or "God" is everywhere. It also states that only Spirit is real and

296

your Soul is divine. Additionally, divine thought (your angel-thought) is a force for good, sickness originates in the mind, and "right thinking" has a healing effect.

Your purpose in life is to make a difference with your words of encouragement, your deeds, and the application of your wisdom. You are an angel using your "right and good thoughts" to help others. You can think happy, positive thoughts and you can think thoughts that make you feel joyous, and you can apply those thoughts to the people around you. You can learn to think about all the good in the world and focus on this good only. All of those right and good thoughts are infectious and will bring happiness to you and your loved ones, as well as to all humanity.

What is heaven?

Heaven is a harmonious state of mind; and of course this harmonious state produces good, right, calm, loving, and charitable thoughts. So again, yes, the angels or right thoughts come from heaven, your harmonious state of mind. Those angel-thoughts protect and lead you, and help you through the rough times. Those uplifting thoughts give you hope and courage. You certainly can call on them anytime you need guidance, as they are within. Isn't your right thought a God-sent message?

Do you ever listen to yourself and know intuitively what is right and wrong? Do you think that you are a victim of circumstances, or do you fully realize that you hold the power to shape your life in your own hands?

The concept of heavenly angels, being exceptional beings, coming down from the heavens to aid and protect you has been all over the world in one way or another. Religious teachings calling the angels "messengers of God" in some mysterious way are outdated. This surely is a material belief in a material world, and there is nothing mysterious about right

297

thinking. However, our world is not material – it is mental.

The teaching about angels needs another look; let's see it in a different light. We know that misinterpretation of the ancient writings in any religion is so common that we constantly must be careful what we believe to be true. Let your heart guide you, but let true reason rule.

Everything in this Universe is mental, always has been, and always will be. So the angels are spiritual visions, produced by our own sense perception as needed. To say it in a few simple words: Look at this phenomenon and realize that the heavenly messenger is you for you, and from within – always.

Giving thanks to the blessings you have received and for the blessings that are coming your way today and every day and saying "thank you" to the Universe with sincere appreciation puts you instantly into a positive frame of mind. Gratefulness will catapult you to a higher frequency and will trigger loving thoughts naturally. Those are your true angels.

September 10

Three keywords in this stage of your unfoldment:

Health, Wealth and Happiness

The three keywords in your unfoldment, at least at this state of your being, are health, wealth (I prefer to call it abundance) and happiness.

Those three little words contain all that is needed to live a blissful life and enjoy the journey of self-unfoldment. We all are looking for the same goal. Knowingly or not, happiness is the goal of all people on this Earth. Of course one would not be happy without health and certainly would struggle without abundance; having said that, health and wealth create happiness.

Later, when greater understanding of Truth has been gained by each of us, we will recognize that what makes us happy now will change. This awakening will shift us into a more intangible realm; one yet to be explored and tested. Our quest to know God, the Universal All-Power, and our desire to reconnect to our source will be the main focus. All other desires will become secondary. This is not a change that will disable you from enjoying Earthly goods, but it will be an enhancement and blissful state.

September 11

Stop being too busy for the right things in life! Most people find time for everything but their own unfoldment. Don't you know that one hour of soul searching is worth far more than an hour of shopping?

Observations of your "style of living"

Make sure you like what you do and how you live. Start with your home. Do you like your abode? Do you enjoy coming home? Do you look forward to hanging out there and relaxing? What about your job? Do you like your profession, your co-workers and your boss? Do you enjoy your friend's company, love going to visit your family, and meet nice people everywhere?

Are the hobbies you attend making you happy and fulfilled? What is your daily routine? Is it calm and organized or are you running around all day accomplishing little? Is shopping a habit, your wish list of things to buy and possess endless? Are you lavishly spending or are you frugal and careful with money?

This list can be endless. Take a sincere look at your "style of living." It will tell you a story and show you where improvements are needed. If you don't like something – and I mean anything from relationship to job to pocket book – change it! Change your sense about it, improve your thought habits, and keep working on it until you get it right. The situation you have created for yourself hasn't been created in a day, so don't expect it to change in a day either. Rather focus on the thought that "I can create the world I desire."

Hopefully you are the happiest person on the planet!

September 12

I thought to write a few "Healing Thoughts" today, here is one:

Nausea is a slight sense of dislike of something that has been presented to you. In a stronger case of nausea, resulting in vomiting, an idea you are fully rejecting is present. You are trying to eliminate this visualization of what you don't want to accept from your thought.

Vomiting is also the rejection of something you don't want to deal with. A feeling of disgust and wanting to get rid of certain wrong or painful emotions triggers this unpleasant heaving and gagging. It's an interesting observation – watch it!

PS: Some pregnant women have far more morning sickness than others ... hmmm?

Think about why are you rejecting an idea? What is it that you don't like about what's presented to you? Remember you have a choice. When you disagree with what you have to deal with, change it. Take a good look at the situation and solve the underlying issue. Why put up with anything that is lesser than good or undesirable?

September 13

People who experience the manifestation called gout are not using enough discrimination between

truth and error. They worry and stew about things constantly and don't discriminate properly. The pain involved includes the longstanding ill feelings and resentments, which is shown in the relationship to inflammatory arthritis. Since it shows up in the feet area it relates to their progress in unfoldment.

Watch your discrimination!

September 14

Listen to yourself carefully. Choose the words you speak and think wisely. Thinking is causative, and your thoughts will create your reality.

How do you know what is a right decision and what is a wrong decision?

I've said it before and I'm saying it again: Any time you are in doubt ask yourself the following questions. Is what I want good for me and all concerned, is it lovely and loving, is it enjoyable, and does it feel right? If the answers to all of those questions is yes then you are making the right decision.

Always listen carefully to yourself, give yourself some quiet time, and you will hear the answer to your calling loud and clear. We have an inert knowledge of everything; it's already there. You don't have to go far to find the answers …. just listen and act with a sincere and loving heart.

September 15

Random act of kindness

What a great story from a reader:

"I just had to share an uplifting moment that happened today at work. A man came through the drive-thru window and paid for his order and also went ahead and paid for the car behind him. We all smiled and thought, 'What a wonderful, random act of kindness.'

Well, it doesn't end there. The next car drove up to the window and when that person found out that her order had been paid for by the stranger in car ahead of her, she turned around and paid for the car behind her! This started a chain reaction and the next FIVE cars after her all did the same thing with one man paying for the next TWO cars behind him!

If this doesn't show how love and kindness can spread and grow from one small seed (action), then I don't know what does. These acts not only spread joy to unsuspecting strangers, but uplifted the entire crew on duty this afternoon. Truly inspiring! I definitely had to share this with my Modern Thought Theories family."

September 16

Aaah ... Patience! Where art thou?

We are tempted to advise and lecture our loved ones. We want to make sure that they are on this journey with us, and we think that we have a better way of enjoying life. However, no one can know for the other, not even for close family members. They have to learn their lessons on their own and in their own time. So be patient and allow them to unfold on their own terms; inching their way towards perfection ever so gently just as the rest of us.

Allowing your friends and family to grow at their own pace and to learn when they are ready is a great gift you can give them. By trying to convince them that your way is the better way you not only interfere in their natural unfoldment, but you also take away valuable energy from yourself.

September 17

Fear is a mental bully, not to be trusted. Face your fears from small to large by saying, "I will not be afraid anymore. I am courage and I am perfect cause."

Facing Fears

We all have fears. We all have worries and doubts. So how do you face your fears? Do you even know what your fears are? Many times they are hidden very deep in our subconscious. You most likely will know when you are afraid of something big like a certain illness, a loved one dying, a fear of flying, or any other phobia. But what about your smaller fears like being "lesser than," being ridiculed about a mistake you made, or your spouse leaving you? Or as small as a fear of being late to work, fear of not passing an exam, and all the other hurry-worry syndromes?

Start with the small ones. Make a list and be honest with yourself. If you rushed this morning and had your adrenaline pumping already, you know that you were afraid of something, maybe just being late sending the kids to school. If you went to the office not wanting to face your boss for one reason or another you realize that there is a fear present. If you don't want to fess up to your spouse about some decision you made that didn't turn out quite alright then you also know that there is a fear of his/her reaction.

After you have worked on those little disturbances you can move up and tackle the larger ones. I, for one, am working on my fear of flying, as I have told you in an earlier chapter. The time of correction is coming up quickly. My flight to my son's wedding is scheduled for October 4th and I have been visualizing flights from the past when I was a young and adventurous girl. I just loved to fly. It represented "freedom" and that was what I strived for at the time. Coming from a small village, with lots of restrictions and cultural set rules, "freedom" meant everything to me. Being above the clouds was exhilarating and uplifting. There was no fear, no terror.

Now being more mature, I have to let go of the stiffer mental attitude and relax, I have to know (not hope) that all will be just fine. Interestingly, I truly know that all is and works for good in the Universe. So what is my worry? Doesn't "ALL" include all, yes, including flying?

September 18

"Hope" should not be a feeling of "maybe" - it should be a certainty of good things to come.

September 19

Keep your visions and aspirations alive. Don't allow anyone to shatter your dreams.

Visions and Dreams
(Ezine Article)

Do you think about your visions and dreams? Do you make a conscious effort to achieve your desires?

Take a few minutes out of your busy schedule and really, really think about your visions and dreams. Have you fulfilled your childhood aspirations? Have you mastered some of your teenage ambitions, or have you even come close to your adult goals?

What are those dreams?

Your minds activity includes desire. Desire is the active spark that presses for expression as part of your natural thinking process. Your mental picture is the blueprint of your experience, good or bad, and this vision will become this experience. Consciousness always assumes a form in the visible; it automatically manifests its convictions and beliefs. There is only one Mind, one

Consciousness. You are Mind, you are Consciousness – you can think. You are aware of your being, you know that you "are," and your sense of self is what is expressed in the form you call YOU.

Many people just exist; they are not fully living. They react to outer circumstances rather than acting in accordance to their God-given power of self-management. Instinctively they reach for a higher goal, a more refined being, but many do not succeed. Only when attuned with the mental force that controls the Universe will they be able to change their destiny and perform the work that needs to be done.

The physical world is merely a reflection of the mental world; it's not the other way around. Unfortunately the reflection is a most imperfect one, as the thoughts produced by us are imperfect as well. Like attracts like, and our thoughts are causative and create everything we hear, see, touch, taste, and smell, and most of all they create everything we experience. It is the Law – it cannot be changed.

The mere fact that you can say "I," "Me," "My" and recognize the meaning of those words show proof of your awareness of self. This one and only consciousness that is within you, and all of us, is the great sea of the Universe and you are part, a particle, of this great mass – a drop in the Universal Ocean.

We, our true substance, are not a changing "thing". We are constant, limitless, powerful, and already perfect. What is changing is our understanding of SELF. Through this change of our understanding, with its triumphs and tribulations, we change the reflection to either good or bad. However, the inevitable growth and self-unfoldment we eventually will experience will reflect the glorious calm and happiness that comes with this understanding.

In order to fulfill our visions and dreams we have to shed the bondage of the ego and leave the restrictions

305

of conformity behind. Ego will always think that we are greater than others and less than we truly are. Ego does not understand the great Truth of our innate heritage of perfection, nor the fact that we are all made of the same substance, imbued with the same Understanding. The only distinction is, and therefore the seeming difference in life experience: We are on different levels of understanding in our quest for unfoldment. But there is within us a power of complete liberation; an ability to rectify our sins. As long as we live and think a certain way, we will continue to do so without progress. However, when once we use this power we are freely given, our visions and dreams will be fulfilled – but remember, only that which takes root in our minds can become fact. It all rests within us.

So cast off all limitations of the ego and improve the quality of your thoughts because what we accept as a permanent mental image, or fact, must manifest in this world.

Can you see the importance? Can you understand that your life has been shaped by your convictions and you are actually living your visions and dreams right now? If you don't like the picture you see, know that you can change it – make it your priority. Set goals, dream big, and know that you can achieve anything you set your mind to because your mind is the most powerful tool you have. Enjoy!

September 20

How do you set your priorities? What is important to you? Do you just go about your daily doings without thinking about it, just shuffling through the day, or do you have an agenda that includes your well-being?

Priorities

When we talk about priorities most people probably think of a work agenda. Maybe your children or your relationship with your partner is high up on that schedule, but I haven't seen a list yet that reads like this:

- Find my true Self
- Learn about the Truth
- Self-unfoldment
- Quiet time and meditation
- Read inspirational books
- Take care of my emotional well-being
- Treat myself well

And the list goes on. What does your priority list look like?

September 21

The Allness of Good

William Walker Atkinson, another great metaphysician and writer of the early 1900ss, finishes his book *Reincarnation and the Law of Karma* with these words:

"...ALL WORKS FOR GOOD... Everything is tending upward, and everything is justified and just, because the END is ABSOLUTE GOOD and every tiny working of the great cosmic machinery is turning in the right direction and to that end.

Consequently, each of us is just where he should be at the present time – and our condition is exactly the very best to bring us to that Divine Consummation and End. And to such thinkers, indeed, there is no Devil but Fear and Unfaith, and all other devils are but illusions, whether they be called Beelzebub, Mortal-Mind, or Karma, if they produce Fear and Unfaith in the All-Good. And such thinkers feel that the way to live according to

307

the Higher Light, and without fear of a Malevolent Karma, is to feel one's relationship with the Universal Good, and then to 'Live One Day at a time- doing the best you Know How – and be Kind' – knowing that in the All-Good you live and move and have your being, and that outside of that All-Good you cannot stray, for there is no outside – knowing that THAT which brought you Here will be with you There – that Death is but a phase of life – and above all that THERE IS NOTHING TO BE AFRAID OF – and that ALL IS WELL with God; with the Universe, and with YOU."

Powerful words indeed!

September 22

Abundance doesn't just mean having money; it is a sense of being abundantly supplied with ALL the good you desire. It represents a wealth of love, patience, courage, health, and all the material things, riches, you need. Not want, need.

How to get more of the good...

In order to create abundance we must take a different look at what abundance means. You also have to know that your mind, and its activity, always makes manifest the image it beholds. You are the only one in constant rapport with yourself; the only one who knows what you really think and feel. Thus you are your own policeman of the thoughts and images you entertain.

I'm sure we can agree on the fact that "you can think what you want to think." No one can dictate your thoughts. You might think someone can influence you, but it is you that allows the other person to persuade you. You need to stand up for your own thoughts with a firm heart. You might feel poor or less than today, but you can change this sense of "not having" by fully acknowledging (and sticking to it, no matter what the appearance) that you have plenty. You are abundantly supplied at all times and you have everything you need.

There is a great story in the book *The Magic in Your Mind* by U.S. Anderson about an oil driller that was unsuccessful for all of his life. One day he sat on a hill, observing the valley below, and his inner eye showed him the valley full of oil. At this moment he knew with certainty that he would succeed. He knew he had finally found the oil field and nothing could stop him – and so it was. All the contrary beliefs and opinions didn't matter anymore. In his mind he was convinced that the day had come and his desire was fulfilled.

There is absolutely no accomplishment or success if you cannot visualize your desire. You have to have vision, imagination, faith, and perseverance. You have to also have courage, boldness and stick-to-it-iveness.

September 23

Daily application to attract abundance

I have mental plenty.
(William W. Walter)

When you hope for riches, yet say: I don't have enough, I'm poor, and I lack money - the Universe will respond saying: OK, you don't have enough, you're poor, and you are lacking money. BUT if you say: I have plenty, I am abundantly supplied, I have everything I need – no matter how the circumstances of your life look at this moment – the Universe will repeat those thoughts and bestow all the goods upon you. However, you cannot say those words without a sincere conviction that "it is so."

You have to believe them with all of your heart. Try it, and you will see a change in your pocket book.

September 24

My business is to unfold myself and through conscious recognition enjoy the goodness and fullness of it.
(William W. Walter)

What about your business?

What do you consider your businesses? Is it the place of work you faithfully trot to every morning? Is it the vocation you chose? Is it the rearing of your children, making sure that they get the best education possible? Or is it your personal unfoldment and welfare?

Be clear about your business and have a plan. We all hear about the importance of a business plan in the corporate world. It is just as important to have a precise outline of your personal business plan. Don't just drift from one occasion or event to another, or be glad that you made it through another day at work or at home. Life is here to enjoy, and a strong plan of action will help you to enjoy your life's work, be it at home or your place of work.

Your most important business, however, is the business of your SELF. The diligent pursuit of health, wealth, and happiness, through rigorous mental house-cleaning and the application of what you have learned so far. It is also your business to live the best possible life, to love the best possible way, and to enjoy your life here on this plane and on all other dimensions yet to come. It's really something to look forward to for someone that understands the importance of self-unfoldment.

September 25

How to stay out of the "others" business?

Very simply – don't get involved in the first place!

September 26

Take command over your own destiny

Taking command is never that simple. We are used to adhering to outside influences and think that we have to blend into our environment. Social dictation is high in our agenda. What if?

I have learned to stand up for what I want and what I believe in. What if you would stand up for your ideas and dreams? Taking this stand would require a firmness and boldness that you might or might not have exercised, and few people actually possess this strength innately. But it can be learned, it can be practiced – the seeds are already within all of us.

You also have to show resistance to defeat and disaster. You have to keep your vision clear and focused with a courage that might yet be unfamiliar to you. This courage comes through reason, culminating in the understanding of Truth; this all-freeing Truth which includes your ability to take command over your own destiny.

September 27

Each and every one of us can contribute to "Sowing seeds of Peace" by making a conscious effort to only acknowledge what is right and abstain from participating in the hype of war and destruction. Your energy should be channeled into all-inclusive love, helpfulness, and kindness, and not into the destruction of war. It should be invested into the creation of peace. Mother Theresa once said, "I will not march against war, but I will march for peace." Think about the difference in viewpoint.

How do you direct your energy into the proper channels? How can you contribute to peace?

It might seem like a daunting task, looking at the big picture with all its world wars and crimes - but this is not what I'm suggesting. I want you to look away from those impressions. I want you to focus on the good and beautiful. I want you to clear your mind of anything that's less than virtuous, lovely, noble, and worthy. There is no gain in absorbing the horrendous reflections we see every day. There is no benefit to anyone in chiming in. Nothing can be won by agreeing with negative emotions.

Since it all starts with you, work on yourself, and sow the seeds of peace within your family and friends and everyone you come into contact with. Make them understand the fact that they are also the "arbiter of their faith" and that they also hold the reign to a more peaceful world. Every tiny step counts. Every loving word will resonate and attract loving vibration.

September 28

Words are so powerful. They can hurt, damage, and sting. Your words should be used only to spread love, embrace, and heal. Watch your words today!

Public speaking and words

I've been thinking about public speaking. I have another book signing coming up in one of my favorite book stores, this time with questions and answers and a mini-workshop. I always look forward to interacting with people which are searching for the Truth. I anticipate their questions and think about the best answers. How can I say what I think and feel aloud? How can I get my point across without sounding patronizing?

The power of words is so little understood. We use them to express ourselves good or bad. They can strike like lightning-rods or provide the soothing balm needed. As a teacher words can be clear and precise, showing the student the way or they can be an intellectual babble with little meaning when not understood by the pupil. I love clear language, I'm a black and white person - there aren't many flowers in my language. But I do try to be kind and understanding, and always truthful. What needs to be said needs to be said. But like with any conversation, be it with a loved one, a business partner, or a teacher, show respect and maturity.

Always remember: We should speak the way we want to be spoken to!

September 29

Creativity resides in each and every one of us. You might not be an artist *per se*, but aren't you creating your reality each day? Are you painting your mental picture of your desires? Are you envisioning the outcome of your dreams? You are creative every moment of your waking hours, because you are the creator of your life.

Creativity

You can be anything you want to be, you can do anything you want to do – how many times have you heard this phrase and how often have you actually acted upon it? Do you believe this statement is true?

We are one mind, one body, one intelligence. We are all connected to that one master mind called Universal Consciousness. Our creativity is already within; we do not have to look outside of ourselves. Many people see

313

themselves as having no creativity but have they ever tried to connect with their inner creative source?

You have to see that every thought you think is creative in itself. Each move you make, each word you speak is creative, because it creates.

September 30

Collective Consciousness

The individual transformation of your mind is not an absolute, but a matter of degree. Each day you are transforming your mind (composed of desire, active thought, past accumulative impressions, and the daily experiences) into a new version of yourself. All impressions and thoughts are stored in your subconscious and transform your understanding as well as your beliefs constantly. Your understanding at this point is relative. It will always be relative to the ultimate Truth.

As stated before, you must give up the ego in order to find your true self, this pure and all-knowing self, which seems had been lost for as long as you can remember. This "knowing yourself," even in a small degree, is necessary as a starting point. Without getting a glimpse of your true Self you cannot understand how Collective Consciousness works.

Start by envisioning that the world is one, that all people are connected. Pretty tough assignment, I know. But you must shed that sense of separateness and realize that Collective Consciousness is more powerful than individual consciousness in the grand plan. As you are the power in your individual world, Collective Consciousness is the power that drives the whole world (don't mistake this with the Universe).

Chapter 10: Wealth Within

October 1

All evil, sickness and discord of any kind must be understood to be the result of wrong mental activity and wrong thinking.
(William W. Walter)

Discovering yourself

The fight is not between you and the outside world, your neighbor, or your family. The fight is within you. It is between what you are accustomed to and what is right and good.

You have to choose to find your true Self. You are far more than your physical body or your accomplishments in this world. You are even more than your current thoughts and emotions. Everything you experience, feel, and think that you are is only a fraction of your true nature.

Think about the times that you talk to yourself out loud. Who are you talking to? Isn't it like you are two people? One "you" that is here and one "you" that listens and advises because it knows better? You don't always trust this inner "you," but you should. And you naturally constantly ask for its guidance, so why not listen to what it has to say?

What is this invisible "you?" Well, it's a more spiritual "you," a more intuitive "you" and a "you" that is in tune with consciousness. Not the perfect "you" yet, but a more connected version of "you."

October 2

We all should be...

Sowing Seeds of Peace

When talking about peace I am not just speaking about world peace, I am speaking about the peace within. In order to contribute to the grand vision of world peace we have to find our individual inner harmony first.

We have to know the following primary facts: Life in itself is intelligent, and we, as part of this intelligence, are composed of this primal substance. We are complete within ourselves. However, we have allowed reacting to outer circumstances rather than acting rightly about them and therefore have lost this natural peaceful demeanor. The fight is not outside of us, it is within.

Most people confuse self-knowledge with knowledge. Humankind and their egos assume that being knowledgeable means to know yourself. But they only act from their ego-consciousness and do not know themselves at all.

The ego is a peace-disturber, a troublemaker. It wants more and more; it doesn't stop or find satisfaction. The inherent and characteristic goal of spiritual unfoldment and growth, always striving to expand, is fully misunderstood by the ego-mind. This ego-mind sees the task of unfolding as an accumulation of material riches and status; worldly powers you might say. However, the spiritual mind knows that the unfoldment of self consists of the humble awakening of Truth within. We have to expand our minds beyond our five senses; to truly "sense" is to go beyond your accustomed limited perception. Mind always seeks to know and to expand its awareness.

"In the last analysis, life is found to be nothing but sense", is stated by one of the great metaphysicians William W. Walter in the early 1900ss. Life, boiled down, hidden behind the veil of all perception leaves a purely mental essence. Truth is mental.

Your work is to observe this inner sensing that is going on at all times. Do you see yourself as the dynamic, powerful, yet peaceful Soul you are? Or do you see yourself as struggling, confused, and always in a hectic state? Where is your inner peace?

Once we have mastered this inner harmony we can start sowing the seeds to include our surroundings and in the end; once we have found this stillness and calm within, it will naturally and effortlessly contribute to a grander picture. It will spread easily and flow with the natural current of the Universe. It will certainly contribute to a better life and manifest into world peace as we are part of Collective Consciousness which is connected to the All-mighty Universal Source.

October 3

Fear is nothing but ignorance, erring supposition, and insecurity. It can only be overcome by reason. You must gain an understanding of the thing you fear and develop the courage to deal with those mental monsters.

Dissolving fear

Remember my earlier admission of my fear of flying? Well the day has come. Tomorrow morning we are on our way to my son's wedding. How did I manage to let go of the frightening memories?

I started to focus on the good memories. I used to love flying. Always sitting next to the window, taking off and seeing the buildings grow smaller and smaller and the clouds come nearer. Once we were above the clouds it was exhilarating to me. I would hum an old German tune "Ueber den Wolken, wo dass Leben so grenzenlos ist" – translated "Above the clouds, were life is limitless". And that is what I felt – limitless, free and powerful.

As I recalled those experiences, and visualized myself back in the window seat, I became more relaxed and I pictured the take-off and the landing perfectly. I started to look forward to the trip. I envisioned the joy my son would feel that his mother had taken this step toward travelling again. It was all working for the good. And so, here I am, the night before my first flight after twelve years looking forward to this adventure. But most of all I am looking forward to my newly found freedom: back to "the window of limitless life."

October 4

Arrival after first time flying, experience - have I worked through the fear yet?

The answer to this question is clear – yes. I admit there were some moments of "what if"- but turning immediately to the Truth that "All is Good" dispelled the moments of fear quickly. After all Faith is a healer. Fear is always a limiting emotion and keeps you in bondage as long as you allow it to rule your life. You have to muster the courage necessary to face your fears.

October 5

Weakness of attitude becomes weakness of character
(Albert Einstein)

Overcoming weaknesses

A weakness is a lesser sense of fear. Maybe you are not sure that you can handle a certain situation. Maybe you are weak in resisting temptations. May it be food or drink, gambling, or other dispositions that need your attention. You cannot run away from your weaknesses. You will have to work them out. You will have to address each and every one of them and honestly face the situation.

We cannot be soft with ourselves and excuse our bad behavior. Only by rigorous correction can we become God-like. We are tested every day of our lives and we must try to succeed. As long as we live on this plane we must make a concerted effort to improve our thought habits and dispositions. One by one we will conquer and grow stronger. The battle field is in our minds; all problems and weaknesses are mental. They only exist in our imagination.

The world belongs to those who dare, try, work on, and aspire to reach higher goals. The drifter or the shifty person will not succeed, but the single-minded and focused individual will bring home the prize.

October 6

Hide not your talents. They for use were made. What's a sundial in the shade? (Benjamin Franklin)

Finding your talents

We all have talents. However, many people have not found their true calling. Family traditions many times play a role in the choice of your vocation. The influences of your friends or mentors might have stirred you in a direction that wasn't your first choice. But now you are an adult and you can look at your chosen profession and you can either love it or make a new decision. "I am too old for that," or "It's too late you change" you might say. Let me tell you – it is never too late!

If you think you can't leave your job, at least take up that hobby you always wanted, write that book or paint that picture you've held in your mind for so long. Allow yourself to make your desires come true. Don't limit your life to what you think you should be doing ... do the things you love!

October 7

Your consciousness is an ever expanding awareness of the already existing Truth. It is your responsibility to stay open-minded and allow this process to take its natural course.

How to expand your consciousness

To awaken to the fact that consciousness is all there is is a great step in the right direction. Once you realize the enormity of this statement you will see that we are not "many wandering souls" fighting for ourselves, but that we are all connected to the one great Consciousness, the source of all life, which makes us "all one."

By recognizing everything you see, objects and events, as part of you, you will further expand this sense of all-inclusiveness and one-ness. This infinite growth of awareness will include not only the immediate persons in your surroundings, but also will include all experiences you encounter and the vast concept of this Universe.

There is a power greater than you or I which orchestrates the workings of the Universe. But we, being part of this power, have a hand in how we are experiencing and applying this force. This is why our mental attitude is so important. "It is not I who doeth the works," Jesus said, "but the father that dwelleth within me." And his most important statement: "I and the father are one."

The creator has given us as his creations, all of his/its potentiality and power. But no individual reigns supreme, as we are a part of this one Universal Intelligence. I hope this example helps you understand the connection from individual Soul to collective Consciousness.

October 8

In order to change your perception of who you are, to who you want to be, you must first create a clear picture of your ideal self. Then and only then can you slowly change your perception of yourself, hence your image and likeness.

How to change your perception of who you are to who you want to be?

We certainly have a picture in mind of who we are, or who we represent. Our self-worth, self-esteem, self-love, beliefs during our upbringing, and other outside influences, or inner accumulated belief system, surely made us who we think we are.

So you think you know yourself pretty well. You are generally satisfied with your moods, mind sets, appearance and productivity, and you created a wonderful home for your family. Good for you!

What about you, the one that feels he/she always gets the short end of the stick? There is always some roadblock, and you just can't get a break. You live paycheck to paycheck and just can't get ahead. Would you like to live better? Of course!

Where and what you are in your life (believe it or not) is not due to outer circumstances, but it is solely the making of your own belief system. It is a complicated

321

structure of accumulated impressions, teachings, mental habits, and most of all beliefs about yourself, over a long period of time. Only you can create a new you, only you have the power to change. But first of all you have to know who and what you want to be.

This knowing takes some diligent thought and soul-searching. Just having more money is not always the answer. I'd say we can all agree that we certainly want health, wealth, and happiness; even though health, wealth, and happiness might have many different meanings to each and every one of us.

October 9

How can you change your mind set from negative to positive? By repetition of good and right thoughts! You have to stop the negative notions at the door of your consciousness and replace them with positive affirmations. Your mind is a sponge that absorbs all impressions, good or bad – so stay on the right side, you will be better off for it.

October 10

The difference between abundance and wealth consciousness is this: Abundance is having what you need, a comfortable home, and enough money to pay the bills, a decent job, and a loving family. Wealth consciousness, however, provides for above and beyond. It is a set state of mind. Not a wishing of being provided for but a demand to the Universe that you get what you are entitled to. It is the knowing that you are Wealth itself.

Difference between abundance and wealth consciousness

Let's start with the sense of abundance. We've talked about it before, but let's get a bit more into the details.

What does abundance mean to you? We all have a different sense of what we need in life to be comfortable. Unless you are poor, living in utter poverty, you will admit that you have everything you need. Maybe not what you want, but certainly what you need. Food, clothing, shelter, enough to pay the bills; but don't mistake this for exuberant spending on credit cards and then not having enough money to pay them off. This is a whole other chapter!

When we desire things for selfish motives we narrow our perceptual horizon. We accept, and believe things as being material and therefore limit ourselves by being blind to the powerful being we are. The only true and lasting abundance comes from knowing that all is mental and achievable through mental means.

Life for each of us is exactly as we construe it to be. You are as rich, or poor, as you sense yourself to be. How often in the day do you say: "I can't afford this," "I don't have enough money" or "I wished I could buy this or that." Watch your word habits and you will be surprised how many times you use negative sentences to tell your (inner) self that you are lacking.

Abundance can also be achieved through gratefulness. Wake up in the morning and think of all the good things that will come your way during the day. Discard the negative notions you might have and only focus on the good. Then remember during the day how wonderful it is that you have family, friends, a home, food and all the things you need to keep you living a good life. But you have to do the work. A complainer will experience exactly the thing he complains about. A person that tends to expect the worst will receive the worst; remember the Universe will give you what you think you are or deserve. It does not differentiate, it follows your command. So make sure that you tell this all powerful provider what you want.

As U.S. Anderson said, "Negative conditions are imperfect perceptions." What a true statement! If you perceive anything as imperfect, you will experience the exact image and likeness, i.e. a negative condition. He also says, that "all lack, limitations, and malfunction that touches our lives is carried in our minds, is literally created there because it is a product if our limited and ego-centered consciousness."

So going back to what is abundance – abundance is your sense, or your perception of, what you think you are worth at this time; and you can change your sense at any time.

October 11

Wealth is more than just money. It is a wealth of love, health, and happiness. Those qualities all belong to wealth.

Wealth consciousness

So you have mastered the art of being abundantly provided for and you are basically happy. You look around and you see that there is so much more. You see the opulence of movie stars or talk show hosts, athletes, and major business owners and you wonder how did they do it? Why are they rich and amassed such wealth? Those are valid questions.

I have my own questions: Why do many of us relate being wealthy to evil? Why do we associate it with ego? How does it relate to being good? Is it really a monetary reward for intelligence, hard work, a lucky break, or what is the driving force in getting more than others?

Our subconscious is a very intricate and complicated system with thousands of belief-layers accumulated through our life. We all are contained within the four walls of our current-ego and it seems to be a huge task to break out of this constrictive prison. And unfortunately, great wealth many times brings with it an expanded ego. This increased sense of ego-self will not help but hinder. It will disconnect you from the real source of power. It might allow you to keep your wealth, but it surely will penalize you in the areas of health and happiness.

The key is to change your sense of abundance to a sense of wealth without increasing the ego. In a matter of fact: In order to not only keep wealth but also health and happiness you have to abandon the idea of ego totally. How?

We can let go of our inflated sense of ego and return to a humble state of mind by acknowledging that we are the eternal thinker. We are connected to the all-powerful source of all. Our ability to imagine, think and feel – this knowledge of our creative power – should give us the self-confidence necessary to let go of this overblown self-image. Once we know who we are, the superficial ego is no longer necessary. Now that we have accomplished a sense of self-confidence, self-worth, and self-sufficiency we are on the way to create our true wealth.

Let's remember that wealth also includes a wealth of love, good feelings, and appreciation. With this new found attitude let's explore further.

October 12

Hang with people that represent who you want to be. Seek out the individual that inspires you, cheers you on, and wishes you well. Stay close to the folks that have the same goals, aspirations, and better yet are already at their best. Learn as much as you can, observe, and know that the power of success is already within you.

Your mind can (when trained properly) perceive all and understand all. Maybe not all there is, because life is limitless, but surely enough for this lifetime. By changing our consciousness from "lack" to a sense of "having" we alter our perception. We are basically brain-washing ourselves by repeating the true statements: I am wealth, I am health, I am happiness. No matter what the appearance, we slowly but surely gain a sense of gaining more. What a lovely tool our imagination is and how great it is to visualize! Yes, visualize morning, day and night on how it would look and feel to live in a grand house, to have all the things you want, and, without greed, how wonderful your new success will make you feel. And most of all think of all the good deeds you can do for others.

Once you have acquired a sense of wealth, you will not have to think about it anymore. You will expect all good and beautiful things come to you naturally and the Universe will respond by giving you all you desire because the desire has become a knowing. Not a wanting anymore, but a rock-steady knowing that you are this wealth. So visualize, idealize, and create your heaven here on Earth! You deserve it!

October 13

Do you value yourself?

Can you truly say that you value yourself and your work? To you feel that others are honoring your worth? You might think that you are a decent and respectable person, full of good intentions, but when it comes down to your value, what do you really think you are worth? Well, take a look at your pocket book. The answer lies within the pages of your register.

Your work is of value. So why take less? Your services should be paid for, so why work for free? Everything, all the good you do has value, be it housekeeping, child rearing, any type of professional work, taking care of an elderly parent or just shopping at the grocery store.

326

Your daily doings have value. You are a valuable mental being. You have purpose.

October 14

One mind, the primal intelligence, seeks expression through nature and all living beings. Become one with this force, by acknowledging that you already are connected and one with this energy. This power is constantly moving upward on the scale of being; and so are you.

October 15

Vision

Today I'm working on a question and answer sheet for a book signing. I'm always envisioning the event beforehand. I'm seeing the people around me and anticipate the questions and my possible answers. This is part of the creation process.

At most locations the audience is shy at first and doesn't want to speak up, so an inviting smile, a thought provoking question, and an encouraging word will make all the difference. The important points of the Q&A will be the basis of all right-thought-teachings; i.e. "mental house cleaning," "what are right thoughts," "how do your thoughts relate to health, wealth, and happiness" are just a few themes to be addressed.

For the more advanced members of the group the topics will include expanding consciousness, the power of your mind, and how are we connected to the Almighty source. Can't wait!

October 16

What prompted me to write this article was the possibility to work on a new film about Yogananda's life.

One of the greatest things I learned was that my soul already knew all of these spiritual truths that Ananda teaches. And not just mine, but that every soul has all knowledge within. It only has to be brought back to one's remembrance and in that process curing us of the spiritual amnesia we had temporarily fallen into.
(John Peters)

Ananda Worldwide
– A continued mission to keep the masters wishes alive

A treasure to visit, located in Nevada City, California, is Ananda Village – whether you stay for a few hours or for the day, its beauty and peace will grab your spirit. If you'd like a longer visit, book a stay at the Expanding Light or the Meditation Retreat. It surely is a delight to the spiritual minded individual and an uplifting and relaxing vacation.

You can enjoy the Crystal Hermitage Gardens, which is the sacred heart of Ananda Village, with its beautiful terraced gardens and expansive vistas. The Meditation Retreat provides the perfect environment for all devout visitors who wish to tap into deep inner stillness.

Ananda Village was founded by Swami Kriyananda, Paramhansa Yogananda's devout disciple. Over the decades Swami has been given many yoga awards; he toured at one point with Louise Hay, orchestrated the Ananda choir performing for the Catholic Church in Rome and wrote over one-hundred books – published by Crystal Clarity Publishers, owned by Ananda. Swami has also participated in hundreds of TV shows all over the world and is a member of a very exclusive club, called Club Budapest, whose other members includes Mikhail Gorbachev and the Dali Lama.

What is Ananda Village as a whole?

First of all, it is a cooperative spiritual community dedicated to the teachings of Paramhansa Yogananda.

The followers attempt to live in active partnership with God.

The group strives to live in healthy harmony with the natural environment. They encourage minimizing the concept of personal ownership — without eliminating it. Ananda Village is a unique blend of ashram, cooperative, and, traditional village with its members placing a strong emphasis on self-reliance.

Even in this somewhat unusual environment, Ananda Village has always encouraged the entrepreneurial spirit. Members have developed a wide variety of businesses that can support themselves and make a contribution to the goals of the community.

Families living at Ananda Village seek to spiritualize the raising of their children and encourage young adults to participate. They acknowledge the fact that young people bring with them high energy, creativity, openness to new ideas, which is needed to attract more likeminded souls. Parents have the option to send their children to a Living Wisdom School from pre-school through college. Music, be it chanting, musical performances, concerts as well as recordings, and the arts including dance, art work, and dramatic performance also play a vital role.

Yogananda's Vision for World Brotherhood Colonies is clear

During his lifetime, Yogananda tried to establish such a colony in the early 1940ss but the time wasn't right. It was his dream however, and in 1968 his faithful disciple Swami Kriyananda and a handful of young friends founded Ananda Village in the Sierra Nevada foothills of California. Swami Kriyananda, even as a boy, before he met Yogananda, had a similar vision of creating communities based on high ideals. This was a perfect match of standards and principles. The journey, however, wasn't easy.

Ananda Village was initially faced with many tests and challenges. Yogananda's motto to create "intentional spiritual communities based on 'simple living and high thinking'" was a progressive one. He envisioned that people could live, work, and seek God together. He wanted to create a harmonious, uplifting environment that encourages the development of spiritual qualities. Swami concurred.

The lack of money, a devastating fire, and too many people's opinions and different ideas made the project difficult in its early stages. But the community held to one principle steadfast: Serving God first, under all circumstances.

Ananda now — fulfilling Paramhansa Yogananda's dream

2012 marks forty-three years of Ananda's existence and it has become one of the world's most successful intentional communities. It has grown into a society, located on 1,000 acres, with eighty-five homes, schools (pre-school through college), businesses, and a mix of 200 residents which vary from families, singles, and monastics.

Swami Kriyananda proudly exclaims in a letter to Mr. Black, one of Yogananda's core followers: "What we have at Ananda now is a real village, with lovely homes, flourishing businesses, schools that have an excellent reputation and an experiment in living that people in many countries admire. We have several branch communities also, including one near Assisi, Italy. Far more important, we have about five hundred devotees who are living joyously for God and Master, who meditate several hours daily, and are dedicated to making Master's message of Self-realization known everywhere."

Currently, about 1,000 devotees, which include 200 at Ananda Village and 800 in other Ananda communities, also live in other areas from Sacramento and Palo Alto,

California; Portland, Oregon; and Seattle, Washington; Assisi, Italy, to Gurgaon and Pune, India.

John Peters, a sound engineer from California, chose to live at Ananda Village for eight years. Here is his fond memory:

"I had been an agnostic all my life. Then I read some books on yoga metaphysics including Yogananda's *Autobiography of a Yogi* which stated that God is absolute consciousness and that we are all manifestations of that consciousness. I thought 'This is the first time I ever heard any description of God that made any sense to me.' I didn't know if it was true, but I felt that if there was the slightest chance then it would be worth practicing yoga meditation techniques to try to find out.

Through practice I came to have some deep experiences that convinced me that these teachings were true. Then I saw a television interview with Swami Kriyananda and was deeply impressed with his wisdom. I visited Ananda Village and had a very blissful time with the wonderful people who lived there and the beautiful mountain forest environment. At first I felt there might be too much 'religion' for this former agnostic to handle. Then I remembered a vision I had where Yogananda came to me and said 'It doesn't matter what our little differences are down there. Up here we are all the same.' With that I was able to relax and enjoy the rest of my visit.

Later that year Swami Kriyananda gave some public talks in my area which I attended. Shortly thereafter he asked me if I'd like to come to Ananda Village to live and be his recording engineer (which was my profession). I said yes. I lived there for eight years, recording Swami's music and helping out in other areas of the community. I enjoyed the community life, meeting with yoga students who visited from all over the world, the chanting and meditating, having fun community events such as putting on dramatic or humorous plays, working

331

with all the musical artists in the community, and much more. Although I eventually needed to move on I have occasionally returned for visits. I have been asked what I have learned while living at Ananda. My answer may sound strange, but one of the greatest things I learned was that my soul already knew all of these spiritual truths that Ananda teaches. And not just mine, but that every soul has all knowledge within. It only has to be brought back to one's remembrance and, in that process, curing us of the spiritual amnesia we had temporarily fallen into."
(John M. Peters)

Swami Kriyananda followed three principles his master taught: The ancient saying "Where there is dharma, there is victory," "Be practical in your idealism," by Yogananda, and "People are more important than things," coined by Swami himself. These are all principles that were taught or inspired and implied by Yogananda. Swami also says: "The most important factor in our success, certainly, has been the fact that every day since our beginnings I have given this whole project to Master, and have asked him to do with it as he would, albeit through our own physical struggles."

Ananda Village is a very well rounded living experience for the seeker of a spiritual life. Maybe I will visit one day!

October 17

We are made to be free.

I do want to clarify that I do not support any religious organization. Even though all of them hold some truth and I studied many of their doctrines, I sincerely believe that churches, religious societies, any closed-minded institutions and clubs, are mere crutches and extremely restrictive. All of them have rules and bi-laws that need to be adhered to in order to fit in. This does not promote free thinking and reasoning. I am a free thinker.

I believe we all are made to think freely, and we always should be able to make choices as we please. Good or bad, we will have to suffer the consequences. However, this puts us into the driver seat and that is where I want to be. How about you?

October 18

Nothing is born without feeling. Feeling is the mother of creation.

The Creation Process

What we see in the world is a constant picturing forth of "thinks" becoming things. The loads of different things created every day reflect the limitless thoughts of the people. Not all thoughts of course manifest. There are quick, fleeting thoughts; the doubtful ones that stop the materialization in its tracks, there are thoughts that aren't thought through properly, and of course the ones that aren't felt. Yes, felt. In order to produce and materialize your thoughts into the visible realm you have to feel your desire. Feeling is the mother of all creation. Nothing would be created, or born, without the feeling that the desire expressed is true and possible of achievement. Think about this!

October 19

Death is the natural transition to another dimension of Life.

Question from a reader:

"Hi Ulrike, Just wondering, what are your thoughts on ghosts?"

My answer:

"I don't believe there are ghosts haunting houses and lingering around as they are portrayed by the media. I think the Soul moves on to the next dimension, continuing its work. However, I do believe that we can be in touch (not physically) with another Soul through intuition. After a loved one passes we have the feeling of their presence lingering for a few days (until they finished their transition). I believe that superior Souls (teachers, guides, enlightened ones) can send you messages and communicate through true 'knowing.' I hope this explains my viewpoint. Let me know if you have any other questions. Thanks for asking - it always inspires me!"

Learn to listen. There are voices that speak within the soul. Learn to tune in. You will know when the voice is real and from the Divine.

October 20

Look at the unpleasant and unkind people that you encounter with compassion. See their pain and struggles and then move on with your own wonderful sense of gratitude. Mentally detach and leave their negativity behind.

From a reader regarding the above quote:

"Deep down I really know that, I just have to work on my conscious mind to agree with this thought so my first impulse on how to act does not get the better of me. My first impulse, my reaction to something mean and horrible is my feeling then? But I would still have to change my thoughts about this to be able to change my feelings about this, don't I?

I mean to be able to change my first automatic unpleasant feeling into a better feeling; I would have to think more positive thoughts to be able to change my upset feelings into more compassionate feelings. This would be how I think it would come about."

My answer:

"You are correct. Your first reactions are always your feelings. However, your thoughts need to be corrected first (through reason). That's actually easier than changing your feelings. After you know what the right thoughts are, which you will know after careful contemplation, you can change your feelings step by step. Reason comes from the 'head' - feelings, or emotions, from the 'heart.' They are your convictions and you will experience what you are convinced of."

October 21

How do you react to (the not so nice) people that live within your family home?

Many times I'm being asked on how to handle the not so lovely one's that happen to be part of the family. As I said in my book *"Better Living...Because You Can!""*:

Include other people in your mental workout

There are and always will be "others" in your experience. Some are here for you to learn from, some are here to reflect or mirror some of your own qualities, and some are here to show you the necessary corrections needed in self. Then, there are your loved ones that you have to deal with on a more emotional level. Those we call "others" are always connected to you in some way and are a mirror of your state of consciousness.

Be kind to everyone you come into contact with. Love thy neighbor as thyself. This doesn't mean that you have to associate with every person you meet, nor does it mean you have to hang out with people who may be unpleasant and alienating. It means that you should feel compassion and love, knowing that they are also a part of the Universal source, and they, too, will eventually find their way. Send them your good and kind thoughts, and walk away tending to your own business.

October 22

Knowledge moves the world.
(U. S. Anderson)

I just found this poem by Mrs. Edward Craster while reading this morning:

> "The centipede was happy quite
> Until a toad had fun
> Said, 'Pray, which leg goes after which?'
> That worked her mind to such a pitch,
> She lay distracted in a ditch,
> Considering how to run"

I love this little gem. It tells you clearly that whatever you know how to do well, you just do. It is not until the seed of doubt is instilled into your mind, this little question of "am I doing it right," that you will start to slip-up and err. This uncertainty will throw you off and make you stop in your tracks.

Do not let anything or anyone derail you from what you are doing. Continue your path that is meant for you. Go for it, conquer, and most of all enjoy whatever you're doing!

October 23

Fear is not inherent in the circumstances. It's our reaction to the circumstance that creates the fear. If we wish to conquer fear of any kind we must develop courage. We have to find out what causes the fear in the first place. We have to free ourselves of the perception of threat and danger. In reality nothing can hurt us as we are mental beings, indestructible souls, and not material human beings.

336

October 24

Healing Thought:
A stiff neck shows an attitude of being unbendable. You are opinionated about something and don't want to bend or look into that direction. Allow your thoughts to flow freely and accept other viewpoints. You are stiff about some idea and want to go with the familiar rather than change. It's alright to change; life is fluid and flexible, not stiff.

How do you let go of opinions?

A reader asked this question today. Well, I think that there is a difference between a fact and an opinion. To have an opinion suggests that you think you are right, when in fact there is always more truth to every opinion ... so in order to let go of an opinion, find out the fact!

October 25

The world and all you see is the expression of Universal Intelligence, the Almighty. You are part of this Intelligence and therefore your immediate world is the reflection of your individual thoughts.

October 26

The question of NOW

What does time mean to you? Are you living in the past or the future? Are you always wondering what's going to happen, or are you craving the memories of the past?

When you realize that all is mental, you will also realize that it is always NOW. Think and imagine the fact, that what I just said, and wrote down on these pages a minute ago, is already the past. What I will be writing in a minute is the future. What you have experienced is what has been thought by you. What you will experience in the future are the thoughts you are thinking now. Time schedules have been created by mankind to keep track of occurrences and they are nothing more than a succession of events.

NOW is the only time there is and always will be. You are reading this now.

October 27

Why do I keep talking about appreciation?

Because appreciation is a multiplier! It will give you back more of the things you appreciate. Your sense of gratefulness will bestow all the good onto you and will make you very happy indeed. This feeling of gratitude is an all-embracing sense of love and goodness; it is overwhelming and invigorating at the same time.

Allow yourself to feel this sensation night and day.

October 28

Self-discipline is a wonderful quality and must be practiced daily. Be disciplined in your mental work-out, your style of living, and your search for the truth. The reward will be peace, calm, and happiness.

Self-Discipline

Saying yes and no to yourself in a balanced way can be an art form. A constant stream of thoughts needs to be observed and sifted through. There are many healthy and good thoughts, but there are also many unhealthy and destructive ideas flowing through our mind. We are the only ones that truly know what we are thinking and therefore we have to stand porter at our door. The entrance to our consciousness must be guarded and

338

only good thoughts must be allowed to enter. This is a life-long task but we can make it a wonderful one.

We can learn to discipline ourselves to also balance our daily doings. A steady and calm demeanor is worth everything as it allows us to think reasonably.

October 29

Healing Thought:
Swelling is an exaggerated thought held in mind; a clogged, stuck thought pattern which includes painful ideas. Take a look at the area that is affected by the swelling to see where this inflated attitude stems from. I.e., arms would represent how you handle things, legs your progress, and so forth. Pinpoint the troubled area and you will see where the correction needs to take place.

Exaggeration is never a good idea. It blows everything out of proportion. Even the smallest forms of embellishing the truth will eventually backfire because it prepares your mind to see exaggeration as acceptable. Stick to the truth and also stay within the realm of balanced emotions. If you let your emotions go wild so will your manifestations of this imbalanced sense. Clear your sense of the stuck thought patterns and be free and accepting of new ideas.

October 30

So many changes

When I look around me, it appears that people change, I change, and my situations and experiences change. This may be true on the outside, but from a mental standpoint a change is more like an awakening to new truths, better viewpoints, and ideas. Change is good when this transformation adheres to a higher sense of life. Keep in mind that progress in life is a Universal Law. So we have to act accordingly.

October 31

You do not achieve your goals by simply wanting them. You attain them by constantly thinking about the objectives and focusing on the end result. Reason about the idea, make it real to you, learn all aspects, and put all of your attention into this endeavor. You will grow to understand the essence and therefore manifest your desire.

Chapter 11: We are all One

November 01

Day of the Dead

Where did this tradition come from?

I thought this was interesting. Originated in Mexico, "The Day of the Dead" celebrations can be traced to rituals celebrating the deaths of ancestors by these civilizations perhaps for as long as 2,500 – 3,000 years. People go to cemeteries to be with the souls of the departed. They build private altars containing their favorite foods, and bring photos and memorabilia of the deceased. The intent is to encourage visits by the souls; they hope the souls will hear the prayers and the comments of the living directed to them.

In many American communities with a large Mexican population like Texas, Arizona, and California, this day is celebrated similarly as in Mexico, with people wearing masks and All Soul Processions. Observances outside Mexico are common in Latin America, European countries with Roman Catholic heritage, and the Philippines, in which it has a more family reunion atmosphere.

November 02

He who has mastered any Law in his private thoughts, is master to that extent of all men whose language he speaks, and of all those into whose language his own can be translated.
(Ralph Waldo Emerson)

From a reader:
"I would like to hear about taking personal responsibility for our actions instead of blaming everyone else."

Taking responsibility for your actions

We hear people playing the blame-game all the time. It was her fault that I failed, or it was his demeanor that destroyed the relationship and so forth. It's the easy way out, but it's also the most destructive approach to oneself. What blaming others, instead of taking responsibility, does is to take away our God-given power. We are basically saying that everything and everyone has control over us. It says that the person that feels the need to blame is insecure, afraid and not mature. It is childlike to say "look Mommy, it wasn't me!"

We, as adults and seekers of truth, have to take responsibility for all of our actions. I will go as far as to say: We are responsible for every thought we think, for all actions we take, and for the outcome or manifestations that we experience every day of our lives.

What to do when we encounter others that behave in such immature fashion? We should feel compassion for them. Feel sorry for their fears and insecurities rather than judgment. Know that they haven't reached their potential and be very grateful that you are at a point dwelling in a higher frequency. You now have the capacity to forgive and feel love toward everyone.

November 03

Animal Rights

Never fight against anything. It's negative. What we should do instead is to support animal rights and causes. I am a big animal lover myself and I can't even look at the photos of abused pets and farm animals that people post on the social media sites. Just this morning I saw another posting that turned my stomach. It sickens me and I have to work on keeping my thinking straight as I sometimes wish harm to the people that are so cruel.

But then I have to remind myself that those people will be severely punished as the Law of Cause and Effect always works. We don't have to be the judge and jury. The Universe works perfectly (and yes, God works in mysterious ways). Always just and fair!

What we should do is focus on helping shelters, people that care, or any good cause which helps animals. Support and Love, not fighting and fueling a war, is the key!

November 04

The world and all you see is the expression of Universal Intelligence, the Almighty. You are part of this Intelligence and therefore your immediate world is the reflection of your individual thoughts.

The ultimate Intelligence

The want to grow, to understand, and to progress in the upward movement of life is a natural process. It is your choice and your ability to draw from your inner source.

You are born intelligence. You are equipped with everything you need to unfold this inherent quality from within; but you have to take the time and make a conscious effort, nothing is gained through laziness and indecisiveness. An inner vision sustains each entrepreneur. A strong drive stirs the successful individual toward his/her goal.

Do not mistake intellectuality with intelligence. Intellectuality is learned, acquired. Intelligence is your substance, your natural composition – your essence. Intelligence is the power that rules all. The Universe is not only composed of but is intelligence.
Life, Love, Consciousness, and Intelligence are all synonyms – they are all one, the one and only power.

I'm reasoning this through: A greater Intelligence rules the Universe, visible through its expressions. This Universe is conscious or aware because Life could not be without consciousness. We wouldn't know that we are alive unless we are conscious. We are intelligent, because we have the power to think, reason, and understand. We have the ability to choose. We have to ability to love. Love, the feeling element of mind, is the mother of all expressions, giving birth to more and more good. Nothing would be born without love or feeling. We are a particle of this great Universe; we are Life, Love, Consciousness, and Intelligence – now and forever! (And 365 days a year of application.)

November 05

We are stronger when we pull together as a group, but we are the strongest when we leave no one behind.

November 06

Those who deny freedom to others deserve it not for themselves.
(Abraham Lincoln)

Election Day

What does freedom mean to you? Write an essay and open your heart about this question.

November 07

**Get thee behind me Satan
(Jesus)**

So many fears

"Get thee behind me Satan" was the reply of Jesus when tempted by the devil, which of course was his own wrong or evil thought when being tested. And in Matthew 16:23 we read: "But he turned, and said unto Peter, Get thee behind me, Satan: thou art an offence unto me: for thou savourest not the things that be of God, but those that be of men."

All fear stems from evil or ignorance, and is manmade. Therefore "get thee behind me fear."

We must condition our subconscious not to be afraid. Fear stands in the way of most everything we do. Much of the suffering in this world is caused by hidden guilt in one's consciousness. Deep down inside is a buried unhappy person that believes the failures of the past. By repressing guilt and shame we have damaged our self-esteem and we have robbed ourselves of the power we possess.

Unfoldment is possible to each of us. As a matter of fact, it is our natural birthright. There is no reason to be guilty or ashamed. The mistakes you made are from the past. They are done and over with. No use to dwell on them or to recall their impact. It's a new day, with new ideas and new hope. A chance to start fresh and with a happy heart, move on to your dreams.

Your immature ego will always warn you of the failures you could be inviting by moving towards an unfamiliar goal. Your ego will also push you to want things that are not in your best interest. Your ego will tempt you to go for material gains in ways that might not be the most desirable. The fears stemming from your ego-consciousness are superficial. They are based on the idea that matter is substance, that this is a material life with material experiences.

Your true consciousness, pure and intelligent as it is in substance, knows the truth. You are a mental being with a powerful mind. You have your right and good thoughts as your tools and you have your ability to choose all the good things you desire. There is nothing to fear. Whatever you can imagine is yours; envision this easily and comfortably. But only when we dwell as our natural selves is it possible to project that power. Search for this inner self and do not give up until you have found it. Dedication and determination are qualities, and you must exert those qualities joyfully and with humor. All doors will open to you – you are holding the key!

November 08

Your basic desires are health, wealth, and happiness. They are intertwined and the reward for your effort to think and live correctly, and with good intention. Keep up this well worthy labor – be a Light-worker!

The basic desires

It is safe to say that our total experience, which is mainly composed of health, wealth, and happiness, is the reflection of our daily thoughts, feelings, and moods and beliefs. We all strive for a better, more fulfilled life. It is natural to want the best for your loved ones as well. But how do we improve this sometimes so drab and repetitious daily rut? How can we stay healthy to enjoy our daily activities? How can we attract abundance despite the picture of lack?

The sense of happiness, of course, is an individual one. Each of us reaches a sense of happiness through different sensory experiences. I, for one, love to hear the birds sing – sense of hearing. It touches my Soul. Maybe overlooking the ocean with its vast sense of freedom and power is your thing – sense of seeing, or that chocolate cookie melting in your mouth – sense of taste. I touched my new luxurious sheets last night – sense of touch, and smelled the freshness of the soft linens. It certainly made me happy.

See, those little things can make you happy. You don't have to reach for the stars right away. Practice with the lesser ideas so you become convinced of the workings. You just have to become aware of every moment. Be awake! This is your stepping-stone; this is how you achieve happiness. Appreciation is part of your mental housecleaning. You let go of the lesser thoughts and replace with your new sense of happy ideas. I've written much about the idea of mental housecleaning. It is absolutely necessary to get rid of those pesky habits and old outgrown beliefs. It is of uttermost importance to replace those bandits with fresh concepts and good thoughts.

November 09

Heal yourself first

The connection of health to right thinking, healthy thinking, is still largely misunderstood and rejected. We still believe that outside circumstances cause our illnesses. We assume that we have no control over our physical ailments. We think that we are the victims of random chance. Nevertheless, no matter what we believe, the truth is, they are intimately intertwined and cannot be separated. Our illness

stems from our unhealthy thinking, moods, and most of all beliefs. Liking it or not, our imaginary "reality" of materialism is what causes all troubles.

Focus on you. Heal yourself first. If you are struggling through life, how do you expect to be of help to others? Your relationship to yourself is what needs attention. Find out who you are, no matter what you see in the process. Be brave and courageous. Fear not! Good or bad, love yourself for who you really are; not the material, corrupt, and destructible being, but the indestructible perfect Soul. I certainly practice this every day, little by little.

November 10

Dreams, how do they work?

I asked my readers to send me topics of interest:

Reader:
"I would like that you write about dreams and the way that we can use them to improve our knowledge about ourselves, please."

Answer:

"Hi Mildred, dreams can be a bit tricky as they consist of current daytime and past experiences, wishful thinking, fears, intuitions, and messages. Since your reasoning ability is sleeping during those hours, your subconscious is running rampant, and does not discriminate between right and wrong. You can use your dreams by observing the pictures, writing them down so they become clear, and without prejudgment dissect the happenings.

For instance, to give you an example, last night I dreamt about being in a house that had many rooms. Houses usually represent your mental household, your mind. The rooms show the different issues, topics you are dealing with.

I didn't know the people but it felt comfortable there. I remember someone saying: We have one hundred chickens and eighteen cats. The house was located in a small town in Austria, which I haven't visited in over thirty years and really never think of. However, subconsciously I have been dealing with a lot of childhood issues.

One room was very messy, which is not like me at all, and the woman – who (I'm certain) represented 'me said to me: 'I'm usually not that messy but I just have been laying on the couch feeling depressed.' I (my true consciousness) answered her: 'Get up and get going, there is a lot of good stuff going on!'

See, I have been a little bit confused over a decision I have to make regarding my personal future in my otherwise very clear head. That's why only one room was messy. And I have been a bit procrastinating on this one issue (lying on the couch) but my subconscious, my true all-knowing self said: 'Get up and get going!'

By seeing it clearly and acting on what you know you can make dreams a tool. It takes a little time to become efficient in this, but it's a fun practice. Enjoy!

November 11

Ilene is still struggling with her weight

Today is Veteran's Day

"I feel like I've been serving in a war against my weight. I started out this year like an eager recruit - poised yet one more time to go out of the front lines and really win this battle. I've recommitted more times than I care to admit to, and yet I still feel in my heart of hearts it's a battle that can be won. Granted, Nixon felt that way

349

about winning the Vietnam War and look what happened there. But the big difference is that I am actually the controller of me - the arbiter of my very own fate - and whatsoever I decree and really believe - therein lies the victory.

I've basically maintained my weight this past month but no serious forward momentum. 'What does it take? What does it take?' I keep asking myself, 'to hurl myself into the realm of overachievers.'

I have to admit, as the year is ending and the pressure to really get it done increases I react with fear, which in turn sets me up for defeat. At least I'm aware of this now. Before I wouldn't even analyze this process - I'd just tune out and turn to food for comfort as I felt more uncomfortable and out of control because I wasn't staying on course. By becoming aware of some of my past negative behaviors I feel at least I put the brakes on before a major binge - and this diffuses the emotional eating part of it.

I renewed my gym membership this week, in another effort to stay on track. Of course, I've not gone very consistently this entire year, but in my defense I will say my back problems made it impossible the first half of the year to contemplate any plausible exercise program. And I've gone here and there, mini startups to get the momentum going. But other things and chores and people seemed to take priority ... which I know is not the case. I must make myself the priority in anything and everything in order to push through and really reach my goals. It's as simple as that. So here it is Veteran's Day and I'm giving thanks to me, thinking I have till the end of the month to lose eight pounds. Boot camp here I come!!!"

November 12

True goals are spiritual

Our goal of living a better and happier life is truly mental, spiritual. True power is effective when used correctly. As consciousness expands and takes on new levels of awareness, so will our power increase accordingly. This power is not restricted to only a few, no, it is available to all people; to all who are sincerely making the finding of Truth their goal.

I posted this comment today and received an interesting response.

Quote:
"God looks at you without judgment or favoritism. He does not punish or reward. He only acts according to Universal Law."

Reader:
"In that case, Universal Law sucks. I get judged, punished, and rewarded a lot."

How do you explain to someone that sees themselves as a victim that the above statement is one of Truth? The Universe, or God, does not pick and choose. It does not favor one person over the other. It is you that must make the choice, change your thoughts and habits and acknowledge the fact that you are the arbiter of your fate. You are the creator of your world. When things look dire, step back and observe your innermost thoughts and then - act accordingly. You can be absolutely certain that the thing that occupies your mind the most will soon be part of your life. So beware what you are holding within your heart.

I finished our conversation with this:

"To your above statement I want to add that 'Nature, the Universe, deals us the biggest blows when

351

it's time to grow personally and spiritually.' There is a reason for everything and when you look back to your misfortunes you will see that they turned out to be blessings. Wishing you well!"

November 13

All possibilities exist within each of us, as we are part of a greater Consciousness. We are manifestations of the God substance.

November 14

We experience only what we are within; meaning that we encounter our inert qualities, good or bad. It is the reflection of our most secret thoughts.

Responsibility of being

You might not like to hear this statement as it puts the responsibility into your court. You might see some character traits that you think you have already altered. That's why it is so important to be honest with yourself and truly admit to those innermost thoughts and feelings. Especially the feelings! People run into the same problems over and over again, because they don't fix the underlying issues. They believe, and think, what they encounter is outside of themselves, or someone else's fault, but you cannot recognize (or sense) anything unless it is already within you.

Life will continue to show us the pictures of our mistakes and bring us into contact with the things we need to correct. As long as our consciousness stagnates and lingers without progress we will be pushed and pushed until we get up and make the necessary correction.

November 15

Once we understand that all manifestations are thought concepts, someone's ideas, we will

understand the cause of all and will be able to go to the source. We will be skilled to shape our future.

Ideas are the stimuli to all creation

Ideas naturally arise in our minds as they are a fundamental core of being. Consciousness constantly produces ideas; it's an idea-producing machine as it is comprised of all knowledge. This knowledge has to express itself constantly and it does this by sparking ideas in the minds of individuals. This world you see is an idea, yes, a mental idea – and each of us sees it differently according to our own distinct understanding.

November 16

**The intellect by itself moves nothing.
(Aristotle)**

November 17

Just because we see something doesn't make it true. Our senses mislead us constantly, telling us that this world consists of matter. This is an illusion. This wonderful world we live in is mental in nature, with consciousness as its master and science has proven this to be true.

We tend to become who "we think we are"

This starts in early childhood and over the years many layers of beliefs, mental impressions, and experiences, which we believe to be true, shape our outward being. We act accordingly and develop into this unique, yet deceived, being.

Our job is to strip our Self of these layers, go deep to the core and reeducate and reshape who we really are. Remember this old "you" didn't happen overnight, so be patient and know that perseverance and focus will get you to your goal. The struggles and mental battles will be well worth it.

November 18

The world we see through our senses is only a partial picture of what exists in mind. As we unfold more of our awareness this picture changes to reflect our new understanding. We only see what we can perceive as true.

Depression seems to be a huge issue with so many people

Where has the love for life gone?

Too many people these days struggle with depression. Not just the alcoholics and drug addicts, but regular folks that go to work in the morning with families and friends and a good living. But when you talk to them there is visible despair. They hold their heads down and always have the attitude of "just getting by," or "I will make it through the day."

I wonder if our society has created this stigma of "you are what you have" and not "you are your character." Is it really necessary that you compete with your neighbor's possessions? Is life only good when you have everything you want (I didn't say need), no - want. Do you want more and more material things?

Don't get me wrong, "having" is good and you should have everything you need. But start focusing on your mental well-being. How good is that boat in the driveway when you feel sad or lonely? How much do you enjoy the new dress or suit when you have no one to take to the dance? Are we really so consumed by material riches that life becomes a struggle if we have a little less than?

Can you appreciate looking at the butterfly and seeing the wondrous transformation from the limited caterpillar, crawling on his stomach, blind, and only out to eat as much as it can, into the brilliant creature soaring in the sky? Ask yourself: "Why do I feel this emptiness?" Ask yourself: "Where has the love for life gone?"

November 19

Visualize, can you see it yet?

Let's do something fun! Let's visualize your future. Find some time without anyone around. Just you and your Self. Sit down in a comfortable chair, or your favorite spot, and make sure it is quiet. No TV, no radio … just your thoughts … comfort, peace, calm, and thoughtful.

Start thinking

Your thoughts will become pictures. Start from where you are at this time in your life, see what you like about it, and depict what you would like to change; anything like relationships, work and career, home situations and so forth.

Write it down

As you get clear on your wishes and desires start visualizing how your life would change if you would get them fulfilled. Feel how it would feel, see yourself in the midst of your longings. Touch them mentally and hear the sounds, get lost in your imagination. Create a vision board or at least write it down. Seeing the words will make it more real to your subconscious.

Make a plan of action

Once you decide what your future looks like, write down a plan of action. Research, get informed, and do whatever it takes to bring your desire into reality. See, it is already real in your mind; it's just a matter of manifesting it into your experience. It takes action to achieve anything.

Keep visualizing

Stay focused, engaged, and do not waiver. You are who you think you are. You have what you think you deserve. You are the maker of your life. Go get it and trust your imagination!

November 20

Practice conforming to Earthly laws, so you can eventually obey Universal Laws.

Mental Laws

There are many mental or Universal Laws, all of them without prejudice. They work always according to the Law and do not discriminate. Idle prayers won't help, faith will. As a matter of fact there is no one to hear you. You are the only one that can hear you. When you pray to God or the Universe, or whatever your "Almighty" of choice is, you are really praying to your understanding of this power which you are part of, and connected to. Let me explain it a bit further.

The average man reacts to the stimuli derived from his senses and therefore does not live according to Universal Law. Most people never realize the power they hold within. They then, after making mistake after mistake, pray to an entity that is personal to them; a personal kind of God, as they cannot see the mentalness of the Universe and understand that even this God is a substance, energy or power – rather than a person or entity. To say it more clearly: God as a person (man with a beard on a throne image) or "someone" to pray to does not exist.

However, once you understand that this power is all-encompassing, all-loving, and all-powerful you will also realize that you, being part of this force, are made out of the same substance and therefore connected to "it" for all times.

You then, as you pray, are only reinforcing your desires and wishes by repeating them in your mind. Your desires spark imagination and action, which in turn will manifest what you are asking for. Now, I can guarantee you, that if you pray to an outside God, hoping that "he" will fulfill your needs, begging and pleading for your yearnings, the result will be zero. There is no one to hear your beseeching but your own mental ear.

"God helps the one who helps himself", said first by Algernon Sydney in 1698, and later accredited to Benjamin Franklin, means, that you are responsible for helping yourself; you are in charge of fulfilling your demands and you, only you, can create your reality. Here is a little story which most of you probably have heard. It's good to be reminded:

"A flood occurred and the old preacher man climbed onto his roof to safety. As the water climbed higher, a whole tree passed slowly by. The man recognized that if he jumped on the tree, he wouldn't drown — however he said, 'God will save me.' A row boat came by and the people offered him aboard, but again he shouted back, 'No thanks! God will save me.' Then a barge came by and urged the man on. His reply, you guessed it, 'No thanks! God will save me!' As the water came over the top of his roof, a helicopter hung in the air offering a ladder. Still, the man said, 'No thank you! God will save me!' Finally, the man drowned. When he came before God he cried, 'God, why didn't you save me?' God replied, 'Save you? I sent a tree, a boat, a barge and a helicopter, and you didn't want to use any of them. I thought you wanted to drown.'"

November 21

What is Spirit but the unseen substance of the Universe? It is the vital principle or animating force within living beings. You are Spirit. You are of this God-substance.

The spirit of the holidays

I'm not really in the mood this year. Besides the eighty degree weather in Southern California, my son spending Thanksgiving in Florida with his new wife visiting the in-laws, and my dwindling desire to participate in the commercial shopping frenzy, I'm really rethinking the Holidays. I celebrated more when my son was little. Back then, decorating was a joy. Seeing his eyes light up and waiting for Santa to arrive made all the cooking and entertaining well worth it. These days Santa arrives in the malls a couple of weeks before Thanksgiving. I thought he was busy at the North Pole, but I guess not!

Even though the actual date of Jesus' birth has not been established, Christmas symbolizes the birth of Jesus. For Christians this is a momentous occasion, but it has been lost mostly by focusing on gift giving and spending money that most people can't afford; leaving them with a bitter taste and anxiety before and after the fact. All religions celebrating the Holidays should regroup and rethink. What did the birth of Jesus mean? What does Hanukah represent? We'll talk some more in December … you can give that some thought in the meanwhile, I certainly will!

November 22

Give thanks all year round, from morning to night. Fall asleep with a grateful feeling of eternal bliss – this is how you enjoy Life!

Thanksgiving

The history of Thanksgiving is rooted in English tradition, giving thanks after a fruitful harvest. Here, in the United States, we trace it back to a 1621 celebration at Plymouth in present-day Massachusetts, staged by colonists and Wampanoag Indians, but was not made an annual practice until 1660. However, it wasn't until 1863, in the midst of the Civil War, that President Abraham Lincoln proclaimed a national Thanksgiving Day to be held each November.

I'm sure you read the full story of the Mayflower, carrying 102 passengers and its calamity, including the landing near the tip of Cape Cod, far north of their intended destination at the mouth of the Hudson River and the first celebration of its kind. But what does Thanksgiving mean to us now in an abundant world? Surely more than a turkey and overeating! What are we giving thanks for?

When asked, everyone is thankful for having enough money or their family. But another priority would be health. Why do we neglect to be thankful for health when nothing hurts? What about your ability to reason and your intellect. Do you take being smart for granted? Do you think that was just a lucky coincidence? Are you giving thanks that you found a more spiritual connection and actually realize that you are a perfect and immortal being?
As my publisher beautifully said:

"I give thanks to the rising and setting of the sun. For all good works completed or begun. For all evil thwarted or undone, on this day these sands have run. I give thanks to passing of the swift silver moon. By all hearts lifted by a happy tune. By good food that fills the supper spoon. May many more days this bright come soon."

November 23

Black Friday

Now here is behavior that shows the opposite from what I was talking about yesterday. Long lines at the malls, overnight tents, and freezing temperature all for a small discount – why? There are hoards of people trampling over each other, hurting and fighting for material things. It's just "stuff" people, just stuff...

Thankfulness also includes humility and kindness. A true thankful Soul is gentle and loving. This Soul is busy with selfless acts and is giving – not selfish and concerned with the ego, and fighting for more and more stuff...

November 24

"Look to this day
For it is the very life of life.
In its brief course lie all
The verities and realities of your existence:
The glory of action,
The bliss of growth,
The splendor of beauty,
For yesterday is but a dream
And tomorrow is only a vision;
But today well lived makes
Every yesterday a dream of happiness,
And every tomorrow a vision of hope.
Look well, therefore, to this day."

~ From the Sanskrit

November 25

Clear thinking

I've been talking about clear thinking a lot, maybe not in these words, but any thought that is consciously thought is a "clear" thought. We spend most of the day like robots. Thoughts are natural but conditioned, not chosen and precise. We rush to conclusions rather than thinking things through. We accept someone else's opinion or we believe the media and buy into the hype of everyday deceptions.

We must learn to think with complete clarity and visualize with focus and positive feelings. When we choose the thoughts we think we choose our lives.

Our experiences are muddled and full of obstacles, just as our thoughts are muddled and unclear. It's like drinking contaminated water, it will make you ill – and so our contaminated thoughts will cause our sickness and demise. Be a clear thinker, a searcher with purpose. Take a broader kind of consciousness. Make sure that you are precise in your quest for a better life, a clear and unblemished life.

November 26

To know is nothing at all, to imagine is everything. (Anatole France)

November 27

Trust life

One of the more difficult things in our journey is to acquire the trust needed to live fully and completely in bliss. Trust in the Allness of Good. How many of us still think that the world is contaminated with bad people, full of evil and wickedness? We see the tragedies in the news and read about horrific acts of mankind all day long. Have you even glimpsed at the truth of this being a mere illusion? Can you be open-minded enough to see its trickery?

Doubt and fear, the big tormenters of life, will constantly parade a slew of awful experiences in front of you. But you must take a stand and say: "Life is good" and mean

361

it, feel it, and act it. You must trust your inner source, which is Universal Intelligence – and won't you agree that Intelligence must be good or it wouldn't be intelligent? Intelligence and perfection are synonyms.

November 28

Doing

Thinking and doing are two actions. It takes both to get things done. You can think all day long but unless you act on it your thoughts will continue to be incubated in mind. Action follows thought. With simple examples like going to the fridge to get a sandwich, you thought of getting that sandwich because you were hungry and then you acted on it. So it is with all thoughts. You think you want a better home and you go online to see what's available and so on.

Your more advanced thoughts pertaining to your unfoldment work the same way. You want more peace? You will have to retrain your thoughts to be more peaceful. You want more love? You will have to acquire a more loving temperament.

Since we cannot stop thinking we are always led into action by our thoughts, even if the action is negative. Fear of failure for example will lead into the action of failure. However, the conviction and action toward success will certainly produce success.

Nevertheless, since you are changing your thinking, it is important to first change your concept of self. You must alter your perception of who you are and slip into this new mind-model of your identity. This can be done. It has to be done to make the transformation complete. If you want to be a doctor, envision yourself being a doctor attending to patients and all the rewards attached to this vocation. If you want to be an artist, writer or such, imagine yourself producing wonderful art pieces or articles. But don't keep it only in mind – act on it. Do what it takes to make this dream come true. Enroll in classes, seminars or take art lessons. Whatever brings you closer to the goal – do it!

And while doing, don't forget to focus, be determined, trust that you can just because you can, and always and steadily chip away at gaining the understanding it takes to succeed.

Good luck!

November 29

A few days ago I read: "Live in daily forgiveness!" What a powerful thought. To have the sense of forgiveness in the forefront of your mind all day, every day, and for everyone is a wonderful application of thought. Cleaning out those pesky feelings of hurt, anger, and resentment immediately and on a constant basis, surely will heal your sense quickly.

November 30

We can alter our environment and our circumstances by disciplining our consciousness. (U. S. Andersen)

How should we think about the Environment?

We can obviously think the thoughts we want to think and therefore create the circumstances and the environment we want to experience and live in. This power of mental choice gives us unlimited freedom, but it also gives us the responsibility to act.

The simple question is: "Where" do we start? Well, right here and right now. With the smaller things that easily manageable yet so important.

Taking care of our planet

I was scrutinized by a friend a couple of months ago when he watched me washing out a ketchup bottle before throwing it into the recycling bin. "What are you doing?" he asked, with a smirk on his face. "Aren't you going a bit overboard? You are cleaning the trash before throwing it into the garbage?" "Nope", I snarled back at him, "we cannot be too caring when it comes down to our environment. Every little bit helps!"

I read on a flyer the sanitation department sent out a while ago that cleansing the cans and bottles of food or debris before discarding them into the proper vessels really will help them out in the recycling process. So why not – it takes two seconds!

Unfortunately, the American culture in general is used to wastefulness and the selfish "someone-else-can-deal-with-it" attitude. I cannot speak about the rest of the world, but I can speak about a small and often overlooked country called Austria, my birthplace.

Even thirty-plus years ago, I still remember clearly my mother and other family members would bundle paper neatly (yes, neatly) before stashing it into a container until the weekly assigned drop-off day had arrived. The food cans and bottles were rinsed out and driven to the nearest recycling center, with the boxes of paper and plastic items. The convenience of trucks picking up those items at your door step wasn't available at the time. However, the City expected all citizens to participate and no one thought that was in any way intrusive or inappropriate. Everyone felt it was their duty.

So let us take another look at how we can make the same commitment to our planet. Each of us, individually, might not have a great impact in this undertaking, but like with all matters a collective effort can move mountains, literally.

Here are some facts about recycling:
The average person uses 650 pounds of paper each year, 2.5 million plastic bottles are used every hour in this country, about 80% of what Americans throw away is recyclable, and our recycling rate is only 28%.

I think education is the key. Do you spend your time researching environmental issues and how to solve the problems? Are you asking yourself, "Is this recyclable before throwing the item out?"" Probably not - but starting right here and now in your household, and teaching your children the importance of living with compassion and concern for our planet is a must. Each and every one of us counts, each and every one of us can make a difference.

Chapter 12: The All-power

December 1

Look at all aspects of your life, not just the good and enjoyable ones. Make sure you are addressing the hidden issues and little annoyances that still pop up every so often. They represent a lack in your still unfolding mind. Balance them all, step by step, and clean up your mental household.

As the year comes to an end...

This has been an interesting and blessed year for me. My husband's health improved, my son got married and promoted, my friends have been well with no major tragedies to report, and I have enjoyed my venture, teaching and writing, to the fullest. It certainly has been a year of spiritual growth.

So to tie up this last month with its daily chapters I will make sure that any topic that I neglected to talk about or only addressed briefly will be included in the month of December. It's important to look at all aspects of our lives, not just the basic ones that come up every day. Maybe there are some areas of our lives which we are already proficient in and no longer need to dwell on. But maybe we just shoved them under the rug? So here it goes...

December 2

No need to feel lost and to wander in doubt and uncertainty. Take a good look at yourself. Aren't you a wondrous being of light and love? Aren't you a perfect Soul with unlimited possibilities? Appreciate yourself!

Feeling lost

Someone wrote me the other day that so many people feel lost. They don't know why they are here on this plane and the reader asked me to comment on it.

People that feel lost haven't found their purpose yet. They are looking in all the wrong places and think that their sense of belonging comes from an outside source. They need others to validate them and their core understanding is rooted in the belief that this world is the real thing. With low self-esteem they are afraid to try new things or open up to new people.

Here is where your appreciation comes in again and again. Appreciation for your own good self, love for your pure Soul, and everything that you experienc, and gratefulness for the world you live in. Once you have a loving sense of self (not just of the other – you have to love who you are) you will find your purpose. Your purpose should always have a component of serving others, be it in a helping way (for example social workers, nurses, doctors, lawyers), or education (teachers of all sorts of subjects for children and adults), or inventing a more convenient tool to make someone's life easier (think of all the manufacturers that produce anything from furniture to gadgets), military, builders, and entertainers.

There are many ways to help and serve others; most professions are designed to be of service in one way or another. You know what's right for you when you find it. Just listen to yourself.

December 3

Today Monday, December 3rd, 2012 ~ Triple-Planet Pyramid

This year was a metaphysical year and the best is yet to come. Following the November 13th total solar eclipse and the November 28th lunar eclipse, December 3rd begins the triple step end phase planetary consciousness activation sequence.

Today Mercury, Venus, and Saturn align in a pattern that precisely corresponds with the Giza Pyramids and Orion's Belt. This alignment will happen for the first time in 2,737 years.

The numerology of 12-3-2012 adds up to an eleven, (1+2+3+2+1+2=11). This eleven-day is repeated on 12-12-2012 and again 12-21-2012. This triple eleven code mirrors the 11-11-11 Aquarian entry date, eleven representing spiritual enlightenment making its way into reality.

December 3rd is eighteen days before Galactic alignment Winter Solstice Day December 21st. Eighteen days times twenty-four hours times sixty minutes equals 25,920. The precession of the Equinoxes takes exactly 25,920 years. The numerology of eighteen is a nine (1+8=9). Nine is the number of completion. We are completing the cycle of galactic powered holographic energetic inserts which are creating the New Age. It will be interesting to observe this shift. Expect the first couple of years to be a "cleansing" experience, a purification process of your old and outgrown concepts so to speak.

December 4

Earning your skills with due diligence and sincere want is the key to all worthwhile pursuit.

Earning your skills

With the start of a New Age on the Horizon, ask yourself: What am I good at? What is it that I always wanted to do but never got the nerve to do? What is my natural ability? Does drawing come easy to you? Do you like to sing or teach? Keep asking yourself until you find something that feels right and good. What do you do in your spare time? Hobbies are always a strong clue since no one forced you to do them. You naturally picked them because they are enjoyable to you. You really like woodwork, but you are a lawyer? Think again!

Don't be too hard on yourself. Condemning yourself for not having followed through with your dreams doesn't solve the issue. I tell my husband all the time that it is never too late. He has had many dreams starting in childhood but was discouraged early on, told he was good for nothing. How damaging and what an imprint it made on his child-mind.

However, we are adults now. We can make the choice to start anew and keep going until we master our new vocation or dream. You too are probably good in everything you love to do. Maybe taking your desire up as a hobby will suffice or it will at least lead you in the right direction.

In my case, I love to read, write, teach, cook, garden, and I love animals. I am great in organizing, planning, scheduling, and marketing – stemming from my years working for a large corporation. New ideas come easily and creating a new project from scratch thrills me. That's what I do; it makes me a creator. Think about it - this is also what you do!

You create new things every day. Be it as that wood-worker creating a new bench or filing documents in an office; teaching young children or designing architectural plans for a building company. Tending to your family is creative because you use your imagination to provide a good and comfortable home. The list goes on and on. We are all creators but we have to earn our skills by diligently learning and working on becoming better at our choices. You cannot be idle and drift; that will only get you into a downward spiral. You can only coast for so long. Don't be a drifter! Be the architect of your life and the designer of your destiny, and most of all enjoy the process!

December 5

You are your own leader. It's as simple as that.

Leadership

Do you take charge easily? Are you always the leader or do you stand behind and observe, do you follow and allow someone else to take the reign?

This is all well and good if the undertaking concerns someone else, or it's a project that you are only partially involved in. But in your own life you have to take charge, you have to assume responsibility, and you have to be the leader. No one, not even your spouse, can take control of even the slightest aspect of your life. You will lose in the process.

It is utterly important that you are self-sufficient, self-reliant, self-loving (not egotistical), and self-confident. Our difficulties include the cluttered up sense of negative emotions, limitations, and fears. We see ourselves as less than, weak, and restricted. We give up too easily and hand over the decision-making to someone that seems stronger and more adept, especially us females. That is the easy way out; but this easy way does not help you in the long run.

The running away from responsibility only makes us weaker. It robs us of all of our courage. We cannot be effective without courage. Courage conquers fear and

370

fears of all kind need to be dealt with. We all know that, we know it deep down in the most secret chambers of our hearts.

December 6

Due diligence and sincere want is the key to all worthwhile pursuit.

Talk about leadership, here is an example on how you can lead as a boss with compassion and inspire your staff.

Inspiration at the job
a real life bosses mission

"Inspirational bosses are few these days and when I was told about this remarkable company, I had to share this story. When you look at their website it's a 'virtual receptionist' operating out of Oregon. Taking a closer look at the operation, there are real people behind the phones that all have the same name 'Ruby.' 'Ruby' is smart and cheerful; she is trained to make a difference in your day and handles each call with care. Ruby is friendly and has a can-do attitude, and most of all she is a professional. Well, Ruby is, in reality, a group of great women who love their jobs.

It all started in 2003 when the founder and CEO, first started the company, and focused on making businesses more efficient. However, the feedback she received from clients centered more on how kind and helpful their staff was, and how their receptionists' cheerfulness helped their clients win more customers. So she trained her people to stay focused on the happiness of her clients and on creating personal connections with them. This attitude earned her several awards, including the 'Best small business to work for," which she is rightfully very proud off.

'Happiness is incredibly important to us,' the marketing person writes me. 'It's definitely played a huge part in making Ruby a success.' Here are some examples of what you can do to improve employee morale: 'We encourage employees to complete daily journal entries for a month in order to create habits of positive thinking. Those who completed the program were entered to win a trip to Hawaii.'

Every Ruby receives a Smile File when they first start. They can fill their folders with compliments, notes from coworkers, and other items that will brighten their days. It helps our staff focus on the positive moments and take pride in their accomplishments.

For every five years at Ruby, employees receive five weeks paid time off, plus a $1,000 grant and coaching session with a well-known positive psychologist. The staff can use these resources to fulfill a dream that they wouldn't otherwise have had an opportunity to realize.

It's no wonder that the marketing person is friendly and efficient. Her job title 'Online Marketing Champion' shows creativity and encouragement to be the best she can be.

With one hundred employees, all answering the phone with a cheerful 'Ruby speaking,' you can be sure that Ruby is never sick, late, at lunch, or on vacation. You can relax knowing that your calls are answered promptly and with care. 'Ruby' is with you around the clock, she is always available.

Another one of the employees coming up on five years with 'Ruby' loves her job. 'We do dress-up Friday's,' she giggles and the photos prove that she is not kidding. There are many perks to working at Ruby's: a reading room stocked with inspirational books, lots of interactive fun, catered lunches and themed events are the norm at this entertaining yet efficient office.

'Our boss even bought us a nap-couch!' grins another Ruby. The morale at 'Ruby' is extremely high, not something you see a lot these days where employees mostly complain about their work places and environments. Not so at Ruby!"

Congratulations to a job well done and to all 'Ruby's', and lots of admiration and thank you to a boss lady with such a big heart!

December 7

A healing thought in itself is healing.

Healing Thoughts

I just finished up my second booklet *The Seeds Will Sprout Somewhere* and my next work will be titled *Healing Thoughts*. It will contain many detailed metaphysical diagnoses on illnesses caused through wrong thinking. I have imbued this book with a taste of what is yet to come. It is my sincere wish that this work will help many a searchers and contribute to the healing of this planet.

Diseases are created by negative thoughts, deeds, and beliefs. Usually, a fatal incurable disease is a wake-up call to look within. Observe your life and your lifestyle. Reexamine your thoughts and stop the mad rush. But even the smaller discomforts need to be evaluated because they are the beginning of a greater risk to manifest a serious dis-ease.

We have to take a good hard and honest look at ourselves. We have to ask ourselves the questions: Are we treating ourselves right? Are we acting as good as we could? Are we thinking healthy and strong thoughts? Do we know that we are cause?

Our thoughts carry the power to create – not just our day to day life experience; they also decide your well-

373

being. By now we have established that our thoughts are powerful and carry a great deal of energy. Good or bad, this energy is released into the Universe and will bring back the mirror-energies be it positive or negative. You are not only the maker of your destiny; you are also your own healer.

Going to the doctor may cure the symptoms for a while but doesn't cut out the root cause. It's only a crutch, a band aid on a festering wound. I'm not sure if the people of this world are ready yet to take on this immense responsibility. But in my mind the time has come, and with courage the Truth must be told.

December 8

I am Love, I am Light, I am Perfection and I am Health – and I know it!

Daily Healing Ceremony

In your daily meditation or quiet time, forgive yourself for all the mistakes, may they be negative thoughts, wrong actions, beliefs, and the expectancy of evil and dis-ease that may have contributed to this illness.

Visualize yourself as happy and healthy, strong, and full of energy. Feel the love and the healing from the Universe. Feel your connection to the Almighty. Be grateful for being alive and give thanks for all of your blessings.

Remember that the Almighty Power is flawless and good; it knows nothing of dis-ease and illness, and it only knows Perfection. So tune into this knowing, and feel yourself perfect.

December 09

A time to heal
A time to break down and a time to build up
A time to weep and a time to laugh
A time to mourn and a time to dance
A time to cast away stones and a time to gather stones together
A time to embrace and a time to refrain from embracing
A time to get and a time to lose
A time to keep and a time to cast away
A time to rend and a time to sew
A time to keep silent and a time to speak
A time to love and a time of peace

Ecclesiastes 3:1

December 10

Your Soul stems from Universal Consciousness. It is your birthplace.

A Clear Channel from your mind to Universal Consciousness

Tune into the frequency of Universal consciousness and don't stand in your way. How? Be quiet for a moment – listen ... feel the good energy and allow the negative to evaporate.

I was thinking this morning about the "Why's." Why those horrific tragedies, people shooting innocent people, and so forth. I went back all the way to 9/11. Why? My head knows it, but my heart still wonders sometimes.

Unfortunately it takes extreme measures to awaken the masses. When times are good, people slip back into their greedy, "it's all about me," little world. Others are forgotten and ignored. We are meant to be together, work together, support each other – act as ONE.

And when we separate and act only in our own interest we breach the "Law of Oneness." The "Law of Individuality" tells us that each of us is responsible for our own actions and that we are in charge of our own lives. Contradiction? Not so fast!

We, as individuals, have the power to create our own heaven and hell. We have proven it many times. We are also responsible for everything that befalls us every day of our lives. However, we are all one as to substance (we are all mental beings) and to quality (we are all good), and most of all we come from the same source. Therefore it is of uttermost importance to treat all people with the same love, respect, and dignity. The Law of Oneness will mean something to you, once you realize this significant fact. You and I, and all people are connected to Universal Consciousness – our father/mother/source. So tune into your birthplace and remember that Individuality and ONE-ness are not contradictory. We are all one as to substance, stemming from the same intelligent source, connected through Spirit. We are individual as to the choices we make, the path we travel. We have to remember this vital fact, as there is power in mass-thinking, and the actions of the "people united" will speak louder when used properly and lovingly. Acting as One great Spiritual Nation shall be our desire and helping/including all people shall be our goal.

December 11

No matter how small... All efforts are rewarded by the "Law of Cause and Effect."

Let me explain: The Law of Cause and Effect is one of many laws active in the Universe. Another name for this law you hear all the time is Karma. Karma insinuates the concept of reincarnation. However, you do not have to believe in reincarnation to experience Karma or Cause and Effect. Universal Laws do not adhere to any religion or belief. It just is, now, and forever. It is not personal but impersonal, it does not acknowledge good or bad, it only acts in accordance to its rules.

I am sure we can agree that there is a cause; a cause even greater than us. We have seen the tremendous power Nature has. We have only barely discovered the creation of the Universe. We instinctively know that there is a cause that is so immense that it created the heavens and the Earth and all that comes with it. This greater cause is known as the Universe, Intelligence, Wisdom, and God. This almighty power causes, and we being part of this power, also cause. We have established the fact that our thinking is causative, and this greater power, which we are connected to, is the motor behind our being.

Get the big picture? Big cause (Universal Power/God) causes for us little causers (us) in accordance to our thoughts and beliefs. Therefore, whatever you think and believe will manifest in the visible and you can accept or reject this picture. You can make necessary adjustments or enjoy the fruit of your right thinking. You have been given choice.

So how do you start? Every little good and right thought counts. The Law of Proportion will manifest your better and improved thinking when it reaches 51% and the scale tips over into the positive realm. Yes, keep on it, keep going, as I like to say one step at a time, and you will see results sooner than later. Do not be discouraged by setbacks and occasional relapses in your thinking. Stop yourself and re-commit, every time to your new and improved attitude. Know that you can, because you can!

December 12

Today I was going back to...

Remember the good old holiday traditions

Every so often I still reminisce about the good old days, growing up in a country that literally gave birth to the Christmas tree. The custom of the Christmas tree can be traced back to the 16th century in Strasbourg, Germany (now part of France), where devout Christians would bring trees into their homes, laden with fruits like apples, nuts, dates, and colored paper. Later, around the 18th century, candles were added to illuminate the tree. However, at the time this custom was largely considered to be a Protestant tradition and only eventually gained wider acceptance as immigrants moved towards other Catholic areas, including Austria.

After the practice had spread throughout Europe it was not until the Revolutionary War that German settlers hauled trees from surrounding woods and decorated them to enjoy the Holidays. Nowadays, the tree is more a symbol of goodwill, hope, and family togetherness and not exclusive to any one religion.

Of course in modern times the trees are decorated with much more than food, besides the occasional American touch of popcorn and candy cane. Imagination and the personal taste of all cultures in our beloved melting pot are incorporated into the decor, and of course the candles were replaced with electric lights. I still get a grin on my face when I think of my first Christmas in Los Angeles in the early '80s. Not knowing any better and wanting to experience a little bit of home, I adorned the tree with real candles, which my girlfriend quickly extinguished and educated me on the danger of home fires.

This year over 33 million American families will celebrate the holidays with a real Christmas tree and countless more with an artificial tree.

Today, countries like Germany and Austria, still being touched by long ago traditions, host a large number of

"Christkindl Markt's" with handcrafted glass ornaments, beautiful arts and crafts, German foods (Lebkuchen, strudel, chestnuts, and special cookies) and Gluehwein (hot red wine with spices) as well as colorful toy Nutcrackers and Advent calendars. Blankets of glistening snow and below freezing temperatures won't keep you away. It enhances the feeling of an era of a gentler, more tender society. The true spirit of Christmas still lingers in the cold winter air. Happy Holidays!

December 13

No need to feel lost and to wander in doubt and uncertainty. Take a good look at yourself. Aren't you a wondrous being of light and love? Aren't you a perfect Soul with unlimited possibilities? Appreciate yourself!

December 14

I woke up this morning, noticing a ray of light shining through my bedroom window, even though it was still dark outside. I was reminded, for a moment, that there is light even in darkness. And I felt this overwhelming sense of bliss, which I wished I could hold onto. "Maybe one day," I thought, but I am OK for now...

Heal yourself and keep yourself well by allowing yourself plenty of rest, a healthy and balanced diet, a soothing environment, and remember to keep a loving and calm disposition, especially during the holidays. Don't react to other people's dispositions and negativity; it's easier than you think. You should be your number one priority! Why am I telling you this over and over again? Because Health is the Treasure of Life!

December 15

Healing Thought:
The symptoms of the common cold are a perfect picture of your overloaded and restless thinking. Mostly occurring during the holiday season, it reflects a sense of clogged up thoughts and a running "on and on about" too much to do. Allow yourself the rest needed, balance your daily routine, and know that all will be done in good time.

Colds and other winter beliefs

During the holiday season many people are down with so-called winter illnesses. The flu runs rampant and you can see the sniffling red noses everywhere. Colds are the picture, or reflection, of your overloaded and out of balance thinking that mostly occurs during the Holiday Season. The stress of "getting everything done" is too overwhelming for you.

To make sure you understand this concept: Anything (including any sickness or disease) you believe can and will come true, because believing is thinking that what you believe is real. So thinking that the winter is a perfect season to catch a cold will make you vulnerable to catch a cold. This does not make it real. It only proves the Law of Cause and Effect.

A so-called "common cold" is the result of too much confusion in your thinking. The runny nose shows the 'running on and on' about something in mind; too much hurry and worry and not enough calm and relaxation. Rushing around all the time, too much to do and not enough time – all of these thoughts are harmony disturbers. They will leave you feeling exhausted and clogged up. Clear up your thinking. Relax. It all will be done in due time.

December 16

What about the flu, sinus infections, and such...

Anytime you experience an infection you can be sure fear plays a role. Sinuses represent the perceptive senses (hear, see, touch). Not being satisfied with your environment or conditions in life will bring on this ailment. You might not see a clear way to better your environment and you are running on and on about it. Maybe you are uneasy and unclear. It's a sense of discontent that needs to be addressed.

Another winter belief is that the cold (temperature) can make you sick. Put on a thick jacket or scarf and bundle up. The cold temperature does not make you sick, your belief does. What about the people in countries like Germany and Sweden who jump into the icy waters of the Artic seas? People are people, their bodies are the same but their (and our) beliefs surely differ!

If you think that the wind, the sun or the cold water make you sick, you make them the Cause, or God. If you think that the smog in the city or the heat of the desert make you sick, you make them the Cause, or God. There is only one Cause, or God, and that is your own good Consciousness with its activity called right thought. And this consciousness is connected to the Almighty, our source, or perfect Intelligence – Universal Godhood.

December 17

We must re-condition our thoughts and habits. This takes concentration and a willingness to change. Since most decisions are made subconsciously, without stopping to think them through, make sure that you are very aware of your "now" choices as they shape your future.

381

What happened to Dexter?

We have followed Dexter's progress throughout the year. He's still in a state of struggle and his progress is slow; sometimes it even seems stagnant. His health has been steady with the same old tweaks and ouches, his drinking has lessened to a manageable degree, and he keeps his distaste for his new boss under wrap. Has he healed? No, but mostly because he thinks he is in the right. He believes that he is right and justified in his negative emotions. He is being stubborn and unless this rigid attitude changes his discomforts will also continue; nothing will change.

No one has the right to be bitter or angry, no matter what the circumstances. A hard one to swallow, I know. And no one has the right to judge others, no matter what the issues are. It's a work-out for sure, but you only have the right to be good, do good, and act according to Universal Law. Amen!

December 18

As long as we think that our sensory experiences are real we will not be the master of our life. We can only become the master if we acknowledge the power within.

How did Ilene Waters faire with her weight loss commitment this year?

As she is checking in with me for a last visit and progress report, let's see what she has accomplished:

"Well here we are - here I am - winding down yet another year. I'm ending this year satisfied on many levels, one of which has been my commitment to losing weight and staying the course for a full year. I am about seventeen pounds shy of my ultimate goal of thirty pounds set back in January, and for the first time, I'm ok with that because I know my commitment is to a

382

healthier life style and this has not been a project that is now ended. It's a new beginning on an infinite timeline - my life. Thanks to friends and family who have supported me on my journey. Thanks to everlasting LOVE that so graciously is extended through this universe. And to myself I give thanks, because I do enjoy the woman I am and who I aspire to be, daily and forever."

December 19

Life is a circulating center in infinity; a merry-go-round, spiraling upwards toward the light of perfect intelligence.

Mother dearest

The time has come to address a longstanding issue that has been on the backburner and heal the wounds inflicted a long time ago.

I haven't seen my mother, who still lives in Austria, for nearly twenty years. For reasons too long to explain in this chapter, we parted with my wish never to return.

Over the years I healed my sense of guilt, resentment, and disappointment. I hold no grudge or any hard feelings. It simply is the way it is and I deeply appreciate the life I have built for myself. I am truly blessed.

The last few years we started to talk once in a while, a letter here and there, all shallow small talk, politeness; nothing in common. Lately, however, she has reached out to me and at eighty-two she is alone and scared of the eminent death. She believes death ends all. What a way to live! I've tried to explain my views and the understanding of life being eternal, to give her some comfort, to no avail. So I let it rest with the calm assurance that she too will find the path when the time is right for her.

I decided to visit her in a few months and she seems pleased. It's a choice I'm making not only because it's the kind thing to do. I am an only child after all. No, it's a choice I am making because it is me, my Soul, which needs the healing and closure. The "I" of me cannot be whole until all dis-easiness is replaced by pure ease and love.

So I will practice patience, kindness, gentleness, understanding, listening and forgiveness and know that all is good – always, and forever.

December 20

Tomorrow is the shift into the Golden Age:

"The Golden Age was first; when Man, yet new,
 No rule but uncorrupted Reason knew: And, with a native bent, did good pursue. Unforced by punishment, un-awed by fear.
His words were simple, and his soul sincere;
Needless was written law, where none oppressed:
 The law of Man was written in his breast"
Ovid (43 BCE - 17 CE) Rome/Italy

December 21

New day, new choice, new chance, new thoughts, and new experiences... How lucky are we?

What's the coming of the Golden Age all about?

Everyone is talking about the transition into the Golden Age and what's to come. The term Golden Age comes from Greek mythology. Legend tells us there are four sequences of Ages of Man, and the first one is called Golden Age. Followed by Silver, Bronze, and Iron; which we currently reside in and is considered a dark or declining age. The Golden Age, the most desirable one, is supposed to bring us peace, stability, harmony, and abundance; surely the long awaited "Promised Land."

There are several different concepts from various cultures concerning this legend. For example, the ancient Hindus saw it as a cycle of Dark Ages and Golden Ages. The Greeks, however, as mentioned earlier wrote about a cycle of four periods, each starting at the Golden Age and getting darker and darker until the Iron or Dark Ages where wars and poverty reigned. Thereafter the Golden Age, or awakening period, returns. The name is not to be taken literally as "golden" but as "good" and "prosperous;" the cycles last approximately 5,000 years.

In the metaphysical and inspirational communities the assumptions are flying high. The theories vary from being "the end of the world" to "a new beginning" led by the awakening of the masses. A cosmic shift of enlightenment and spirituality is expected by the positive scholars, New Age teachers and metaphysicians.

Astrology holds 2012 as an important extension of the Aquarian Age, which is called the Communication Age – already being seen by the extreme advancements in technology and communications since the year 2000. The Age of Aquarius promotes also peace, love, and understanding. Observing the masses of people that are looking for groups of like-minded spiritual searchers on the internet these days surely confirms this trend. Let us make this new period in time the best we have experienced so far!

December 22

What can we do today to make someone's life a little better? How can we support and nurture a person that might be feeling less than and help them get back to a more positive outlook? The law of attraction will give back to you in exact proportion. So remember: When you do good, good will return to you.

December 23

Be aware that we over-extend ourselves in this busy holiday season. Keep your calm and know that the most precious gifts are love, friendship, giving of your time, emotional support, and caring.

December 24

Be kind and compassionate. You never know when you need the same treatment from others.

Thoughts on friendship

What are true friends? I pondered this thought this morning and here is what I came up with. Friends are two Souls that support each other on their journey.

Encouragement, stimulating conversation, and companionship is part of friendship. Quality time and creative communication should be the norm, not complaining about experiences gone wrong and gossiping about others. Gossip is hurtful and damages the gossiper.

Friends look out for each other but are not critical or judgmental. They understand that each still has to work out some challenges and they know that each is on their own path. Friends acknowledge the Godhood in each other as Children of the Light – think about that one for a moment.

Look at your friend and see what he/she really is. No matter what the appearance, he/she is a being of perfect intelligence; just like you on the road to gain perfect Understanding.

Each person approaches their journey in a different way, uniquely as they are individuals. But remember, he/she is in your experience, they are playing a role in your life and therefore they are (must be) on your frequency. Your friend mirrors you. He/she mirrors parts of who you are, parts of who you want to be, and parts of the corrections necessary. This of course works both ways. They also see themselves in you. They see in you parts of who they are, who they want to be and what corrections are needed.

So it all works perfectly together, as always.

December 25

Life always moves forward and upward. Even in your darkest hour there is a movement towards the Light. So stop hindering yourself by being inflexible and scared. Move with it and trust in the Allness of Good!

Sacrifice

What does sacrifice mean? What do you mean when you say "I sacrificed?" If you do things for others with pure intent and good motivations without expectations of getting something in return, you will never feel that you sacrificed something.

The word sacrifice means "offering." So did you sacrifice years of your life or did you offer to stay in a relationship that wasn't to your liking for example? Did you sacrifice the time spent or was it your choice? Did you give something up (freedom, enjoyment etc.) in order to gain something (security, money, etc.) in return? Think about it!

How can you sacrifice if you gained something in return? That would be an even exchange, wouldn't it? If you didn't gain anything in return, then why didn't you make another choice and leave the relationship? Do I hear "I didn't have a choice!"? Yes, you did or you gained something in return that made you stay. See the wheel spinning?

387

Don't regret your choices. Be observant yet neutral and fair toward yourself. If you decide that the choice you made no longer works for you, change it. You can do so anytime!

December 26

Many people experience depression during the holidays, but carrying spiritual burdens such as grief, sorrow, and self-pity are mental disasters. They rob you of your natural good energy and drag you down into the dark chambers of despair. Don't allow those harmony disturbers to influence your daily practices and remember that you are in charge of your moods and habits.

December 27

Many times decisions are made on a pure emotional basis. Make sure that your reason is present without attachment to the issues, so you can see the picture is clear and without bias. It takes both reason and feeling to come to the right conclusion.

Relationship with Self

The only true relationship you can ever have is with yourself. You, your true essence, is all you will ever really know. You, is all there is in your world. Strong statements you say? Well, let's talk!

Since I can only have a relationship with myself (I am the only one I truly know) I will start by explaining how my thought process works. Please apply this line of thinking to yourself when going through this exercise and ask yourself the same questions. See how you feel about yourself. So in my case, when I think about my relationship with myself, what comes to mind? I must admit, the more thought I give this question, the more I see that I have a great relationship with myself. I don't

388

annoy myself, I don't ignore myself, I enjoy myself when alone, I take care of myself, and most of all I like myself. I can keep myself busy easily, I'm never bored, and I spend lots of quiet time to reflect upon myself. I like to improve myself, educate, and treat myself well. It doesn't take much to do all of the above. It doesn't take money or a lot of time.

How do you find periods of quietness in a busy day, you ask? Yes, I have a fulltime job between my workshops and my writing commitments. But to me it's all as natural as breathing. I have trained myself to think that way. I work it into my daily schedule. It's all about your priorities. Instead of going to the mall, I read a book ... instead of going to the beauty parlor, I work on my goal list ... you get the point.

I focus on myself without being egocentric. I enjoy without grandeur. I take care by allowing myself plenty of rest. I keep busy by practicing right thinking and studying. I always put myself first without being selfish. Everything I do is focused on the mental, not the physical process.

Who do I think I am? I have always wondered who I am and why I am the way I am and you probably have too. Many of us ask that question at some point in our lives. We must realize that we have been, at least in our younger years, shaped by parents and family, community, religion and ethnicity, and education. Yet as we mature, we often divert from those influences that had seemingly made a lasting impression. We all decided to make unique life choices and start drawing our own conclusions that may indeed vary from how we were raised; even so we keep many of the old beliefs. This certainly shows in the experiences we now encounter.

This is what I've learned: What I am is a mental being, looking for my purpose as I unfold the inherent intelligence within me. And if, as I am certain, the purpose of my life is to enjoy myself, then I am on the right path. I am consciously trying to accomplish this daily. What I am is a unique instrument born of the Universe, expressing life and serving my purpose by contributing to the Allness of Good.

In reality this process is already accomplished. The Allness of Good is already all there is. What I mean by this is that the Universe is made out of goodness and therefore we do not have to add to or interfere in it. However, we have to find and acknowledge, and then externalize all that is already positive within us.

So, how is your relationship with yourself? Do you like yourself? Do you spend time with yourself? Do you have alone time and how do you handle those quiet moments? Do you escape into activities to avoid yourself? Do you struggle with feelings of loneliness the minute you are alone? Are there times you really want to be alone but fear hurting someone else's feelings? Do you treat yourself well? Are you taking care of yourself physically and mentally? Do you acknowledge your Godhood? How well do you know yourself?

In your daily mantra, say to yourself "I am all there is in my world" and live accordingly. Realizing that your world consists out of your perception of your world will bring your life experience to a different perspective. The realization of your importance, in an unselfish way, will make you a better person. It will give you the strength to move on gracefully and enable you to take care of your immediate environment. This newfound empowerment will ripple out affecting everyone that comes into contact with you. You will truly know yourself and enjoy your life, which is your purpose on this plane of existence.

December 28

Once we identify ourselves with our universal God-source it will lead us to actions that are more in

line with our true nature. We will have a more universal viewpoint than our small ego self.

As we are nearing the end of this year, I wanted to reiterate the importance of our connection to our universal God-source. We have talked a lot about "who and what" we are during the year and it is simply time to apply what we have learned.

Wake up and smell the roses...

Looking at spiritual publications, the social media, and talking to people throughout this year, it has become clear to me that the awakening of the masses is on the agenda of this new era. Searchers are joining groups of likeminded people in the hopes of lifting their conscious awareness to a better understanding and to help enlighten all brothers and sisters. All efforts are welcomed and certainly a step in the right direction. At this point however, many – or shall we say most – people are still in a state of delusion; an unconscious sleep of what life really consists of.

The daily grind and long held beliefs are gripping those Souls, seemingly with no way out. Hurry, worry, nagging, envy, fear, to name a few and many other ugly dispositions are on the day's agenda. And even though glimpses of hope occur every so often, most of the day is spent with reacting negatively rather than positive action according to Universal Law.

The time has come that each and every one of us has to start taking responsibility for our own lives. We have to see the fact that how we have lived, acted and believed, up to now, is no longer good enough. This way of living has not produced the bliss we are capable of experiencing. So in finishing my year of sharing my daily thoughts I am urged by my own understanding to reiterate strongly and with great love:

Wake up! It's time to smell the roses! It's time that these glimpses of Truth you have experienced, become the full-blown "Rose of Life" it is meant to be.

December 29

Why is it that we have such a personal sense about everything? Do we think everything that is said and done pertains to us? Let go of this mistake. Only what you think and do is about you. What others say and do is about them and has nothing to do with you. It's only an opinion, someone's perception. Shed this personal sense and free yourself of buying into someone else's viewpoint. You will be better off for it.

Goal setting and goal achieving for the New Year

We started the year with dreams, goals, and hopes of achievement. Have we accomplished at least in part what we set out to do? Have you reviewed your progress during the last months? I just reviewed my goal list and want to share the results with you. I published my second booklet *The Seeds Will Sprout Somewhere and* held twelve workshops with a dear friend and life coach over the past year. I found the classes and the lovely people I met absolutely fulfilling and I am looking forward to many more. I'm still working on getting my legal papers in order, but I have drafted a will and the rest is in flux due to a change of property. We did repave our driveway. My patience with my husband still needs work and lots of practice, but I am aware of my short-comings and it's a daily task and I have been much better in allowing the Law of Individuality to work.

We all have an easier time to set the goals than to achieve them. It's the focus and the commitment to stay with the project that veers during the course of the year. But believe me, once you have trained yourself to stay "with it" and to be single-minded, all things fall into place easily. So in review of how to achieve your desires, I will reiterate: Start with a thorough mental house cleaning. Set your goal. Visualize all the details, including colors, smells, feelings, and sounds. Use your perceptive senses to make it real. Then bring it into your "now" experience. Believe that you already have it. Don't put it into the future, say and feel: I have, I do, I am.

It will be yours – I guarantee.

December 30

Our imagination cannot grasp the vastness of the Universe at this time. This universal concept stretches far beyond our ability to understand. However, the Universe works according to Universal Laws, which are perfect and good. Therefore flow with it - not against it, by trusting the Allness of Good.

Healed at last

Healing your Soul – what does it mean to you? Is your Soul sick, misguided or deceived? Your Soul cannot be sick. It is the pure substance sent to this Earthly dimension in order to learn more of truth. Our consciousness fell into a mist of misunderstanding when born on this plane. Misguided by our parents and loved ones, taught wrongly by our teachers and clergy, and even well-meaning friends along the path encouraged ignorance, due to not knowing any better.

Not to see the light, or the truth, has kept us in bondage long enough. It's time to awaken the sleeping Soul and restore it back to its Glory.

We believed that sickness is real and we accepted the lie that we are powerless creatures. We believed that we have no choice than to adhere to outside forces and give in to circumstances beyond our control.

But at last we glimpsed at the truth, now knowing that we came from the source of all sources, called

Intelligence, mass-consciousness. We awakened as an individual thinker on this plane, knowing only one small piece of truth. We know that we are alive, we are conscious and we know that we "are" or "exist."

All other knowledge is still in the dark, hidden behind the veil. It is our job now and forever to search, find, and gain understanding. As we evolve toward the light, we clear up many of the wrong concepts. It is a lifetime task, yet our Souls stay pure and only the mud (misunderstanding) that we have thrown upon ourselves stays glued to us until we commit to rigorous mental housecleaning and wipe away those lies step by step.

Healing our Earthly pains should be high on our list, as all dis-ease is caused by wrong thinking and wr wrong believing, giving cause to outside forces. Once you have cleared your mind of fears, with this new understanding of the Allness of Good, the road is ready to be travelled. The heavens will be open to embrace you, the lost child, to come home once again.

December 31

This is all you need to know; I mean "really" know. So say to yourself:

"I am Love, I am Light, I am Perfection and I am Health – and I know it!"

In closing...

A year is but a bleep in timeless motion. But on this plane of lower frequency it is a speck of our work needed, day after day, month after month, test after test. It has been a pleasure to write every day, to research other philosophies, and to learn so much about the already existing Knowledge of Truth. It is my privilege to share what I know and to reveal what I found in my pursuit of more understanding.

We have to acknowledge what's already good and improve that what is still lacking. We have to become aware of our limitless possibilities. The key to a better life is diligent study and the search for the truth. We are the Light Workers of this nation called Universe.

Join us at http://www.modernthoughttheories.com/ and get on ULRIKE's mailing list for inspiring videos, current happenings and weekly uplifting motivations from ULRIKE herself!

You can also find ULRIKE at:
FACEBOOK:
https://www.facebook.com/ModernThoughtTheories
TWITTER:
https://twitter.com/ThoughtTheories
GOODREADS:
https://www.goodreads.com/author/show/1954337.Ulrike
If this book has touched you, please consider leaving a review.

Other Books by ULRIKE

Because You Can

Inspire Your Day

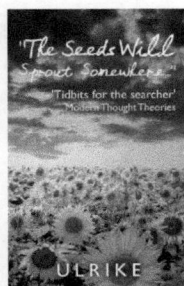

The Seeds Will Sprout Somewhere

www.ingramcontent.com/pod-product-compliance
Lightning Source LLC
LaVergne TN
LVHW051222080426
835513LV00016B/1364